SIMPLICIUS

On Epictetus Handbook 27-53

SIMPLICIUS

On Epictetus
Handbook 27 - 53

Translated by
Tad Brennan & Charles Brittain

Bloomsbury Academic

An imprint of Bloomsbury Publishing Plc

50 Bedford Square	1385 Broadway
London	New York
WC1B 3DP	NY 10018
UK	USA

www.bloomsbury.com

Bloomsbury is a registered trade mark of Bloomsbury Publishing Plc

First published in 2002 by Gerald Duckworth & Co. Ltd.
Paperback edition first published 2014

British Library Cataloguing-in-Publication Data
A catalogue record for this book is available from the British Library.

ISBN HB:	978-0-7156-3069-3
PB:	978-1-4725-5736-0
ePDF:	978-1-7809-3903-2

Library of Congress Cataloging-in-Publication Data
A catalog record for this book is available from the Library of Congress.

Acknowledgements
The present translations have been made possible by generous and imaginative funding from the
following resources: the National Endowment for the Humanities, Division of Research Programs,
an independent federal agency of the USA; the Leverhulme Trust; the British Academy; the Jowett
Copyright Trustees; the Royal Society (UK); Centro Internazionale A. Beltrame di Storia della
Spazio e del Tempo (Padua); Mario Mignucci; Liverpool University; the Leventis Foundation;
the Arts and Humanities Research Borad of the British Academy; the Esmée Fairbairn Charitable
Trust; the Henry Brown Trust; Mr and Mrs N. Egon; the Netherlands Organisation for Scientific
Research (NWO/GW), Dr Victoria Solomonides, the Cultural Attaché of the Greek Embassy
in London. The editor wishes to thank Brad Inwood, Christopher Gill, Doug Hutchinson and
Teun Tieleman for their comments and Han Balthussen for preparing the volumes for press.

Typeset by Ray Davies

Contents

Preface

The writings of Simplicius are now extant. His physical and meta-physical commentaries on Aristotle have passed away with the fashion of the times; but his moral interpretation of Epictetus is preserved in the library of nations, as a classic book, most excellently adapted to direct the will, to purify the heart, and to confirm the understanding, by a just confidence in the nature both of God and man (Edward Gibbon, *Decline and Fall of the Roman Empire*, pt. V, ch. 40).

Gibbon's casual condemnation of the 'physical and metaphysical commentaries on Aristotle' – i.e. of most of the volumes in the Ancient Commentators on Aristotle series that has given our own translation a home – now seems merely to illustrate the fashion of his times: translations of ancient commentaries on Aristotle's *Physics* or *Metaphysics* no longer need to justify their appearance in print. A translation of an ancient commentary on Epictetus' *Encheiridion*, however, perhaps does require a bit more justification than Gibbon's pious encomium, particularly when it is appearing in a series on the exegesis of Aristotle. Although it is not included in the *Commentaria in Aristotelem Graeca*, we think that there are good reasons for the inclusion of this commentary in the series that will assure it of appropriate readers. For Simplicius was an ancient commentator on Aristotle, and this work tells us a great deal about him, the other ancient commentators on Aristotle, and the Platonist milieu in which they worked; and, though nominally devoted to a Stoic text, it is perhaps the most concise encapsulation of the Platonist vision of the world that survives. Thus, by including this volume, the series will eventually contain all of the extant commentaries by Simplicius, and a work that is extraordinarily informative about the larger intellectual project that underlay the commentaries on Aristotle that are its principal constituents.

Our translation is to a great extent the product of our predecessors: Johannes Schweighäuser, whose commentary on Simplicius' commentary is a model of philological and philosophical incisiveness; and Professor I. Hadot, whose dedication to Simplician studies is likely to remain unmatched, and from whose editions, books, and articles we have learned a great deal (and continue to learn: her second edition of the first half of the commentary in the Budé series unfortunately reached us too late to be of use for this translation). Where our predecessors failed to enlighten us, a wealth of detailed comments were provided by the readers co-opted by Richard Sorabji, including Christopher Gill, Margaret Graver and Brad Inwood, as well as six others who remain anonymous. Susanne Bobzien and Tony Long gave us further necessary comments on Simplicius' logic and on the style of our translation, respectively. We have also received valuable editorial and indexical assistance from Han Baltussen, Eleni Vambouli, Andrew Chignell, and Kate Woolfitt. Richard Sorabji, the general editor of the series, assisted us at every stage; his willingness to include this volume in the series made it possible for us to focus on Simplicius without the distractions of a pressing press. We are honoured to have played our small part in his tireless efforts to inform the scholarly community about the philosophers of late antiquity. We are profoundly indebted to these scholars and friends. We also gratefully acknowledge a generous grant for collaborative research from the Society for Humanities at Cornell University and a grant from the Frederick W. Hilles Publication Fund of Yale University.

T.R.B. would like in addition to thank colleagues at King's College, London, where he began this work, as well as at Yale University, where he finished it. Richard Sorabji, M.M. McCabe, Sylvia Berryman, Michael Della Rocca, Shelly Kagan and Bob Adams deserve special mention. His children, Alexandra and Lincoln, lightened the difficult years; and, as always, his deepest thanks go to Liz Karns.

C.B. is indebted to Michael Frede for suggesting Simplicius' work as a text for a reading group, and to Stephen Menn, George Boys-Stones, Susanne Bobzien and his colleagues at Cornell, particularly Hayden Pellicia and Jeffrey Rusten, for their help and encouragement over the years. He is very grateful to Sophie and Helena, whose births punctuated the translation, and to his delightful copyeditor, Harriet Brittain.

New Haven & Ithaca   T.R.B.
                                                                     C.B.

Introduction

1. The interest of the work

In [Simplicius' *Commentary on Epictetus*], you have clearly before
you the whole philosophical scheme from which Christianity took
its outlines, so that this book, written by a 'pagan' philosopher,
makes the most Christian impression conceivable (setting aside
the fact that the whole realm of Christian sentiment and pathology
is absent, i.e. 'love' in the Pauline sense, 'fear of God', and so on).
The betrayal of all reality through morality is here present in its
fullest splendour – pitiful psychology, the philosopher reduced to a
country parson. And Plato is to blame for all of it! He remains
Europe's greatest misfortune!' (Nietzsche in a letter to Overbeck,
7 January 1887).

The Commentary on the Handbook of Epictetus is a valuable source for
the history of Platonism. It contains a series of lengthy digressions on
some of the central philosophical issues in Platonist ethics, treating the
metaphysical structure of the world, the nature of evil and free will.
These essays are particularly valuable because they are designed for
novice philosophers – hence Nietzsche's 'country parson' jibe – and thus
accessible in a way that most of our surviving evidence for late Platonism, which often seems obscure and unduly exuberant, is not. The work
also provides useful information about the Platonists' theory of emotion,
about their interpretive and pedagogical practices, and about Simplicius' own reaction to an increasingly hostile political order.

The commentary is equally informative on the history of ancient
Stoicism. It is an extended epigraph on a school which had been dead for
several hundred years, revealing that the Platonists were tacitly engaged in harmonising Plato and Zeno no less than Plato and Aristotle,
by introducing their students to ethical virtue using a Stoic handbook.
It thus provides a precise gauge for the degree of knowledge of Stoic
ethics and psychology still current in the philosophical schools of the
sixth century AD.

The commentary is also of some significance for the history of Christian theology. For despite its defiant enunciation of pagan principles,
there is – as Nietzsche scornfully remarked – something eerily Christian

about the work. But Simplicius' arguments do not appear to require the positing of any Christian influence: his text is discernibly a systematic working out of a few Platonic dialogues supplemented with a Platonised exposition of Stoic ethics. The extraordinary coincidence in their end-products makes it hard to reject Nietzsche's conclusion that Christian theology is inextricably linked to this pagan milieu.

2. Biography and historical background

The author of this idiosyncratic work is fairly well known to us from a variety of sources, although some important details of his life remain controversial.[1] It is clear that Simplicius grew up in the Roman province of Cilicia, studied in Alexandria under Ammonius, and lived for some time in Athens as the intellectual heir and confidante of Damascius, the last Platonist 'scholarch' of the Academy.[2] He was certainly active in the 530s AD, and probably through at least the 540s and 550s.[3] Of the other treatises he is known to have written, his commentaries on Aristotle's *de Caelo*, *Physics* and *Categories* survive; treatises on Euclid, Iamblichus and Hermogenes (the rhetorician) do not. A commentary on Aristotle's *de Anima* has also come down under his name, but its authorship is disputed; if scholarship eventually credits it to Simplicius, then we may also credit him with a commentary on Aristotle's *Metaphysics*, which it mentions in passing.[4] Rather surprisingly, Simplicius appears not to have written commentaries on any of Plato's dialogues.[5]

The *Commentary on the Encheiridion* (or 'Handbook') provides very little personal information about its author. Apart from telling us that he once saw a statue of the Stoic philosopher Cleanthes in the latter's hometown of Assos (Hadot 451 / Dübner 137,20), and suggesting that he had an interview with a leading Manichean (H325 / D71,48), Simplicius offers only a few hints about his life or times. The conclusion of the work notes that he writes in 'tyrannical circumstances' (H454 / D138,19) – i.e., it seems clear from an earlier comment (H257 / D35,34), a period during which anti-pagan laws were being effectively enforced. Accordingly, though he rarely attacks the Roman state or Christianity directly, several passages in the commentary are plausibly interpreted as indications of political dissent. Among these are his condemnations of currently popular theological misapprehensions (e.g. H219 / D15,51-16,03, on 'cheap' views of the divine, and H387 / D106,3-20, on 'forgiveness'), and his digressions on the role of philosophers in worth-less states and on friendship (see Section 3 below).[6]

The controversial questions about Simplicius' life depend on whether any of these details can be used to assign a more precise date or provenance for this commentary or any of the others. It has long been thought that there is some relation between Justinian's order for the closure of the Athenian philosophical 'schools' in 529 and the voluntary exile of the leading Platonists of the time – Simplicius, Damascius,

Priscian and a few others – at the court of the learned Persian king Khusrau (or Chosroes), recorded in Agathias' *Histories* 2.30-1.[7] Agathias reports that the philosophers quickly found that life under a barbarian philosopher-king was not to their liking, and returned to Roman territory, after cleverly securing a coda to the treaty being drawn up between Rome and Persia in 532, to the effect that they could 'return to their accustomed haunts and pass their lives without fear amongst themselves' (2.31).[8] These episodes – Justinian's order and the trip to Persia – are clearly relevant to the circumstantial material in the commentary on Epictetus, but they do not obviously tell either way on the date or provenance: the remarks in the commentary might show why Simplicius had left Athens, or why he was going to leave.

In the last 20 years, however, Michel Tardieu has argued that the circumstantial evidence from Simplicius' commentaries, in combination with some recondite facts about Syria in the sixth century, point to the beguiling conclusion that Simplicius *et al.* settled in Harran (Roman Carrhae, on the Syrian border with Persia) in about 532, and there inspired a school of Platonist 'Sabians' that survived the Islamic invasion, and only closed in the eleventh century.[9] On the basis of his research, Tardieu concludes that all the extant commentaries were written in Harran and after 532. His argument in the case of the *Encheiridion* commentary is simple: Harran was one of only two cities in the Roman East of the sixth century in which there was Manichee activity that we know of – the other was Byzantium, which is an unlikely place of refuge for a banned Platonist – and hence is the most likely place for Simplicius' interview with a Manichee 'wise man' (H325 / D71,48), and one where Simplicius' extended attack on Manichean dualism (in ch. 27) was appropriate.[10] In support of this identification are various ingenious arguments drawn from the other commentaries – Simplicius' knowledge of the Harranian calendar, of Syrian methods of transportation by river, and of various Syrian place names and divinities – the indirect attestation of a Platonist Sabian sect in Harran by at least 717-20, and the implausibility of Simplicius' return to either Athens or Alexandria in the 530s.[11]

Tardieu's thesis is learned and intriguing, and has had the beneficial effect of making the Eastern connexions of Simplicius and Damascius relatively well-known. But it suffers from several undeniable weaknesses. For the dating and provenance of the commentary on the *Encheiridion*, the problem is obvious: from the fact that we know of only two active communities of Manichees, we cannot infer that Simplicius' exposure to the sect was similarly limited.[12] Nor can we infer from the sarcastic and polemical tone of his attack on dualism that he expected his readers to be Harranian, or even familiar with Manichaeism: the attack on dualism is a set-piece of Platonist metaphysics, made entertaining by the absurdities of his unnamed opponents.[13] His supporting arguments look equally insecure. First, the calendrical argument appears to rely on a misunderstanding of Simplicius' remark.[14] Secondly, since we know that Simplicius accompanied Damascius to Persia (or its environs), and that Damascius came from North Syria, it is not unlikely that he gleaned his knowledge of the area from travelling through it with his teacher.[15] Thirdly, the 'Platonist school' is not in fact attested until 200 years after Simplicius' trip to Persia: it is rash to infer from the silence of our extant and discovered sources that there were no subsequent Platonists who settled in Syria.[16] And finally, we do not know enough about Athens (or other Greek cities) in the middle of the sixth century to be certain that Simplicius did not return there – or to his native Cilicia.

The precise provenance and date of the commentary thus remain unclear, though Harran in the 530s has not been ruled out.

3. Simplicius' interpretative methods

The choice of Epictetus' *Encheiridion* as a text-book for an introductory course on Platonist ethics strikes the modern historian of philosophy as rather strange, since it is a Stoic manual, and hence incompatible in obvious ways with Platonism. The strangeness of this choice is made very clear in Simplicius' general remarks on the nature of the text in the brief introduction to his commentary. For there he picks out various features that might recommend the *Encheiridion* as an ethical manual – it is emotionally powerful, consists of concise, but thematically organised 'precepts', and is aimed at the moral improvement of fairly ordinary people (H193 / D1,36-46) – and immediately sets them in a Platonist framework. The appropriate audience is defined by reference to the Plotinian-inspired theory of grades of virtue, in which the civic or political virtues instilled by Epictetus are not the ultimate goal (H195 / 2,30-3,2); and Epictetus' 'hypothesis' that a human person is a rational soul using a body is rapidly demonstrated by an argument from Plato's *First Alcibiades* (H196 / D3,3-54). (See Section 4 below.)

The external context of the commentary provides some explanation for Simplicius' choice of text. The *Encheiridion* was a popular work in late antiquity, excerpted at length in collections such as Stobaeus', and adapted several times by Christian writers.[17] It was also known to many, perhaps even all, Simplicius' fellow-Platonists, including Hierocles, Proclus, Damascius and Olympiodorus.[18] In his commentary on the *Gorgias*, for example, the latter cites precepts from the *Encheiridion* five times explicitly mentioning Epictetus, and on two other occasions repeats or paraphrases chapters from it.[19] The general function of the *Encheiridion* for these Platonists was thus as a simple, but memorable, source for first-order ethical rules. But their ultimate motivation for adopting this text was the normal pedagogical one: it was the best course-book available to fit their curricular needs. For, as Hadot and others have shown, the late Platonist curriculum, in theory at least, involved a strenuous programme of Aristotelian lectures, starting with the *Categories*, to be crowned by the detailed study of Platonic ethics, logic, physics and theology, starting with *First Alcibiades*, *Gorgias* and *Phaedo* (cf. *Anon. Prol.* 10).[20] But since the study of philosophy was conceived by the Platonists, as by most ancient philosophers, as an *ethical* search for wisdom or perfection, it wouldn't have done to set students onto the *Categories* without any moral guidance, for reasons set out in Plato's *Gorgias* (447-60). Hence, there was a need for introductory texts that gave useful advice in a memorable form, and thus supplied the true beliefs that the ethical part of the Platonic cycle of study would demonstrate and explain.

Even if this explains the basic motivation for using texts *like* the *Encheiridion*, however, it doesn't explain the choice of that *Stoic* text, with its inevitable 'false' doctrines. Simplicius tacitly allows as much in his introduction, when he notes that Epictetus' book has the 'surprising' feature that it inculcates virtue even on the (false) supposition that the soul is mortal (H194 / D1,47-2,14).[21] Olympiodorus is more circumspect in this regard, since he keeps silent about the false doctrines in the *Encheiridion* throughout *in Gorg.* and only disavows Stoic materialism at *in Phd.* 6.2, i.e. towards the end of the first Platonic cycle. The general problem here is nicely illustrated by the vignette in Damascius' *Philosophical History* on Theosebius, a pupil of Hierocles.[22] Theosebius is characterised as someone primarily interested in moral exhortation rather than 'scholarship' – we learn of an exorcism through the powers of Helios and the Jewish God, and of his wife's continence – who took 'much of what he said from the discourses of Epictetus', and also wrote his own Epictetan-inspired works. As a result, Damascius reports, Theosebius became 'the modern Epictetus, *but without the Stoic doctrines*.'

So why did Simplicius choose the *Encheiridion* rather than one of Theosebius' works, or the Pythagorean (and so Platonist) *Carmen Aureum*, which Theosebius' teacher Hierocles used for precisely the same introductory purpose? One possible answer is that Simplicius may not have fully understood the incompatibility between his and Epictetus' views in ethics (see Sections 4-5 below), perhaps because Plotinus had incorporated many Stoic doctrines and terms into Platonist ethics, or perhaps because Simplicius was an inveterate syncretiser.[23] But the commentary itself suggests a more interesting answer: that Simplicius used the *Encheiridion* because he thought it the most powerful text for his purpose, and one that could be pressed into the service of Platonism without damaging side-effects. To see how he might have thought this, it is necessary to examine the structure and methods of the commentary in a little more detail.

The *Encheiridion* consists of 53 chapters, which Simplicius divided into 71 lemmata for commentary, prefaced by a brief introduction and crowned with a final prayer (see the table on pp. 149-50). The chapters are each discussed in a single lemma, except where they are too long or contain distinct sections (*Ench.* 1, 5, 13, 14, 19, 33), are absent from Simplicius' text (*Ench.* 29), or re-interpreted by him as a single chapter (*Ench.* 21-2).[24] Following up on his hint at an order behind Arrian's apparently loosely-structured selection of maxims (H194 / D2,19-24), Simplicius explicitly divides the text into four distinct sections:

I: What is up to us and not, and how to deal with external things: chs 1-21
   (a) chs 1-2: what is up to us and not and the consequences of choosing either;
   (b) chs 3-14: how to deal with external things (Epictetus reins the reader in from them);
   (c) chs 15-21: how to use external things correctly and without disturbance.
II: Advice for intermediate students: chs 22-8
   (a) chs 22-5: the problems of intermediate students;
   (b) chs 26-8: varia – the common conceptions, badness and shame.
III: Technical advice for the discovery of 'appropriate actions' (*kathêkonta*): chs 30-3
   (a) ch. 30: appropriate actions towards other people;
   (b) ch. 31: appropriate actions towards God;
   (c) ch. 32: appropriate actions about divination;
   (d) ch. 33: appropriate actions towards oneself.
   (e) chs 34-47: various precepts on justice, not well related to each other by Simplicius.
IV: Conclusion on the practice of the precepts: chs 48-53
   (a) ch. 48: conclusion of Epictetus' advice and his division of kinds of people;
   (b) chs 49-52: the practice of the precepts;
   (c) ch. 53: quotations for memorisation.

The rationale behind the division between sections I and II is a set of distinctions of 'kinds of people' with respect to their progress in philosophy. The basis for these is set out lucidly by Epictetus in ch. 48, where the ordinary person and (perfect) philosopher are distinguished with respect to whom they anticipate harm or benefit from, and the progressor is assessed by his approximation to the philosopher's position, i.e. expecting good and bad only from himself. But Simplicius discerns a further subdivision of the category of progressors, into beginning and intermediate students (H441 / D132,32-4); and it is on the basis of this subdivision that he marks a new section of the *Encheiridion* in his comments on ch. 22 (H301 / D58,39).[25] Simplicius explains his subdivision as that between any human beings who want to improve themselves and (ordinary) 'philosophers', as we would call them, i.e. those actively engaged in the pursuit of philosophical knowledge; and he sees his subdivision as marking two distinct kinds of advice Epictetus gives in the course of the work.[26]

Section III is introduced as the section in which Epictetus gives, with admirable concision, 'the technical method dealing with appropriate actions', i.e. with the content of the precepts given in chs 1-28, (H346 / D83,4-29). Its initial four chapters are taken by Simplicius to present a systematic general theory of one's duties, which he discusses at some length; the remaining chapters (34-47) are less clearly ordered, in his view, but sufficiently tied to the promotion of justice to be numbered in this part.[27] Simplicius plausibly takes section IV to be distinct from the rest of the text, since it exhorts us to enact the preceding guidance, and explains how to do it (H441 / D132,23). Such, in brief, are the 'orderly relationship' and 'logical sequence' of the precepts of the *Encheiridion*, that Simplicius discerned in his introduction (H194 / D2,17). On his account, the work presents the beginner with a carefully graded approach to the kind of life that befits an (ordinary) 'philosopher', which culminates in a systematic canon for the discovery of one's duties and some exhortation to ethical practice.

Some insight into the way Simplicius uses the *Encheiridion* is provided by the features he praises in his commentary. Most prominent among these are four points he identifies in his introduction: its order (described above), concision, emotional power and practical applicability.[28] All four are conspicuously praised in ch. 30, where Simplicius compares traditional works on 'appropriate actions' – presumably by the Stoics, and figures like Theosebius, although he names only Nicolaus of Damascus – with Epictetus' treatment 'in a few lines using effective illustrations and soul-stirring vividness' (H346 / D83,12).[29] The emotional power of the work is located by Simplicius in various elements. He admires its use of imagery: the analogies of the voyage (ch. 7), inn (ch. 11), banquet (chs 15, 36), acting in a play (chs 17, 37) stepping on a nail (ch. 38), shoes (ch. 39), and the two-handled jars (ch. 43).[30] He is impressed by Epictetus' use of often trivial examples, that are 'from life' and hence familiar to, and effective on, the reader: the broken jug (ch. 3), the trip to the baths (chs 4, 45), Epictetus' own lameness (ch. 9), the loss of a child (ch. 11), the price of a lettuce (ch. 25), etc.[31] And he praises Epictetus' use of exemplars, particularly Socrates (chs 5, 32, 33, 46, 51, 53), but also Diogenes and Heraclitus (ch. 15), and Zeno (ch. 34).[32] The practicality of the work is proven through Epictetus' emphasis on various techniques for self-improvement: for instance, his suggestion for distancing oneself from one's impressions (ch. 1), his use of the phrase 'Remember' (ch. 2 *et passim*), and his stress on prior consideration of misfortunes (ch. 4).[33] In all these respects, Epictetus is a truly 'admirable' or 'astonishing' preceptor.[34]

But a deeper insight into Simplicius' use of the *Encheiridion* can be gained from the points at which Simplicius believed that Epictetus' arguments require supplementation: the seven excursuses or essays, which provide the doctrinal framework for Simplicius' commentary.

1. ch. 1, H199 / D4,52-H217 / D15,2: on the soul, against various determinists.
2. ch. 8, H257 / D35,48-H272 / D44,22: that god is not the cause of the bad.
3. ch. 24, H313 / D64,53-H316 / D66,36: on the role of the philosopher in city-states.
4. ch. 27, H322 / D69,46-H342 / D81.18: on the derivative nature of the bad.
5. ch. 30, H346 / D83,30-H348 / D84,37: on the relations that reveal 'appropriate actions'.
6. ch. 30, H351 / D86,20-H357 / D89,28: on friendship.
7. ch. 31, H367 / D95,17-H392 / D109,6: on providence.

Two of the shorter essays, nos 3 and 6, concern political or ethical subjects that Epictetus ignores, but Simplicius finds important enough to discuss in some detail. The essay on the state is a diatribe drawing on *Republic* 6, and perhaps reflects Simplicius' own experience of voluntary exile (though if it does, it does so via Epictetus' move to Nicopolis to avoid Domitian's tyranny). The essay on friendship is more of an encomium, drawing on the *Symposium*, Aristotle and Pythagorean sources, and emphasising the divine favour that graces intellectual friendship (H354 / D88,2-8); but here too Simplicius stresses the disappearance of friendship in the present times (H357 / D89,25-8). It is notable that Simplicius does not suggest in either essay that Epictetus was remiss, though a more polemical commentator might well think that his omissions are the result of dubious Stoic doctrines.[35] The third short essay, no. 5 on 'relations', is still more revealing of the way in which the *Encheiridion* is treated by Simplicius, since it supplies the 'technical method' for discovering appropriate actions – a remarkable example of Simplician scholasticism – that its author ascribes to Epictetus.

The four longer essays, nos 1, 2, 4 and 7 (whose content is discussed in Section 4 below) make Simplicius' philosophical approach to the work explicit. A brief model for his technique in these essays is given in the introduction, where Simplicius frankly explains that Plato demonstrates in the *First Alcibiades* what Epictetus took as a 'hypothesis', that the rational soul is the true human being (H196-7 / D3, 3-54). The first essay thus justifies Epictetus' starting with the distinction between what is up to us and what is not by setting out the status of the soul in a Platonist theology, and arguing for its 'freedom' via a series of anti-determinist arguments drawn from Aristotle's *NE* 3.[36] The second essay demonstrates the Platonic thesis that 'god is not the cause of the bad' (cf. *Tim.* 42d3-4) through an examination of sublunary existents familiar from Plotinus' and Proclus' treatises *de Providentia*. It is introduced explicitly as a defence of Epictetus' unargued thesis in ch. 8 (H257 / D35,48), and justified as an excursus necessary for both Epictetus' theodicy and his doctrine of the nature of the bad in ch. 27 (H272 / D44,19). The fourth essay, on ch. 27, spells out Proclus' version of the theodical claims in ch. 8, in the form of an argument against Manichean dualism (with striking echoes of Augustine's Plotinian solution to 'the problem of evil' in *Confessions* 7). Simplicius justifies this excursus in a single sentence on its utility for a proper conception of divinity (H322 / D69,46). The final essay defends three Platonic theses from *Laws* 10 that Simplicius finds in ch. 33, that the gods exist, are providential, and are just; the first thesis is demonstrated via a series of Platonist 'ascents' to the first cause (subsequently codified by Aquinas); the second and third are demonstrated directly from *Laws* 901-4. (The argument for the third thesis contains his anti-Christian polemic against the notion of 'forgiveness', though Simplicius' own position is identical with e.g. Augustine's; see H389/D107.19-108.06.) Here again Simplicius justifies his excursus as a demonstration of theses that Epictetus merely assumes.[37]

Even this brief review of Simplicius' supplementary essays – which constitute about one third of the commentary – is perhaps enough to make it clear why he was able to select a Stoic text for his introductory work for Platonist novices: the *arguments* for all the substantive metaphysical and meta-ethical theses in the commentary are Platonist arguments, not only where Simplicius and Epictetus disagree (e.g. on determinism and in their theologies), but also where they agree (e.g. on the nature of the bad and on providence).

Simplicius explains the purpose of his detailed comments on the content of each chapter of the *Encheiridion* in two remarks that frame the work (H194 / D2,24-9 and H454 / D138,15-21): by explicating the text in detail he hopes to assist its interpretation by students who are unaccustomed to such writing and to confirm his own grasp of the ethical truths they contain.[38] His typical approach to these tasks is straightforward: (i) he explains how the chapter or lemma in question relates to its context; (ii) he summarises its content; (iii) he remarks on any unusual vocabulary it contains; (iv) he corrects any misapprehensions students might be liable to concerning its claims; (v) he elucidates its content by formalising its argument or spelling out its metaphorical terms; (vi) he responds to objections he anticipates; and (vii) he concludes by remarking on its position within the overall argument of the work (by explaining how it fits into the four sections he has identified or for which kind of person it is primarily intended).[39] The results of this familiar approach are mixed. These procedures often yield valuable insights into the structure of the work ([i] & [vii]), for example;[40] or the level of literary or intellectual learning he expects to find in his students ([iii] & [vi]); [41] or Simplicius' own understanding of the arguments ([iv]

& [v]).[42] But their overall effect, particularly in stretches of the commentary that are not broken up by Simplicius' digressions, is frequently rather dry.[43] This result is hardly surprising in a serious text-book (ancient or modern), if unfortunate, since Simplicius chose Epictetus' *Encheiridion* for its concision and emotional power. But the contrast between a primary text praised for its vitality and a commentary that mutes the feature of the text it most admires by the exhaustive application of a scholastic methodology is one that has rarely been avoided in the Platonic tradition.[44]

4. Simplicius' presentation of Platonism

Simplicius presents a systematic outline of Platonist metaphysics in the commentary, intended to introduce novices to the philosophical doctrines that are necessary for a rational understanding of ethics. The following paragraphs sketch Simplicius' treatments of theology, human psychology, freedom and determinism, the problem of evil, and theodicy.

4.1 God and the hierarchy of being

Simplicius outlines the basic contours of his theology in the first and last of his essays, on chs 1 and 31.[45] The views he presents are in general the orthodoxies of post-Plotinian Platonism, though some details remain more controversial.[46] He takes the visible world to be the base of a pyramidal structure whose apex is the highest divinity. That divinity, God or the One or the Good, is the fount and origin of all things, to whom all the traditional appellations of divinity apply: God is the greatest, the best, the wisest, the most-powerful, the creator.[47] Beneath God are a rank of primordial origins (*arkhai*) that are good in themselves, and stand as the unique simple paradigms (henads) of all the pluralities below them. (These henads are theoretical descendants of Platonic forms in the Platonism of Proclus.) Directly below this level are the highest kinds of souls, e.g. the World-soul of the *Timaeus*, and the souls of the heavenly bodies, which cause the rotation of the heavens, and are thus responsible for the workings of fate in the sublunary realm. Below this level of divine souls are the angelic and daimonic souls, and still further down are human souls.[48] Below human souls there are the souls of irrational animals and of plants, and at the very bottom is matter, which is completely lifeless and inert when considered in its own essence.

Every lower level is less good than the level above it, but only at the lowest four levels is the less good able to be bad. Thus, since all badness comes from the badness in material bodies, their effects on plants and animals, and the results of humankind's excessive preoccupation with these bodies, the cosmos would have had nothing bad in it, if God had stopped at the level above human souls.[49] Yet without these lowest levels the universe would not have been as good as it could be for two reasons. First, the lower levels do contain some definite positive good, even though it is a lesser good than that contained above, and accordingly they do add some increment of goodness to the whole construct. Secondly, without these bottom levels the entire system would have been incomplete, since the higher levels would have been 'impotent' – i.e. lesser goods – had they not been higher than something else (H212 / D12,3, H333 / D76,1).

Simplicius sketches this pyramidal structure most explicitly in the course of four 'ascents to the origin' (H375 / D99,35), which are presented as demonstrative proofs of God's existence. These ascents are reflections on the nature of origins or principles, as well as on the sorts of origins required to account for the causally posterior, moving, manifold, and changing world around us. The arguments occupy the following passages (though the boundaries are not completely clear):

1. cause: H369 / D96,5-H369 / D96,45
2. motion: H369/D96,45-H371 / D97,20
3. simplicity: H371 / D97,20-H374 / D99,5
4. change: H374 / D99,6-H375 / D99,34

The germs of these arguments can perhaps be traced to Plato, though their development owes more to Plotinus and Proclus.[50] Although Simplicius tells us that certain steps in his exposition of the ascent from lowest to highest have been omitted (H378 / D101,41), it seems unlikely that this indicates that he has suppressed references to some entity higher even than the One or the Good mentioned above, since he tells us on the same page that there is no origin higher than this one.[51] The point seems rather to be only that he has passed over some of the intermediate subspecies of the lower orders, which tended to proliferate in triads in the fuller expositions of e.g. Proclus.[52] If so, this may be a point at which Simplicius differs from his teacher Damascius, perhaps in deference to the more canonical presentation of Proclus, which he may have found more suitable for the audience of this work.

4.2 The nature of God

We learn several things about the highest God from the commentary. He is the cause of subsistence for all things, and the demiurgic Father of all (H193 / D1,23, H333 / D76,20, H215 / D13,40);[53] he is present as a whole with all his powers everywhere at once; and he enfolds all things in his providence (H383 / D104,10).[54] The operation of divine providence, however, is distinct from fate, or rather, is an overarching force in which fate is one element (primarily the element controlling the dispostion of sublunary bodies).[55] Thus the human soul's powers to resist the attractions of the material world are owed to providence (H276 / D45,53); but souls that fail to use these powers are chastised by divine 'punitive justice' working through the consonance of their desires with the operations of fate (H264 / D39,30, H382/D103,40, H388 / D106,45). The purpose of 'punitive justice' both here and in Hades is the purification of the soul so that it can achieve virtue and knowledge (H390 / D108,10).[56]

Simplicius emphasises the absolute transcendence of God by insisting on our inability to obtain adequate conceptions of the highest divinity (H375 / D99,40), and on the literal inadequacy of any positive characterisation (H378 / D101,30).[57] Yet the same God is also given a variety of more personal epithets, such as 'Father' (H193 / D1,23) and 'Lord' or 'Master' (H454 / D138,22), and made the addressee of a fervent concluding prayer.[58] Simplicius has two interesting proposals to make about how we should reconcile our belief in divinity's transcendence with our need for something like personal interaction. The first is the suggestion that our rites of prayer, repentance and entreaty give us the illusion of bringing about changes in God, by producing genuine changes in ourselves (H390 / D107,45). The second is that those who have purified their souls through reason may also be able to partake in divine illumination through religious and theurgical rites (H364-6 / D93,30-94,33). If these reconciliations sit uneasily together, that is presumably because the late Platonist doctrine of 'divine grace' is as obscure to human reason as its Christian counterpart.[59]

4.3 Human psychology

Simplicius begins his discussion of psychology and anthropology with a definition adopted from the *First Alcibiades*: a human being is a rational soul that uses the body as an instrument (H197 / D3,30).[60] Perhaps the most important effect of this definition is the exclusion of two competing pictures, according to which the human being simply is the body, or is composed of body and soul together. Were either of these other two pictures correct, our perfection as human beings would either amount to or at least include the perfection of our bodies, and bodily goods would have a claim to be goods simpliciter, i.e. goods for us qua human beings. By insisting that the human body is merely an instrument of the human being, Simplicius insists that our good is completely disjoint from its good.[61] Since this is the central thesis on which the practical ethics of the work depends, the phrase 'using the body as an instrument' forms a leitmotif throughout the commentary

But the picture at the level of metaphysics is slightly less clear. The body that a human being uses is no part or constituent of the human being; and the compound of soul and body is a 'mortal animal' (H337 / D78,12). But is the soul's *use* of the body essential to its being a human being, as the presence of the second clause in the definition would suggest? Does that soul cease to be a human being when it ceases to use the body? Some passages suggest that a human being is simply a rational soul, whether using a body or not (e.g. H197 / D3,47). If we ask of two disincarnate rational souls what it is that makes one of them a human soul and one an angelic or more divine soul, Simplicius' response is that the human soul has a nature such that it is able to involve itself in the material world of bodies and generation in a more intimate way (H202 / D6,40, H336 / D77,40). The more divine soul has its attention and striving always directed upwards towards the Good; the human soul is capable of attending to the Good, but also capable of directing its attention downwards towards bodies (H340 / D80,8). The consequences of this view for responsibility and theodicy are considered below; here it suffices to say that this is probably the more accurate and deeper account of what a human being is. If so, the *Alcibiades* definition is an approximation suitable for beginners: a more scientific definition would assert that a human being is a rational soul that is *capable* of using a body as an instrument.

The rational soul, which in its disincarnate state is simple and without irrational emotion, animates an earthly body by projecting irrational 'lives' into it (H199 / D4,42, H208 / D10,5, H258 / D36,20, H337 / D78,10). From a functional perspective, these irrational 'lives of the body' can be construed as the various psychological sub-routines required for the employment and maintenance of an earthly body – e.g. the capacities for sight, ambulation, digestion, and so on, which are required to activate a creature fitted out with eyes, feet, and bowels. (In the materialist psychology of the Stoics, they are conceived as literal pneumatic conduits following the vessels and nerves, like an octopus' tentacles.) 'Lives' are thus quasi-autonomous capacities for animating particular portions of body; they represent the soul in its most mundane aspect. But Simplicius' ascription of 'lives' to the soul is complicated by his exegesis of the lower kinds of 'soul'. For he remarks that the souls of plants are more accurately described as 'lives' than as souls (H261 / D37,4); and his view that souls of the lowest kind simply follow the determination of their bodies, as shadows follow and are determined by the opacity that cast them, suggests a curious and inconsistent materialism. Even in his unequivocally dualist account of the souls of human beings, their irrational psychological elements are standardly described as 'lives of the body', i.e. as something attributable to the body, or at most to the soul's entanglement in body, rather than to the soul's intrinsic nature.

The ultimate sources of these apparently inconsistent views on 'lives' are Plato's superficially incompatible accounts of the nature and status of the 'parts' of the soul – i.e. the tripartite soul of *Republic* 4 and the unitary soul of the *Phaedo* and *Republic* 10. The Platonists discerned various hints in the dialogues pointing to Plato's own solution to this problem: *Republic* 518 and 612 suggested that the soul is simple in its own nature, and hence that its 'irrational parts' are a by-product of its union with the body; and *Phaedo* 66, and more clearly *Timaeus* 42-3 and 77, suggested that the body itself might be a mortal living thing of some kind. The theories that the Platonists constructed to accommodate these Platonic insights, as well as embryological and other more strictly psychological data, are remarkable and complex; but since Simplicius does not elucidate his remarks on 'lives' much beyond noting that the 'living thing or body' is supplied to the rational soul by fate (H212 / D12,15-20), it is not clear to which he subscribed.[62]

Having touched on the metaphysical status of the soul, we should now inspect its behavioural repertoire. Rational souls are self-movers and the causes of motion in the bodies they govern.[63] They move themselves, and the body, through such psychic motions as desire, aversion, impulse, choice, belief and knowledge. Simplicius sometimes appears to accept the Stoic analysis of these categories, according to which they are all reducible to assents to impressions, and certainly subscribes to the view that all actions for which we may be held responsible involve assent.[64] The way in which he prefers to express this, however, is by saying that all psychic motions involve 'choice' (*hairesis*).[65] Simplicius appears to consider this a merely terminological matter; but the shift from Stoic assent to Platonist choice is probably a central development in the evolution of a more familiar medieval concept of the will.[66]

Yet Simplicius still takes it as an axiom of psychology that all desire is for the good or apparent good (H203 / D7,1, H271 / D43,25, H330 / D74,45). Accordingly, he tends to think of human error or badness as a failure of cognition rather than a perversion of the will. The general preference of embodied human souls for the lesser good of bodily preoccupation and pleasure over the greater good of contemplating God is thus not a contravention of the *sub specie boni* axiom; rather, human souls somehow forget what their good consists in, and mistake the good of the bodies for their own good (H262 / D38,35). This partial account of the origins of moral evil is far from clear or muddle-free (see below). But it aligns Simplicius with the Stoics in the rationalist tradition deriving from Plato's *Protagoras*: practical irrationality is essentially a failure of theoretical rationality, rather than a corruption in human desires or a brute perversity in the will, that makes us unable to be moved in the right way by even a clear-eyed view of the good.

Simplicius differs from the Stoics, however, in ascribing – at least in his practical ethical psychology – the irrational activities and motions of the 'mortal body' to the rational soul. Since these irrational motions are affected by factors external to the soul, they are not entirely self-determined.[67] Simplicius can thus allow both that irrational emotions are not *strictly* up to us (H199 / D4,45), and that we are responsible for them (H441 / D132,30), presumably because we are responsible for the dispositions that give rise to them.[68] Hence, he follows Aristotle in the non-Stoic view that there are degrees of responsibility, since one action can be more up-to-us than another, if it is less affected by irrational emotions; and, like Plotinus, he considers actions to be fully free only when they are the products of pure reason, unsullied by sensual inclination.[69]

The consequences of this disagreement with the Stoics are evident when we turn to Simplicius' theories of emotion and of virtue. The early Platonic tradition had criticised the Stoic view that virtue required '*apatheia*' or the eradication of emotions such as anger and fear (though the Stoics could point to Socrates in Plato's *Phaedo* as a model of what this might look like); and their view that virtue requires '*metriopatheia*' or moderated emotion that has been made tractable to reason was elaborated in Aristotle's theory of 'ethical' virtue. But Plotinus' resolution of Plato's apparent inconsistency on the nature of the soul allowed him to combine both theories by distinguishing between different grades of the virtues.[70] In Plotinus' view, Stoic *apatheia*, the life depicted in the *Phaedo*, characterises the 'cathartic' virtues of a rational soul that aims to transcend the body altogether, while Aristotelian *metriopatheia*, the life analysed in *Republic* books 1-4 and 8-9, characterises the 'political and ethical' virtues of a rational soul that is using its body to order the world. A soul that possesses only the latter kind of virtue will experience emotions as it responds to the affections of the 'mortal compound', but these emotions will be under the control of reason, and employed to make its bodily activities and interactions more efficient.[71] Plotinus' reconciliation of *apatheia* and *metriopatheia* was subsequently codified by Porphyry and elaborated by Proclus and other late Platonists.[72] Simplicius alludes to this theory (see H234 / D24,1), though since his work is directed at aspirants for the first grade of virtues, the mechanism by which he might reconcile Epictetus' inculcation of *apatheia* with his own advocacy of *metriopatheia* is rather hidden from view in the commentary.

4.4 Badness and theodicy

Simplicius' task in his comments on chapters 8 and 27 is to vindicate the claim of Plato's *Timaeus* 42d3-4, that God is not the cause of anything bad. But since he also holds that God is the cause of everything that exists, he can vindicate Plato only by defending the intuitively less plausible thesis that the bad does not exist. Simplicius employs two strategies to show that the bad does not exist. The first is to argue that alleged bads are in fact not bad, or that evil is an illusion. This strategy is most prominent in the commentary on ch. 8, and applies most successfully to the non-moral case – e.g. physical illness or bodily destruction.[73] His second strategy is to argue that bad things do not exist in the sense that they have an ontological status subordinate to existence: they do not *really* exist because they are not primary or *per se* subsistents: they have only a derivative subsistence (*parhupostasis*, H342 / D81,27). Neither strategy, however, can account for the case of human turning away from the good; but here Simplicius can plausibly argue that God is not properly speaking the cause (H338 / D79,1-H342 / D81,20). For in this case God is responsible for the production of a class of self-determining substances, human souls, whose perfection in human virtue is a great good. The existence of such a good requires the possibility of human corruption, since God could not have brought about the conditions under which human virtue can exist, without at the same time creating the conditions under which human vice could exist (or subsist). When vice does exist, however, it is the fault of those human beings who themselves choose to use their self-determination to turn downwards (H272 / D44,1).

Simplicius' theodicy is thus remarkably close to more recent elaborations of the free-will defence. He explicitly endorses the three attributes of divinity that are standardly employed in setting out the problem of evil: omniscience, omnipotence and benevolence (H380 / D102,30). And his argument is no clearer than some of its contemporary descendants about whether the occasional fall is a necessary concomitant of God's creation of self-determining creatures of this sort or a contingent one. (It looks necessary at H339 / D79,35, which threatens to implicate God in a foreseeable evil; but elsewhere it looks as if he considers it possible that human beings could have had an eternally unactualised potential to fall, which threatens the intelligibility of his explanation of actualised badness in our world; see e.g. H272 / D44,5.) Nor does Simplicius show why God's decision to create souls of this sort is not open to the critical assessments of probability that he deploys against other agents. When a human agent in pursuit of the apparent good accepts a high probability of considerable badness in exchange for a low probability of a trivial good, Simplicius condemns him: this is the means by which the vicious choices of the adulterer and thief are analysed in the theory of the commentary (H331 / D74,50). Yet, when he applies this analysis to God's choice, he is content to assert the positive balance of the good without seriously attempting to weigh the costs of corruption as his criterion of assessment demands, despite his prior recognition of the magnitude of those costs (H257 / D35,25-47).

Simplicius sets out his views on badness partly in the context of an argument in ch. 27 against the Manichees that contains a good deal of material that is original to him (in comparison with rival Platonist and Christian polemics).[74] But their philosophical basis is not new: the same lines of argument are found earlier, both in Hierocles and subsequently in Proclus.[75] Since there are many literal echoes of Proclus' arguments, this seems to indicate something beyond the rare unanimity of late Platonists on this topic. The range of Simplicius' references to discrete works of Proclus, however, suggests that he may have followed a post-Proclan treatise, perhaps by Damascius or Ammonius.[76]

4.5 Freedom and determinism

Since the apparent evils of natural decay and physical destruction are easy to dismiss as illusory, the core of the theodicy outlined above is Simplicius' attempt to show why human beings, rather than their creator, are responsible for moral evil. His views on human freedom and responsibility, however, are difficult to untangle, perhaps partly because their sources are so various. The basis of his theory seems to derive from Plotinus' reconciliation of Plato's exposition in *Laws* 10 with the Stoics' psychology of action and determinism. Plotinus distributed freedom to agents in accordance with their place in his scale of virtue (see above on the grades of virtue), so that real freedom is reserved for the One, and even ethically virtuous human action is constrained by circumstance or fate. But Simplicius' conflation in the commentary of an Aristotelian theory of deliberated choice and a Stoic theory of causal responsibility depending on assent appears to lead to confusions that are original to this work (see Section 5 below).

The nature of Simplicius' position can perhaps be illustrated briefly by comparison with a partisan sketch of what might be Augustine's temporal variant of it. In the *City of God*, the complete freedom of God is followed by the apparently indeterminist free choice of the angels, leading to the separation of the good from the fallen angels. This allows for the fall of man in Adam, which looks indeterminist but is qualified by the additional circumstances of embodiment and a temptor; the result is the current enfeebled capacity of choice of fallen humans. Humans who are saved by divine aid will eventually have the uniform freedom – currently possessed by the good angels – to choose only the good in heaven. Some points of similiarity in Simplicius are:

1. The apparently indeterminist pre-embodied choice of the less good over the good.[77]
2. The change in the nature of human choice that occurs after embodiment (including both a non-rational soul and the disappearance of the unaided ability to choose the good).[78]
3. The claim that both fallen man and confirmed angels (and the saints in heaven) have 'free' choice, although the former choose between goods or apparent goods, and the latter have no choice but the good.[79]
4. The claims that the soul is not determined by physically determining causes, while the body and hence much of human life and many actions are subject to fate or providence.[80]

The heart of Simplicius' difficulty lies in the 'diversion' or 'turning away' (*paratropē*) of the disembodied rational soul from the Intellect.[81] From a teleological perspective, this word describes a beneficial and desirable event: the human soul's fulfillment of its function as the 'bond between the things that always remain above, and the things that always remain below' (H202 / D6,45). On this score human souls are the emissaries of divinity to the sublunary material world, bringing order, beauty, and goodness to matter, since it is through the human soul's intimate interaction with bodies that the lowest level of reality is made as beautiful or good as it can be; without our activity, all would be an ugly, lifeless chaos down below.

This teleological explanation for the 'turning away' of human souls does not require corruption or a fall, or that the bringing of order to bodies should also be the bringing of evil into the world. The need to explain the origins of moral evil, however, demands a different perspective, for which Simplicius requires a second sense of 'turning away', making it the source of all subsequent vice and depravity:

> the soul keeps company with things that are being generated and perishing and are declining towards the privation of the good, and surrenders itself to them (H203 / D6,53) ... [when the soul] no longer treats [the body] as its instrument, but rather embraces it as a part of itself, or even as though it were itself, then the soul is made irrational by the body and shares affections with it. Then the soul believes that the desires of spirit and appetite are proper to it, and by being subservient to them, and finding means for getting what they desire, it becomes bad ...(H2262 / D38,20).

This second interpretation of the soul's 'turning away' raises two problems. First, it is unclear why the human soul cannot perform its teleological task without becoming corrupted, if, as Simplicius says, it has been 'graced' with powers to resist the temptations of bodies (H195 / D2,48-54). Secondly, it is unclear at which stage the corruption occurs – i.e. whether it is an unfortunate effect of excessive immersion in the material world, as the passage cited above suggests, or whether the fact of the soul's descent shows that it has already fallen prior to its incarnation. Simplicius unfortunately gives conflicting responses to these problems. Some texts emphasise human freedom and self-determination in order to exculpate God, and thereby suggest that bondage to sensory pleasure is not the inevitable price of acting as the bond between high and low: at H272/D44.15, for example, he claims that human beings can remain undiverted as long as they wish to (cf. H337 / D78,34). But elsewhere Simplicius suggests that the soul had somehow already fallen prior to incarnation (H226 / D19,42, H336 / D77,53); and in one passage he seems to claim that the very activity of engaging with matter makes the human soul incapable of maintaining its correct relation to the higher goods (H203 / D6,46).

But, on this score, Simplicius is not himself guilty of any original sins; he has either inherited incoherences already found in Plotinus, or has fallen victim on his own account to the twin temptations of the pre- and post-incarnate falls in Plato's *Phaedrus* and *Laws* 10.

5. Simplicius and Stoicism

5.1 Simplicius' knowledge of Epictetus

The opening pages of the commentary suggest that Simplicius may have read two important sources of information about Epictetus that are now lost to us. The first is a letter by Arrian describing his method of assembling the *Encheiridion*. Simplicius concluded from this letter that the *Encheiridion* was a selection by Arrian of material from his earlier compilation of speeches by Epictetus, the *Discourses* – a finding that tends to confirm the orthodox view of the authorship of these works.[82] Secondly, it seems likely that Simplicius had access to parts of Epictetus' *Discourses* that are no longer extant. For Simplicius reports that 'practically all' the material in the *Encheiridion* may be found verbatim in the *Discourses*; but since this is no longer true, it suggests that he had more of the larger work than now survives.[83] Simplicius no doubt found the anecdote that Epictetus adopted a friend's child, and employed a nurse to look after it (H406 / D116,50), from one of these sources.[84]

There is, however, some reason to doubt that Simplicius had the *Discourses* to hand as he wrote. For he never gives the impression that he is reading the longer work, either by telling us where a line from the *Encheiridion* can be found in it, or by supplying quotations or paraphrases from the context in the longer version; and there is at least one passage in the commentary where a broader familiarity with the *Discourses* would have resolved difficulties he finds in the *Encheiridion* (see H440 / D132,10 with note). A natural inference is that either Simplicius had read the *Discourses* at some earlier time and did not have it in front of him, or his information about that work comes from Arrian's letter. But since Simplicius' commentary was for beginners, it is also possible that the lack of scholarly reference reflects only the genre of his work.

5.2 Simplicius' knowledge of Stoic doctrine

Although Simplicius exhibits a fairly extensive knowledge of Stoic metaphysics in his commentary on Aristotle's *Categories*, the breadth of his reading in Stoic ethics is less manifest in his commentary on Epictetus. His comments on the soul's immortality in a brief parenthesis adverting to the Stoics' 'rather peculiar views' (H212 / D12,15), for example, suggest that he knew that some Stoics believed the soul to be perishable; but since he does not expand on his remark, it is difficult to judge how much he knew of the Stoic controversies on this issue (though here again he may have thought the details were irrelevant or unsuitable for a beginning audience). His more extended reports on 'appropriate actions' (notably in his comments on ch. 30) and the 'common conceptions' (chs 11, 26), two further subjects for which the commentary is often regarded as a useful source for Stoic doctrines, present similar difficulties.[85] Since the correct way to inculcate 'appropriate actions' had been a topic for controversy amongst Platonic commentators from at least the second century AD, it seems quite likely that Simplicius' information about Nicolaus of Damascus, and the detailed inventory of natural and prohairetic 'relations' with which he prefaces his discussion of ch. 30, are mediated by the Platonist tradition.[86] Simplicius' intriguing remarks on the articulation of our 'preconceptions' about God, and on the role and content of the 'common conceptions', however, may represent more direct evidence for the Stoic use of these notions.[87] But here again the fact that Proclus appeals to rather similar ideas in analogous contexts at least gives reason to doubt the immediacy of his knowledge, if not its authenticity.[88]

Some of Simplicius' comments about Stoicism, however, especially concerning their logic, epistemology and moral psychology, suggest a surprising lack of knowledge. A notable example is furnished by his commentary on *Encheiridion* ch. 36 (H423 / D124,15 et seq.), where he confuses conjunctions with conditionals, statements with syllogisms, and propositions with first principles (see e.g. his gloss on the Stoic term '*axiôma*' at H423 / D124,26-8). Although his mistakes here can be paralleled by other late authors on logic, and his version of the lemma differs from ours in ways that are related to his misguided interpretation, it appears that his knowledge of Stoic logic was very slim indeed.[89]

A similar conclusion seems inevitable concerning his understanding of Stoic epistemology. In his comments on *Encheiridion* ch. 45, for instance, Simplicius *equates* 'receiving' a cataleptic impression with 'grasping' and 'perceiving' something, although the purpose of the chapter is to *contrast* the cataleptic impressions one 'receives' with the non-cataleptic impressions one assents to, and the Stoics take 'grasping' and 'perceiving' something to entail assent to a cataleptic impression (H435-6 / D129,44-130,20). Simplicius' grasp of the Stoic conception of assent is put further in question elsewhere when he describes assent as if it were a speech-act, or a public, observable act of affirmation, rather than a private act that the Stoics thought was sometimes tacit or even obscure to its agent or subject.[90] The allusive comment at H216 / D14,3 equating assents with the 'vital extension' of the soul may, however, hint at a more sophisticated understanding of the psychological role of assent (see Section 4 above). For here Simplicius applies the Stoic term to the fundamental form of psychodynamic activity – i.e. the soul's going for something, whether by taking an impression to be true or pursuing an object as desirable. His view that every desire (*orexis*) is an extension of this sort (H198 / D4,25) is thus parallel to, and perhaps identical with, the Stoics' doctrine that desire and impulse are kinds of assent.[91]

Simplicius' understanding of Stoic moral psychology is also questionable. In a puzzling passage starting at H198 / D4,30, Simplicius tries to make sense of the false Stoic view he takes to be asserted in

Encheiridion 1, that impulse comes before desire and aversion.[92] But his question is misconceived, since none of the Stoics believed that impulse and desire were the names for sequential stages in a single psychological process. The early Stoa used 'impulse' (*hormê*) as the name for the genus of psychological motions to which desire, aversion and the emotions belong, so that anyone who is having a desire is *eo ipso* having an impulse; and Epictetus, for reasons that are obscure, observed a differ-ent terminological convention, so that 'impulse' is used in his works for what the early Stoa had called 'selection', which was a further and distinct species of the original genus of 'impulse' in the earlier schema.[93] Accordingly, Epictetus thinks of impulse – i.e. the 'selection' of indiffer-ents in the early Stoic schema – as what one should employ *in place of* desire, which is directed at goods; but here again neither precedes the other in a single psychological process. Simplicius' attempt to resolve the anomaly at H199 / D4,38 by suggesting that the Stoics 'saw the motions of the soul that are prior to desire and aversion', is perhaps a distant reminiscence of the Stoic doctrine of *propatheiai* – i.e. of psycho-logical motions or events that do precede assent and so do precede impulse, selection or desire.[94] But if this was his intention, it reflects a further misunderstanding about assent, since when Epictetus enjoins us to use 'impulse and counter-impulse', he must be referring to psycho-logical events that lead directly to action, and hence are assents, since we are supposed to do everything that ordinary life requires us to do merely by using them.

Underlying this apparently terminological confusion is the central point of difference between Simplicius and the Stoics: their disagree-ment over the sources of psychological events. The Stoics rejected the Platonic (and so Platonist) notion that rational adults have irreducibly 'irrational' desires or emotions that are ineliminable even in the state of virtue, and so insisted on the complete eradication of all emotions (*apatheia*) in their 'sage'. But Simplicius, following the Platonic tradi-tion elaborated by Aristotle, accepted the usefulness and necessity of moderated emotions (*metriopatheia*) for a politically virtuous life. The distance between his view and the Stoics' on this issue can be gauged from his comment at H337 / D78,20, that no one, 'particularly of the purer sort, would endure to spend so much time eating and excreting like an irrational animal if he weren't provoked to it by irrational desire'. Thus, on his view, no matter how pure one is, one needs to employ irrational desires to motivate even the activities that maintain one in an embodied state: incarnation requires irrational desire.[95] The Stoics, however, denied that a virtuous person could ever be 'provoked by irrational desire'; what motivates the sage to eat is not, in their view, irrational desire, but the rational judgement that it is reasonable to eat. The gulf between these views is palpable; but whether Simplicius was aware of this crucial difference between the psychological theory he expounded in the commentary and the theory presupposed by the text he chose to comment on, is less clear.

5.3 Prohairesis

Simplicius' understanding of prohairesis is of particular interest in regard to his psychology and ethics. This term first became part of the philosophical vocabulary in Aristotle's ethical treatises, where it means, roughly, 'settled choice' or 'decision'. For Aristotle, it is the outcome of an antecedent process of deliberation, in which one considers the best means to attain a certain end, and it eventuates in action without the need for any further psychological steps on the agent's part (when the particular means to be employed are evident to perception). Prohairesis is of central importance in Aristotle's ethics as the cause of the actions for which we are most fully responsible, and the distillation of our antecedent deliberation, shaped by the ends we value, the means we are willing to employ, and the practical wisdom with which we accommodate each to each. Thus Aristotle calls virtue a 'prohairetic disposition' (*EN* 2.6), because it is the state of one's soul – with respect to one's knowledge and emotions – through which one makes the concrete choices and decisions that add up to a virtuous life.

The word 'prohairesis' plays no special role in the early Stoa, and there is no reason to think that the Stoics were influenced by Aristotle's use of it.[96] The central influence on Stoic moral psychology was rather the cognitivist theory of emotion in Plato's early dialogues, which Aristotle had rejected in *EN* 7.2. As a result, the basic notion in Stoic psychology is 'impulse' (*hormê*), which covers 'irrational' emotions – i.e. false practical beliefs, such as fear, greed and lust – no less than the carefully deliberated rational desires of the virtuous person. The differences between Aristotelian prohairesis and Stoic impulse at this level of psychological theory are clear: Aristotle does not consider fear, greed and lust to be instances of prohairesis; and the Stoics make no particular connection between impulse and deliberation.[97]

There is, however, considerable overlap between the roles of impulse in the Stoa and of prohairesis in Aristotle. For both Aristotelian prohairesis and Stoic impulse are thought of as the psychological event that correlates to and underlies the fully voluntary actions of a rational agent, because the agent's actions stem directly from prohairesis or impulse, and these in turn emerge from and express his or her character as an agent in the world. Hence, just as Aristotle said that virtue is a certain prohairetic disposition, one might expect the Stoics to have said that virtue is a certain impulsive disposition – as they more or less did. But since their cognitivist view that impulses are occurrent evaluative *beliefs* implies that virtuous impulses just are perfected occurrent beliefs, the Stoics defined virtue not as an impulsive disposition, but as (dispositional) knowledge of value. Thus, while Aristotelian *prohairesis* and Stoic impulse are the products of incompatible theories of emotion and desire, they play analogous abstract or meta-ethical roles in connecting up character, virtue, action and responsibility.

Epictetus' frequent use of prohairesis was probably an innovation in the Stoa, and is clearly different from, and perhaps completely unconnected to, Aristotle's. Its technical meaning is something like 'general disposition to assent', where this includes our dispositions to assent to ordinary, non-ethical impressions as well as the dispositions to assent to evaluative impressions that constitute the virtue of the sage and the vice of the rest of us. But since our dispositions to assent are equivalent to our dispositional beliefs, an agent's prohairesis also signifies the totality of his beliefs – i.e. his 'self' or (the governing part of his) rational soul. It seems that Epictetus arrived at this conception of prohairesis by focusing his ethical teaching on the correct 'use of impressions' rather than the ultimate goals of virtue or happiness. The process of developing the correct use of impressions depends entirely on one's habits of, or dispositions towards, assent and suspension of judgement: one starts off with false beliefs about value, but gradually learns to suspend judgement about them. But instead of taking this change as progress toward virtue, Epictetus invited his students to view it as a change in their pattern of assents. One advantage of this description is that it does not make any reference to vice or virtue, which are not useful measures of their progress in the employment of impressions, since students will be equally vicious throughout their training.[98] Even in the ideal case, when the training is completed, it is still possible to understand the change from virtue to vice entirely in terms of the patterns of assent. For even here the terminus is reached precisely when the student's dispositions to assent become fixed and harden into a psychic disposition that is incompatible with assenting to any non-cataleptic impression or any impulse that is not virtuous. Accordingly, Epictetus de-emphasised the distinction between virtue and vice, and found a term that applied equally to the vice of the vicious, and to the virtue of the virtuous, when both were considered as dispositions to assent to impressions: 'prohairesis'. Using this term allowed him to stress the centrality of having the right beliefs – i.e. the right dispositions to assent to and suspend judgement about impressions – and thus keep students focused on the concrete task of using each of their impressions correctly.

With these sketches of their views in mind, we can now try to clarify the relation between Aristotelian and Epictetan prohairesis. An Aristotelian prohairesis is an event, a decision made at a particular time, rather than a disposition (although the agent's virtue or vice is the disposition from which an agent's individual acts of prohairesis arise). As the outcome of the agent's deliberation, it reflects the agent's non-evaluative beliefs, practical wisdom, and other cognitive capacities, although Aristotle is more concerned with the way that the prohairesis reflects the habituation and shaping of the agent's irrational desires. An

Epictetan prohairesis, however, is a disposition – or the set of the agent's dispositions – to assent to impressions: it *is* the agent's beliefs, or virtue or vice, or (the governing part of his or her) soul. Since every impulse is a belief, Epictetan prohairesis includes the agent's disposition to have Aristotelian prohaireseis. An agent's Epictetan prohairesis will give rise to the Aristotelian prohairesis to perform some deliberated action, but it will also give rise to rage, self-pity, true or mistaken perceptual or intellectual beliefs, etc., since they all involve the agent's assent to impressions.

Simplicius clearly inherited the Aristotelian theory of prohairesis.[99] He was also the heir to the Epictetan theory, at least in his commentary on the *Encheiridion*. Unfortunately, he appears not to betray any awareness that the use of this word in Epictetus raises difficulties or requires comment by someone who also employs the Aristotelian notion.[100] Perhaps he had a theory about the relation between the two senses of the word something like the one we sketch above; and perhaps this theory, too, was judged too complicated, or insufficiently relevant, for the uses of beginners. But it is difficult not to suspect that he was unaware of the differences. The most charitable conclusion that we can draw is this: when the subject is narrowly ethical, so that the Epictetan prohairesis that is of interest is a disposition to assent to impulsive impressions about serious affairs requiring deliberation, the distinction between the two sense of prohairesis narrows to the distinction between potential (Epictetan disposition) and actual (Aristotelian choice), which to a Peripatetic is the nearest approach to unity that two distinct things can make.[101]

(Since the word is at once important and problematic, it is left untranslated in this translation. We hope that others will make a detailed study of Simplicius' use of prohairesis, and either substantiate or supersede the tentative suggestions made here.)

As with the *Discourses*, so too with the remainder of the Stoic corpus: Simplicius does not cite Stoic views taken from other sources that might elucidate Epictetus.[102] It is thus hard to believe that Simplicius had any Stoic text open in front of him other than the *Encheiridion* itself. Is Simplicius then of no use for understanding the Stoics? Perhaps his theological outlook provides a salutary corrective to the view of the Stoics that one tends to derive from more secular presentations such as that in Cicero's *de Finibus*, which is designed to appeal to eclectics, and so emphasises the conventional and uncontroversial aspects of the system. Simplicius provides a rather different perspective, from which the Stoics are seen as theistic naturalists, another link between the Socrates of the *Phaedo* and the Platonists. If Simplicius perhaps misunderstands, and certainly misinterprets, some central views of Epictetus and of the earlier Stoics, his portrayal of Stoic ethics remains of considerable historical interest.

6. Remarks on the translation

Our translation follows, with a few exceptions noted below, the excellent text of Hadot's *editio maior*. Anyone who has used Schweighäuser's 1799 edition (or Dübner's reprinting of it) – the text available before 1996 – will appreciate how great an improvement Professor Hadot has made in the state of Simplician scholarship. Since we had already drafted roughly half of our translation from the Dübner text before Hadot's became available, we are acutely aware that the new manuscripts she used have restored words, phrases, and whole lines to the text in several dozen places. Her new witnesses also bore out many of the brilliant conjectures of Schweighäuser (whose commentary on Simplicius remains an invaluable tool). For ease of reference, however, particularly in connexion with electronic searches, we have retained the page and line numbers of Dübner's edition in our translation, as well as Hadot's page numbers.

The translation printed below diverges from all texts of Simplicius in one glaring respect: before each lemma and its accompanying commentary, we have inserted translations of the entire chapter of the *Encheiridion* on which Simplicius is commenting, along with the more meagre lemmata that appear in the manuscripts. The utility of having before one's eyes the entire text that Simplicius himself is referring to will be evident to the reader. It brings out forcibly the degree to which his vocabulary and turns of phrase are influenced by Epictetus: long stretches of the commentary may be seen to echo key phrases from the *Encheiridion* that would not appear in a translation of the lemma alone, or might be hidden from the reader who consulted a separate translation of Epictetus. Our text for the *Encheiridion* was Schenkl's edition; where it disagrees with the lemma printed in the manuscripts of Simplicius we have noted this and sometimes discussed it.

Our method of working was thoroughly collaborative. Each of us produced a first draft of roughly half the *Commentary*; after a first revision by the collaborator, a second revision fixed a common vocabulary and level of diction and the construal of particularly recalcitrant stretches. This draft was sent to nine anonymous readers by Richard Sorabji, and the readers' often extremely detailed comments were incorporated into a fourth draft. The final version was revised again for consistency and smoothness. Thus neither of us can now say which parts we worked on at any stage, though every part has been worked over several times by each.

Our aim has been to produce a work that reads like contemporary philosophical English and reproduces the philosophical content of the *Commentary* with as little distraction as possible. Since few things are as distracting as the constant awareness that one is reading a translation, we saw it as our job, as translators hoping to bring Simplicius to a wider audience, not to represent his Greek, but rather to represent his sense, and to deliver it to the reader in an easy, smooth, and uninterrupted flow. (An extremely faithful representation of Simplicius' Greek may be found in Hadot 1996.) Accordingly, we have not hesitated to divide up straggling sentences, to reorder their parts if doing so produced in English the logical sequence and rhetorical emphasis that we found in the Greek, or to put a passive construction into the active and supply a person for an impersonal Greek verb if it read more smoothly. Some ambiguities in the Greek are not preserved in our text; some passages which we first translated with trepidation now present an innocent appearance to the unwary; and anyone who delves into the original text will find that we made questionable or controversial interpretive choices. But we hope that the result is throughout a translation rather than a paraphrase; where we have diverged from the literal, our principle has been to make the philosophical content as transparent as possible.[103]

So much by way of apologia. Some of any translator's choices inevitably prompt reflection; a handful of terms forever evade happy translations, but offer equally strong (or weak) alternatives. Among the latter in this translation are the Greek word *eurrhoia* and its cognates. Etymologically, this clearly means 'a good flow', but Zeno and Epictetus used it to describe the condition of happiness enjoyed by the Stoic sage, and Simplicius sometimes used it in this sense as well. So a translation guided by etymology leads to the claim that 'virtue produces a good flow', thus promising regular elimination as the reward for good conduct. But a translation guided by the concept's philosophical application yields 'happiness', which conflicts with a better candidate for that English term – *eudaimonia* – and disguises the fact that *eurrhoia* was a characteristically Stoic technical term, where 'happiness' is not. We settled dyspeptically for the second set of defects.

A more significant set of interpretive questions is exemplified by the word *hamartia*. In Christian theological texts, this word is naturally translated as 'sin'; but in most pre-Christian contexts it means something closer to 'error', since it often has no connotations of culpability, much less the particular cluster of doctrines suggested by the word 'sin'. Thus it seems best to avoid 'sin' altogether in pagan philosophical contexts, and stick with 'error'. However, Simplicius presents a special problem in this regard for two reasons. First, since he lived in a world that was increasingly Christianised, for much of his audience the central meaning of *hamartia* was probably closer to the Christian 'sin' than the rationalist 'error'. Secondly, Simplicius himself has a view of the soul's choice of good and bad that seems to presuppose some of the peculiar doctrines that underwrite a notion of 'sin'. So when one reads his description of the soul's fall from God through its willful choice of sensual pleasures, the word 'sin' does not appear out of place. Nevertheless, we decided to err on the side of caution, by avoiding 'sin', in deference to the non-Christian context.

Finally, there is the case of *prohairesis*. As noted above, it proved impossible to choose an English word that would usefully represent this word; so we did not.

Notes

1. In the Introduction and Notes we refer to the text of Simplicius' commentary by means of a double numeration, for reasons explained in Section 6 below. A reference such as '(H357 / D89,27)' directs the reader to the text that appears on p. 89, line 27, of Dübner's reprinting of Schweighäuser's text, which is located on p. 357 of Hadot's 1996 text. Hadot's edition also includes Dübner's line numbers, so that readers who have only the Hadot text will still find the Dübner line indicated on the Hadot page given.

2. The principal external source for Simplicius' life is Agathias *Hist.* 2.30-1, on which see below. His Cilician origin is noted by Agathias at 2.30; his study with Ammonius in Alexandria is evident from his citations of Ammonius in his *Physics* commentary, and made explicit in his *de Caelo* commentary at p. 462.20 Heiberg; his relations to Damascius are evident from his comments in his *in Phys.*, Suida II 3.28 (*sub* Damascius), and Agathias 2.30-1.

3. Since his *Physics* commentary names Damascius (18 times) and criticises him gently, it presumably post-dates the latter's death, which is placed after AD 538 by a dated epigraph from Hims in Syria ascribed to him in the *Palatine Anthology* (VII.553); see Hoffman 1994 section 10.

4. Against Simplicius' authorship of the *de Anima* commentary, see C. Steel in Huby and Steel 1997, 105-40; more or less in favour, see Hadot in Sorabji 1990, 290-4 (= Hadot 1987, 223-7), which slightly corrects Hadot 1978, 193-202; agnosticism is perhaps appropriate until the work – and its relation to Simplicius' other works, such as this one – has been studied in more detail, as Blumenthal concluded in his 2000, 1-6. There may be traces of Simplicius' commentary on the *Metaphysics* in a few late scholia, as Hadot argues in her 1987, 225-45.

5. Two cross-references, however, may suggest a work on the *Phaedo*, or parts of it concerning the immortality of the soul, as Hadot 1996, 6 n. 17 argues – cf. *in de Caelo* 369,4-6 and *in Ench.* H212 / D12,15. But even if these references are to a work by Simplicius rather than one of his teachers, they may well come from his commentary on Iamblichus' work on the Pythagorean sect.

6. Simplicius is very enthusiastic about friendship (H357 / D89,27), and even recounts his own experience of the value of friends who looked after his family when he was away (H354 / D87,40), though unfortunately he does not tell us where he or they were.

7. See e.g. Cameron 1969 and Glucker 1978, 322-9. On Khusrau, see Tardieu 1994.

8. On the controversial final clause, we follow Foulkes 1992, who argues that it demands only that the philosophers should be able to practise their 'religion' privately (*contra* Hadot 1987, 7-10 = Sorabji 1990, 278-90).

9. Tardieu 1986, 1987, 1990, 1994, followed with less or greater enthusiasm by Hadot 1987, 1990 (see previous note); 1996, 28-50; 2001, xiii-xxxiii.

10. Tardieu 1986, 24-5 n. 106; Hadot 1987, 17-21; 1990, 286-9; 1996; 2001, xiv-xviii.

11. Tardieu's arguments are usefully summarised by Theil's *Simplikios* 1999 and in Hadot's various accounts.

12. Simplicius may have met his Manichee source at any time and anywhere on any of his travels. Augustine's report of his long wait for the Manichee 'bishop' Faustus in *Conf.* 5.10-12 suggests that such figures were or might be peripatetic (though this is evidence from the West and 100 years earlier).

13. Tardieu 1987, 24-5 and Hadot e.g. 2001, xiv-xviii note that Simplicius' anti-Manichee predecessors – such as Alexander of Lycopolis and Titus of Bostra (both in Migne's *PG* 18) – as well as the anti-dualist arguments of Plotinus *Enn.* 2.9.10 – though not obviously of Proclus *de Malorum Subsistentia* – seem to have had in mind specific audiences affected by Manichees or dualists. But Simplicius' commentary does not seem to have any particularly situated audience in mind, unlike these figures, whose audiences are known, unless one presupposes that he was writing in Harran. And if the expected audience were Harranian, one might expect that Simplicius' comments on the life of a would-be philosopher would reflect it in other ways too.

14. See Van Riet 1991 and Foulkes 1992.

15. Damascius' epigraph (n. 3 above) was found in Hims, not in Harran; there is no reason not to suppose that he went home to Damascus, at least temporarily.

16. Our historical grasp of the intellectual life of this period is just as likely to be confounded by surprising new epigraphic evidence as our predecessors' understanding of Epicureanism was by the new evidence from Diogenes of Oenoanda; the recent discoveries concerning Empedocles and Posidippus suggest that there may be more to come even on paper or papyrus.

17. See Boter 1999 for an excellent new edition of the *Encheiridion* and its three Christian versions. Boter gives an extremely valuable conspectus of the ancient authors who cited or paraphrased the *Ench.* on his pp. 432-3.

18. See Boter 1999. Hierocles alludes to *Ench.* 9 and 11 at *in Carm. Aur.* 11, pp. 42 and 44 Koehler; Proclus to *Ench.* 5a and 5b at *in Alc.* pp. 288.8-10 and 287.3-9 Segonds; and Olympiodorus to *Ench.* 1.5 at *in Phd.* 6.2, p. 99 Westerink, and to *Ench.* 1-2, 3, 5b, 17, 21 (and 11), 30 (and 43), 33, and 47 at *in Gorg.* pp. 198, 144, 131, 97, 252, 130, 96 (and 98), and 99 Westerink, respectively. (Boter also detects a probable allusion to *Ench.* 17 at Plotinus *Enn.* 3.2.17 lines 18-19.)

19. The two uses not marked as Epictetan are of *Ench.* 1-2 at p. 198,9-18 and *Ench.* 30 and 43 at p. 130,17-21; the latter is remarkable, since a reader unfamiliar with Epictetus would infer from the context in Olympiodorus that it is a citation from Plato's *Laws*.

20. See the excellent introduction to Westerink 1990, and Hadot 1978 ch. 7.5 (= Hadot 2001, ch. 3.5).

21. Cf. H212 / D12,13-15. Simplicius does not point out other Stoic errors explicitly in the commentary, though he mentions minor points of interpretation, e.g. at H204-5 / D7,53-8,6 on the scope of Epictetus' division of existent things into those up to us and those not up to us. He never alludes, for instance, to the Stoics' determinism, or allows that their psychological theory is inconsistent with his Aristotelian and Plotinian framework (see Sections 4-5 below).

22. Frr. 45-6 Athanassiadi = 106 and 109 Zintzen.

23. The first alternative is perhaps the view of Hadot 1978, ch. 7.1-4 (= Hadot 2001, ch. 3.1-4, cf. ch. 4). In favour of the second alternative is Simplicius' status as the most prominent exponent of the 'harmony' of Plato and Aristotle, and his implausibly Platonist interpretations of the Presocratics.

24. Simplicius argues that *Ench.* 21 and 22 form a single unit because ch. 22 explains how to deal with the problems of ch. 21; he suggests supplying an 'and' to link the two syntactically (H300 / D58,14). He argues in the same fashion for chs 5a and 5b (in Boter's edition), suggesting an additional 'for' in that case (H246 / D30,6).

25. Simplicius presumably took ch. 22 as his dividing point since it is there that the student begins to worry about being mocked for being a philosopher. If so, he probably misinterprets Epictetus' notion of a 'philosopher' – i.e. someone interested in ethical progress – for his own – i.e. someone sufficiently interested in philosophy to attend a pagan philosophical 'school' or 'circle'. But his division is not the pure fancy Hadot 1996, ch. 6 takes it to be (and requires less special pleading than her favoured model for the partition of the *Ench.*).

26. Simplicius notes various differences between the two groups. Most important is that the beginner should not attempt to select external things even as incidental to their progress, while the (ordinary) philosopher may do so (H233 / D22,34, H254 / D34,2-8). He also explains and contrasts *Ench.* chs 23 and 24 with chs 13 and 12 respectively, on the grounds that the former are appropriate for beginners, and the latter for intermediate students (H303-4 / D60.34-49, H306 / D61.15-27).

27. At H346 / D83,15 Simplicius discerns four categories of 'appropriate action': [a] relating to other people; [b] to our superiors; [c] to our inferiors; and [d] to ourselves. He treats [a] in his comments on ch. 30, [b] in 31 (H361 / D91,24-6), [d] in 33 (H397 / D111,46), and takes ch. 32 on divination to be a category intermediate between [b] and [d] (H392 / D109,7-11); he may have considered divination to concern [c], since it is consulted for advice on external things. Simplicius links the remaining chs to justice at H425 / D125,21 (ch. 36), H426 / D125,41 (ch. 37), H429 / D127,10 (ch. 39), and H436 / D130,20 (ch. 45); and at H431 / D127,48 he notes that ch. 41 explains 'the just distribution of our appropriate actions' with respect to bodily functions, thus showing that he considers all of chs 30-47 to be concerned with both (Stoic) 'appropriate actions' and (Aristotelian, specific) 'justice'.

28. See H194 / D2,15-17, H193 / D1,30-5, and H194 / D2,19-29, respectively.

29. Simplicius praises Epictetus' concision at H253 / D33,32, H297 / D56,33, H 367 / D95,19, H397 / D112,10, and H398 / D112,34; cf. Epictetus' own advice, mentioned at H451 / D137,11-17.

30. See e.g. H254-5 / D34,9-35 on ch. 7, and H293-4 / D54,46-55.4 on chs 15 and 17.

31. See e.g. H236-7 / D24,55-25,45 on ch. 3, H241 / D27,25-43 on ch. 4, H275 / D45,34-45 on ch. 9, H280 / D48,11-15 on ch. 11, and H319 / D68,9-18 on ch. 25.

32. Simplicius comments on Socrates at H243-4 / D28,14 (on ch. 5); H395 / D110,48 (on ch. 32); H397 / D112,5, H405 / D115,47, H415-17 / D120,45-121,50 (all on ch. 33); H438 / D131,6 (on ch. 46); H449 / D136,8 (on ch. 51); H453 / D137,48-138,14 (on ch. 53).

33. See H227-8 / D20,2-46 on 'harsh impressions', H226 / D19,38-46 on 'Remember', and H239-40 / D26,9-27.24 on 'prior consideration'.

34. See H264 / D39,44, H305 / D60,51, H367 / D95,17 and H406 / D116,48.

35. The Stoics seem to have rejected Aristotle's theoretical emphasis on the value of friendship for philosophical and moral progress, in favour of the older Socratic and Platonic model of an erotic and unequal relation between a mature lover and a naive beloved; see *SVF* 3.625-35 and 716-26. A familiar modern criticism of Epictetus' (and Seneca's) universalist conception of personal ethical progress is that it is apolitical or even reactionary; something of this sort can perhaps be gleaned from the charges levelled by Plutarch against the early Stoics in *St. Rep.* chs 5-6.

36. Simplicius explains his motives for this excursus at H199 / D4,52-5,3, H204-5 / D7,50-8,16, and H217 / D14,54-15,5.

37. See H367 / D95,17, H368 / D95,47, H379 / D101,38-46 and H391 / D108,38-45.

38. Since Simplicius ties his own profit from the study of Epictetus to the 'tyrannical circumstances' in which he wrote in the second passage (H454 / D138,15-21), it seems plausible to interpret both as intimating his own need to confirm the priority of 'internal freedom' over external circumstances. Neither passage suggests that the practice of writing commentaries, or this commentary in particular, was seen by Simplicius as a 'spiritual exercise' as such (*contra* Hadot 1978; 1996): as Epictetus points out (chs 49, 52), what matters for moral improvement is not interpreting texts but putting them into action.

39. Two examples that give the flavour of Simplicius' interpretative methods are lemma ix on ch. 4 and lemma lxvi on ch. 48. The former goes through stages (i), (ii), (v) – though the formal argument for ch. 4 is actually given in ch. 5, Simplicius thinks –, (vi) and (iv); the latter progresses through stages (i), (ii), (v), (iv), (vii), and terminates at (iii).

40. See e.g. the passages mentioned in nn. 25-7 above.

41. The range of references that the readers are expected to be familiar with does not seem very broad; the most frequent references of this kind are to Euripides' *Medea* (H225 / D18,49, H247 / D30,37, H252 / D33,20) and Demosthenes (H239-40 / D26,1-49, H444 / D134,1).

42. See e.g. his comments on the balance of Epictetus' division of existent things (H204-5 / D7,50-8,6), his note on the contribution of the soul towards gaining external things (H218 / D15,26), and his reconstructions of Epictetus' argument about the nature of the bad in ch. 27 (H342-4 / D81,19-82,19).

43. Notable examples are Simplicius' scholastic divisions of people into 'fortunate' / 'of good fortune' and 'unfortunate' / 'ill-fortuned' in lemma vii on ch. 2, and of types of things people enjoy in lemma viii on ch. 3, etc. The acme of scholasticism in the work is his division of 'relations' at H346-8 / D83,30-84,37.

44. As Sedley 1999, 134-40 notes, the Platonist commentators had a long tradition of attacking the Stoics for their dull presentation of 'appropriate actions' via rules rather than dramatically as Plato represented them in his dialogues. They do not seem to have noticed the context of their criticisms in their own works.

45. H199 / D4,50-H217 / D15,1 (on ch. 1) and H367 / D95,10-H392 / D109,1 (on ch. 31).

46. One controversy that now seems happily dead concerned the alleged distinction between 'Alexandrian' Platonism, supposedly exhibited in Simplicius' *in Ench.* and Hierocles' *in Carmen Aureum*, and the 'Athenian' Platonism of e.g. Proclus' commentaries and *ET*. Hadot 1978 and 1982 has shown that this distinction, presented in Praechter 1927, rests on a misunderstanding of the genre of these introductory works, as well as misapprehensions about the relative simplicity of their doctrines.

47. See H376 / D99,34-49 and the caveats at H378 / D101,17-28, discussed below.

48. On angelic and daimonic souls, see H270 / D42,53, H276 / D45,55, H340 / D80,7. The passages containing the hierarchy of beings are set out in tabular form in Hadot 1978, 168-73.

49. H333 / D76,16

50. For simplicity, see *Parmenides* 157c and Plotinus *Enn.* 6.9.1, 5.6.3, Proclus *ET* 1 and *Th. Pl.* 2.1. For motion, see *Laws* 894b-895b, and Aristotle's *Phys.* 8.5, Proclus *ET* 14, *El. Phys.* 2.19, and *in Tim.* 3.9. For cause, see *Philebus* 27b, Plotinus *Enn.* 5.4.1, 5.5.3, Proclus *ET* 7, and *in Tim.* 1.259. (See Dodds' edition of Proclus' *ET* ad loc. for these and further references.)

51. See H378 / D101,27, *contra* Hadot 1978, 62-5.

52. See e.g. Proclus, *ET* 64, though the instance itself could be multiplied.

53. Specifically, he gives human souls their subsistence (H271 / D43,35), and hence like one's parents, God is the cause of our subsistence and goodness (H351 / D86,19).

54. God's pervasive control of the universe is expounded with reference to human beings in various Epictetan similes: he is pilot of the universe (H253 / D33,40, H254 / D34,16); director of the play we are in (H294 / D55,1), and so on.

55. The distinction between providence and fate is central in both so-called 'Middle' and 'Neo' Platonist accounts of freedom and determinism (though it is not observed in Alcinous) – see e.g. ps-Plutarch *de Fato* 572-573. Apuleius *de Platone* 1.12 and Nemesius *de Natura Hominis* 36-7, as well as Plotinus *Enn.* 3.3.5 and Proclus *de Providentia* 13.

56. God wants the human soul to see the truth for itself (H395 / D110,50), and become virtuous 'not through fear but by choice' (H264 / D39,30).

57. In the latter passage (H378 / D101,30), however, Simplicius resists criticisms that might tend towards advocating a method of negative theology.

58. The final prayer seems to allude to the three kinds of virtue that Simplicius mentions elsewhere in the commentary (e.g. H195 / D2,35): first he prays for purification from the body, so as to acquire ethical and political virtue; second he prays for the correction of his reason so that he can acquire cathartic virtue; third, he prays for the complete removal of the 'mist' before his psychic eyes so that he can acquire theoretical virtue. Note that the *Iliad* quotation in the third prayer comes from a prayer to Athena, the goddess of wisdom, i.e. the goddess who controls the philosophical path to wisdom: there is no reference to theurgical *virtues* here or elsewhere in the commentary (despite the mention of theurgic practices at H364-6 / D93,30-94,33).

59. Simplicius uses the terminology of 'divine grace' only at H195 / D2,51; like Plotinus and Augustine, he favours the language of 'illumination' instead – see the passage cited above, and H354 / D88,2-8, on the power of friendship. (The exactness of the parallel in the latter passage makes it clear that Simplicius is not interested in highlighting theurgy.) For Platonist theories of 'grace', see Plotinus *Enn.* 5.5.8 and Augustine *CD* 10.29 on Porphyry's recognition of 'grace', and the comments of Smith 1974, 102-21.

60. Since the *First Alcibiades* was usually the first Platonic dialogue students were given to read (cf. *Anon. Prol.* 26), Simplicius' assumption that his students have not yet read it (H196 / D3,13) is a good indication of their status as absolute beginners.

61. The conception of the 'real' self as a rational soul also goes some way towards explaining the attraction of a Stoic text like the *Encheiridion* for Platonists like Simplicius, since the Stoics thought that there was no more to an adult human soul than 'reason'.

62. See e.g. Plotinus *Enn.* 4.3-4, Porphyry *ad Gaurum*, and Smith 1974. The Platonists' various theories of the soul's 'astral body' or bodies – see e.g. Proclus *ET* 198, 206-11, and Smith 1974, appendix 2 – are designed to accommodate some of these insights. Another route was the theory that the soul is a 'double entelechy' in e.g. ps-Simplicius *Commentary on the de Anima* – see Blumenthal 1996, chs 7-8 and Steel in Huby and Steel 1997, 117-18.

63. See e.g. H215 / D13,50, H271 / D43,37, H336 / D78,5, H372 / D98,5.

64. At H216 / D14,5 he equates assent with 'vital extension', a phrase common in Damascius; see Section 5 below.

65. Simplicius construes choice as the genus of the other psychological motions through such phrases as 'our desires or aversions, or in general our choices', e.g. at H206 / D8,.38, or H208 / D9,41. For choice as the mechanism for responsibilty or 'what is up to us', see e.g. H338 / D78,52.

66. See Bobzien 1998, 396-412.

67. See H199 / D4,40-52 and H260-1 / D37,32-38,6 on animals.

68. More precisely, we are responsible for the dispositions of ourselves or rational souls that give rise to our false beliefs that the motions of the 'mortal animal' are our own – see e.g. H261-2 / D38,6-44. Simplicius' basic strategy for vindicating responsibility follows Aristotle in *NE* 3.1-5.

69. See H204 / D7,20, and Simplicius' remarks on the higher kinds of being than the rational soul, at H202 / D6,30-40 and H211 / D11,42.

70. See Plotinus *Enn.* 1.2, and Dillon 1990.

71. Plotinus' view that the 'cathartic' person *also* has the ethical virtues, and thus can combine *apatheia* and *metriopatheia*, is problematic. But this is not a problem Simplicius deals with, since his commentary is only directed at aspirants for the first grade of virtues.

72. Porphyry *Sent.* 32, Proclus *Vita Marini* 3-22; see Schissel von Fleschenberg 1929.

73. See H258/D36.25-H260/D37.30 & H334/D76.30-H335/D77.28.

74. On Simplicius' report on Manichee cosmology, see Hadot 1996.

75. See e.g. Proclus *de Decem Dubitationibus* 5.26-32, *de Malorum Subsistentia* 2.11-4.57, *de Providentia* 2.3, 4.10, 4.24, 6.35, and *in Tim.* 1.373.22-376.15 – cf. Hierocles *de Providentia* at Photius *Bibliotheca* cod. 251, 460.b.22-466.b.24. Some of the twenty or thirty exact parallels between Simplicius and Proclus on this topic are specified in the notes.

76. See previous note; Hadot 1996, 88-102 and 2001, lviii argue for Damascius.

77. See H336 / D77,53 and the remarks below on Simplicius' conflicting accounts of the fall of rational souls.

78. See H214 / D13,10, where Simplicius explains our general dispositions or characters as the result of the choices of our previous lives, and hence as 'up to us' only over the course of more than one incarnation.

79. For the uniform choice of the goods-in-themselves and angelic souls, see H202 / D6,30-40, H211 / D11,42.

80. See H212 / D12,20, H215 / D13,25 (cf. H261 / D37,40).

81. See H270 / D43, 1, H332 / D75,44, H333 / D76,14, H340 / D80,6 et seq.

82. Dobbin 1998, xx-xxii argues that Arrian did not transcribe speeches given orally by Epictetus, as the standard view has it; rather, Epictetus wrote the *Discourses* himself, as a literary work, and fathered their composition on Arrian. The veracity of Simplicius' report of the dedicatory letter is supported by Gellius *NA* 1.2.6 and 19.1.14, which rely on the evidence of Epictetus' contemporaries.

83. The extant books of the *Discourses* provide more or less direct parallels for less than half of the chapters of the *Encheiridion*; see Boter 1999, xiii. Evidence that the *Discourses* were once more extensive is supplied by Aulus Gellius, who refers to 'the fifth book of Epictetus' *Dialexeis*' at *NA* 19.1.14.

84. Simplicius gives further information on Epictetus' life at H274 / D44,53-4 (he was lame); H275 / D45,35-40 (he was lame, a slave, and ill), cf. H295 / D55,30; and at H314 / D65,35 (he moved to Nicopolis from Rome to escape Domitian's tyranny). But he is the unique source only for the story of his adopted child.

85. See H346-8 / D83,4-84,37, H279 / D47,36-43, H319-21 / D68,19-69,45.

86. See Sedley 1999, 134-40; Proclus *in Tim.* 1.18-19 shows that Porphyry wrote extensively on 'appropriate actions' in Plato.

87. See the passages cited in n. 85 above. Simplicius' first example of a common conception in H319 / D68,19-25, concerning the relation between goodness and benefit, appears to trace back to a Stoic source – cf. Diogenes

Laertius 7.94 (*SVF* 3.74), Stobaeus *Ecl.* 2.69 (*SVF* 3.76), and Sextus *M* 11.22-7 (*SVF* 3.75). However, even here, there may be a connection to Porphyry, whose views on 'common conceptions' Simplicius cites at *in Cat.* 213,8-28. The 'articulation' of our preconceptions about God is mentioned at H368 / D95,40.49, H391 / D108,42, and connected to the common conceptions at H368 / D95,30, H379 / D102,11 (cf. H335 / D77,8 on badness).

88. See e.g. Proclus *de Decem Dubitationibus* 1, where he ties 'preacceptiones communium conceptuum' to the 'common Mercury'; cf. H441 / D132,40, and the passages cited in the notes above.

89. Susanne Bobzien is preparing a monograph on the history of propositional logic in antiquity which will shed a great deal of light on the question of the knowledge of Stoic logic among the Platonists. The comments above reflect some of her preliminary observations, though the summary judgement is our own.

90. Simplicius gives a related, non-Stoic usage of 'assent' at H424 / D124,40, where he remarks that 'two negations make an assent'.

91. Cf. e.g. H210 / D10,43, H210 / D10,50, H231 / D22,22, H218 / D15,12.

92. Simplicius contradicts the claim he misascribes to the Stoics both here at H198 / D4,30 and again at H232 / D22,32-4.

93. See Inwood 1985, 115-19.

94. On the early Stoic theories of *propatheiai*, the Posedonian doctrine of *pathetikai holkai*, and Seneca's doctrine of 'first movements', see Graver 2000, Cooper 1998, Sorabji 2000, 66-75.

95. Hence Simplicius is able to vary his usual leitmotif, that political virtue requires us to 'use the body as an instrument' (a sentiment with which the Stoics did not disagree), by saying at H194 / D2,4 and H454 / D138,26 that we use the body *and* its emotions (*pathê*) as instruments.

96. There is an obscure and isolated use of it in Stobaeus' list of *eupatheiai* in *Ec.* 2.87 (*SVF* 3.173), which indicates that it was one of the impulses that a Sage might experience. But any such experience that was restricted to the perfectly virtuous could not be much like an Aristotelian prohairesis; see Inwood 1985, 240-2.

97. The Stoic account of deliberation seems drastically underdeveloped, if it has not been lost in transmission; see Brennan 2002a, 2002b, and the response in Barney 2002.

98. A second advantage is that it is not beneficial for students to dwell on their own vice and virtue, because even the sincere desire for virtue, when felt intensely by aspiring students, can have the counterproductive effect of inducing emotional disturbances, and thus interfere with their ability to accept the dictates of nature and fate. The path to virtue seems to lie in the complete disregard of any explicit assessment of one's virtue (hence advanced students can turn into sages without even being aware of the transition). See Cicero's *Disp. Tusc.* 3.77 for the story of Alcibiades, discussed in Brennan 1998.

99. See e.g. H202 / D6,38, H216-17 / D14,25-53, H338-9 / D79,2-24, H348-9 / D84,14-85,2. Although he does not seem to have written any commentaries on Aristotle's ethical writings, the commentary on Epictetus shows that he was thoroughly versed in their doctrines.

100. H277 / D46,46 shows one unmistakably Epictetan usage, but otherwise his typical usage tends towards the Peripatetic, esp. where he equates prohairesis with hairesis (choice) as at H202 / D6,38, H204 / D7,25-H206 / D8,40.

101. *de Anima* 412b6-9.

102. He does tell us, what we would otherwise learn from Seneca, that the trimeter lines in the last chapter of the *Encheiridion* are a quotation from

Cleanthes, but it seems clear that he did not have any other access to the poem itself (H451-2 / D137,17-30).

103. In the first sentence of the commentary, for instance, we learn that Arrian compiled the *Discourses* of Epictetus '*en polustikhois bibliois*'. A literal translation might be 'in books of many lines'; but the reader who encounters this phrase will be meeting something that seldom occurs in English and raises a distracting question in his or her mind. Having raised the question, a footnote might explain how ancient book-rolls were quantified by counting lines of writing, but at the cost of multiplying the obstacles to the reader's easy progress through the prose, for the sake of a trivial and irrelevant historical point.

Simplicius
On Epictetus
Handbook 27-53

Translation

Textual Emendations

References at the start of each entry are to Dübner page and line numbers, given in the margin of the translation. This list also signals differences between Simplicius' text of the *Encheiridion* and our standard text

Simplicius' Commentary on the
Handbook of Epictetus

[*Encheiridion* Chapter 27 (= Lemma xxxv): A target is not set up[1] to be missed: in the same way, there is no nature of the bad in the cosmos.]

xxxv: 322[1a] A target is not set up to be missed: in the same way, there is no nature of the bad in the cosmos.

[Commentary on Chapter 27, Lemma xxxv]
An improperly articulated theory of the form of existence[2] of the bad is responsible for impiety towards the divine; it disturbs the first principles of a proper ethical education; and it drives anyone who has not properly worked out the cause for its existence into many insol-   69,50
uble difficulties.

   If someone claims that the bad is an origin, so that there are two origins of existent things, the good and the bad, then many serious absurdities follow. Where do the origins get this originative status of theirs from – which is one and pertains to both of these opposites in   70,1
common – if not from one cause which is prior to them both? How could they be opposites at all if they weren't ordered under one common genus? Mere difference does not make things opposites: one wouldn't say that white is opposite to hot or cold. Instead, opposites are those things that stand at the furthest remove from one another in one common genus;[3] e.g., white from black – where the common genus is colour, since both are equally colours – or hot from cold –
where their genus is the quality of tangibility in respect of tempera-   10
ture. Thus it's actually impossible for opposites to be origins, because their common genus necessarily precedes their existence. Another reason is that it's necessary for the one to be prior to the many, given that each of the many things must either be one thing by **323** participation in the first One, or not be anything at all. Further, if, prior to every particularity, there is necessarily an originative monad from which every particularity shared in by multiple things gets its form of existence (since all beautiful things proceed from the divine and originative Beauty, and every truth from the first divine Truth), then the many origins also necessarily reach back to one Origin. And   20
that won't be any partial origin like all the others, but the Origin of origins – something which excels and transcends them all, collecting each of them into itself and providing from itself to each of them the

originative status connate with the level of descent[4] belonging to each of them. So this is one way in which it is absurd to claim that there are two first origins (or any number more than one).

But those[5] who claim that there are two origins of existent things, the good and the bad, are also compelled to give up the claim that the good – or God, as they call him – is the cause of all things; nor can they rightly proclaim him the universal ruler, or ascribe to him the highest and complete power (but only half of complete power, if that), or believe that the 'fount of light and goodness' (as they call him) illuminates everything and makes it good. Consider the kind and number of blasphemies against God which necessarily follow from what they say! They make him a coward, afraid that the bad which has come to be near to his borders will get inside them. On account of this cowardice, unjustly, and without benefit to himself, he threw his own parts and limbs – i.e. souls, on their view, which had not previously erred in any respect – to the bad, in order to save the rest of the goods. This is like a general, they say, sending forward a part of his own army against the enemies coming upon them, in order to save the rest. (These are the things they actually say, even if perhaps not in the same words.) But, in their view, in throwing away souls (or ordering them **324** to be thrown away), he 'forgot or failed to notice'[6] what the souls given over to the bad were going to suffer: that they are set alight and fried, as they put it, and become bad in every respect, although they had not previously erred in any way and are parts of God. The final result, they say, is that souls which have become impious – and, in their view, these are not the souls which have committed murder or adultery or done something abominable as a result of a perverted life, but rather the souls who do not admit that there are two origins for all things, the good and the bad! – these souls, then, they say, no longer turn towards the good, but remain glued to the bad, so that God remains incomplete owing to his loss of parts of himself.

So he is also stupid on their view – please don't think that this view is mine! – since he wasn't able to calculate what would benefit himself and didn't understand the nature of the bad. How could the bad have got into the sphere of the good when their territories had been eternally discriminated, as they report, and were separated according to their natures? (What did it come from anyhow? They don't say. Well, it's clearly either from chance – in which case chance will be the origin of all things on their view – or from some single thing which is superior to both of them. But however that works, prior to the generation of their cosmos, they make a distribution of parts as though they were already on the earth, giving three parts – east, west, and north – to the good, and the south to the bad. They also suppose that the Five Stewards of the bad are caverns of some kind; and they fashion trees and animals there – both land and sea animals –, which

are continually fought by and eaten by their Five-shaped Beast,
although they claim that all these are indestructible, just as the first
goods are.) In any case,[7] if the places have been marked off according
to their natures from the beginning, how was it possible for the bad
to penetrate into the sphere of the good? And how was it possible for
something to receive its opposite while itself remaining opposite **325**
and not perishing? In that case, white could be black and remain
white, and light could receive darkness and remain light.

So if this is impossible, how can it not be stupid, in addition to being
cowardly and unjust, for God to have thrown the soul to the bad and
to have a problem from that time to this, as they say, because he is   30
unable to recall the soul completely, and won't be able to since, as I
mentioned before, in their view some souls will remain in the bad for
the infinite eternity of the future? And on their account he didn't even
foresee this! And yet the bad did foresee the embassy which was going
to be sent against it, and devised stratagems against it.[8] It would have
been far better for him to leave the bad to itself than to have mixed
himself with the bad given that he was unable to overcome it – at
least, they say that the bad is also ungenerated and indestructible,
just like the good. One could also criticize them for saying that the   40
attributes of ungeneratedness and indestructibility, of being without
beginning or end, belong equally to the good and the bad (what is
more revered than these attributes?).

Next, consider what they say about the creation of the cosmos!
They claim that there are some pillars, not the ones 'which keep earth
and heaven apart'[9] (they don't think it right to pay attention to
mythological accounts), but rather, as one of their wise men explained
it to me, ones they take to be made of hard stone and sculpted at the
top; and they claim that there are twelve doors, one of which opens   50
for each month. Again, their causal explanations for eclipses exhibit
an astonishing superfluity of wisdom! They claim that, because the
bad elements which were bound together in the creation of the cosmos
cause disturbances and uproar **326** in their movements together, the   72,1
Lightbearers project a kind of curtain from themselves so as not to
participate in that disturbance – and this is their eclipse: being
hidden by curtains! Then consider the enormous absurdity of honouring only two of all the Lightbearers in the heavens, claiming that they
are portions of the good, while despising the others as portions of the
bad! They don't believe that the light of the moon is from the sun,   10
either, but think it to be souls which the moon draws up in the period
from the new to the full moon, and then channels towards the sun in
the period from the full to the new moon.

But why go on enumerating such views? Having fashioned mon-
strous things which it's not right even to call mythical, they don't use
them as myths or believe that they point to something else, but take
what they say to be the truth itself.[10] They fashion the bad into some

five-shaped animal (composed of a lion and fish and eagle and I don't
recall what else) and are frightened at the onset of such a creature!
20   That's the degree of impiety towards the divine in such views. And
the astonishing thing is that they actually devised all these things
owing to a pious worry. Since they didn't want to say that God was
the cause of the bad, they posited the existence of a specific origin of
the bad, taking it to be equal in honour and strength to the good (or
rather, even stronger, since up to the present the bad has obviously
been superior in all its undertakings). And, in their view, the bad can
be seen everywhere clinging[11] to the good and devising all kinds of
30   means not to lose it; while the good, so they say, voluntarily mixed
itself in with the bad, and its behaviour up to the present has been,
in their view, cowardly, unjust, and stupid. The result is that in their
flight from saying that the good is the cause of the bad they portray
it as utterly bad – and so, **327** as the proverb has it, by running from
the smoke they fell into the fire.[12] So that's how this theory of the form
of existence of the bad is impious towards the divine.

   This theory also corrupts the origins of ethical well-being (to the
extent that they depend on it) by in fact destroying what is up to us.
For it makes the origin of bad things ungenerated and indestructible
40   and powerful, something which shoves souls to the bad by force, so
that it's no longer up to us to err or not, since what is compelling us
is so powerful, in their view, that it hasn't even been conquered by
God. Yet they ought to have realized that if souls were to commit
murder or adultery or do anything considered bad while compelled by
shoving and not voluntarily, they would be without error, since things
done by force and involuntarily are forgiven by both God and the laws
as actions which are not errors. If someone supposes that we do such
50   things compelled by more powerful causes, then error and badness
simply no longer exist at all. So if they posited an origin of bad things
because they were seeking for the cause of such actions *qua* bad
actions, but, because the origin posited is a compelling one, there is
no longer anything bad, their argument is pleasingly self-defeating.
73,1   For it follows that, if there is an origin of the bad, there is nothing bad
at all; but if the bad doesn't exist, there won't be an origin of the bad
either; so that, if there is an origin of the bad, as they say there is,
neither the bad nor the origin of the bad will exist.[13]

   Now that this hypothesis has thus been clearly refuted, if someone
dares to say, in order to avoid this refutation, that God himself is the
cause of the **328** bad *qua* bad, he too will be refuted, somewhat more
10   briefly, as impious to God and mistaken. (After all, how could a view
be true which is impious to God, the composer of truth?) First, how
will God, who is good according to the highest and incorruptible
goodness, produce the bad from himself, if the bad is opposite to the
good, as the people who have this difficulty believe? How will an
opposite be produced from an opposite? And secondly, anything that

produces something from itself and is the cause for its being, produces
it because it possesses its cause and is itself constituted in accordance
with the cause, being itself as cause what the other (produced) thing
is as an existent. So this position fails to observe that, in addition to
being plainly impious to God, it introduces both an origin of the bad   20
and a first bad thing, like the previous position.

So if the bad does not have an origin and God is not its cause, where
does it come from? After all, it's impossible for anything to be generated without a cause. Perhaps we should first articulate *what* it is
that we call bad. Only then will we be able to inquire *where* it comes
from, since someone who doesn't know what some particular thing is
can't discover its cause either. Well, the first thing to say is that this
bad, the one conceived of by those who posit an origin of the bad and   30
by most people having difficulties about the bad – i.e. the bad conceived as some kind of substance, having a primary[14] form of existence
just like the good, and equal in power to that of the good, and opposite
to it as an equal (since they also think that the bad so conceived is a
substance whose nature is unmixed with respect to its opposite, the
good, as black is with respect to white or cold to hot) – a bad of this
kind, then, doesn't exist at all in the nature of existent things. For if
it had been a primary substance, like a man, say, or a horse, then it
would have had some **329** perfection and form in accordance with its
nature, in virtue of which it is the thing it is. But every form which   40
has the perfection in accordance with its nature is good, not bad.
That's why the Manichees say that their bad desires the good, and
participates in it, and is benefited by it, and loves its participation and
does everything so as not to lose it.[15] So how can we conceive of such
a thing as bad *simpliciter*?

But the bad in virtue of which we are called bad and erring, and
submit ourselves to justice on the ground that we are bad, is an
accident, not a substance, given that it arises and passes away
without the destruction of the substrate, and does not subsist *per se*.[16]   50
For what badness could there be which did not belong to something?
The good which is contrary to this is itself likewise an accident.
Further, the good is what is in accordance with the nature of each
thing, in virtue of which it has its perfection, while the bad is the
disposition of the thing that has it which is contrary to its nature, in   74,1
virtue of which it is deprived of its natural state and of the good. For
if the bad had also been a natural disposition and perfection of the
form which had it, it would have been itself good, and no longer called
bad.

As a result, there is no primary nature or subsistence[17] of the bad,
as there is of the good; rather it has a derivative existence,[18] derived
from the good, as a falling away from and deprivation of it. The vice
or badness[19] of the soul is related to virtue as disease is related to   10
health. Just as walking correctly is a primary activity of an animal,

which it sets as a target and has an impulse towards, whereas limping and lameness while walking happen instead[20] of the primary activity and derive their existence from it (since they are motions contrary to nature), so the same holds for every bad with respect to the good contrary to it. Hence you can't say that these are alike primary, or of equal standing with each other just like the white and the black are. Black and white are **330** both equally forms, and the one has its own

20   natural perfection no more or less than the other, and neither is the privation of the other. For a privation is a confusion or failure of the form, like lameness in walking, but each of these has its own distinct form as much as the other. In the case of good and bad, however, while one of them is in accordance with nature the other is contrary to nature, and the unnatural derives its existence from the natural quality (i.e. the bad from the good, obviously, not the good from the bad). Similarly, one wouldn't say that attaining the target derives its

30   existence from failure to attain it, or health from disease, but rather that failure derives its existence from attaining it, and likewise disease from health. After all, the primary goal of the archer is attaining his target, since it's on account of attaining it that he shoots; and the primary goal of nature is health, since it's on account of its safety and health and in general what accords with its nature that an animal does every act it does, and the primary goal of every activity is the thing on account of which the activity arises. Failure happens instead of[21] the target of attainment when the activity doesn't achieve its target or acquire the goal on account of which it acts, but acquires a failure instead of the thing itself. But what happens involuntarily

40   and instead of[22] the primary goal could rightly be said to derive its existence from the goal, not the primary goal from what happens involuntarily and instead of it.

Now if everything strives for the good[23] and it's on account of attaining the good – whether the real good or what seems so to it – that everything which is acting acts, it's clear that the primary goal of every activity is the attainment of the good. Yet the bad sometimes happens instead[24] of the activity, when the striving is not for something good in reality, but for an **331** apparent good which is

50   accompanied by something bad. Someone commits adultery because he is striving for pleasure, or someone steals and plunders because he desires financial ease. He is primarily striving for his apparent good, and acting on account of that, but he is compelled to take along with it the bad which accompanies it. After all, no one desires to commit

75,1   adultery on account of the adultery itself, or to steal on account of stealing, or desires any other bad thing on account of its badness, because no one strives for the bad *qua* bad. For if it had been the origin and cause of the things that depended on it, it would also have been their goal and an object of striving, as the good is. Again, if that's how it was, it would have been good, not bad, since anything that is

an object of striving is good, and anything good is an object of striving. So all things desire their own benefit, whether real or apparent – and even then, they desire it as if it were real. For no one is voluntarily deceived into taking the false instead of the real or the image instead   10
of its archetype. Rather, through our excitement[25] about an apparent good, we sometimes don't see the bad accompanying it, and sometimes, even when we notice it, we make a mistake in our calculations as if the good were greater and the bad accompanying it less than it is. (Of course, we often choose the greater good along with a lesser evil, just as we endure surgery and cautery because we believe that health, the good which comes about from them, is greater than the badness in them.)

But that everything strives for the good is also clear from the fact   20
that the bad itself, even if it actually existed and acted in some way, would act for the sake of its own benefit, which is to say, for the sake of its proper good. For this reason, even those who posit it say it does the things they say it does for the sake of participating in the good and possessing it itself and not losing it.[26] So if nothing strives for the bad, its **332** form of existence is not a primary one. But given that it exists at all and comes about in the way we've said, it makes sense to say that it subsists derivatively, not that it subsists.   30

All right, someone may say, maybe the bad is an accident, a failure to attain the good, something whose subsistence is derivative from the good. But granted that's the *kind* of thing it is, what can its *cause* be? For the question under discussion is this: given that everything generated is generated by some cause, where did the bad get any sort of entrée whatsoever into existent things, if God – which is to say, the origin of all existent things – is good? Well, something has been said about this earlier, both in our discussion of what is up to us[27] and in my exegesis of the text 'Do not seek for what happens to happen as you wish.'[28] But we can say now, somewhat more briefly, that God,   40
because he is the fount and origin of all goodness, did not produce just the first goods – the goodnesses-in-themselves – nor just the intermediates – which remain eternally with them in the good – but also the lowest goods – which are by nature able to turn away from what is in accordance with their nature and from the good, towards what is contrary to their nature – which is in fact what we call the bad. For after the eternal bodies (which are always in accord with their nature and always situated in the good), things that are generated and perish came to subsist; and after the souls that are always situated in the good, souls able to turn away came to subsist. <This was for   50
four reasons.> [1] So that the wealth of the productive goodness could produce all the goods that were capable of subsisting. [2] So that the cosmos **333** would be made perfect – i.e. having not just the first goods and intermediates, but also the lowest (which is the specific property of perfection). [3] So that the first goods, or the intermediates, which   76,1

are wholly good, should not be found to be lowest, without honour, and impotent, by no longer giving subsistence to things that are generated and perish, although they themselves transcend such things; <but so that it would be> things that are generated and perish <which were found to be lowest>, since such things are necessarily the lowest.[29] [4] Because, given that the first and intermediate existents were such that the former are unchangeable in both their essences and their activities, and the latter have an unchangeable essence but change their place with respect to their parts, it was impossible for the lowest things below the revolution of the heavenly bodies (the things under the moon) not to subsist as things essentially capable of change and able to be disposed contrary to their nature.

For these reasons, then, and for others which are obviously much more awe-inspiring than these, there came to subsist the sublunary things and the mortal place[30] where there was room for a turning away from the good – because the lowest good had also to subsist, and the lowest must necessarily be of such a kind as to be able to turn away. Therefore there is nothing bad in the things above this place, because it is the nature of the bad to be a kind of turning away by the lowest good (the thing which by nature is able to turn away) and to be down here where the lowest good is. Hence the soul too, when it has its nobler and unchanged essence – i.e. when it exists by itself – participates in nothing bad. But since by nature it comes to be in this place in accordance with its relation,[31] and is interwoven with bodies – since in his providence the father and demiurge of the whole produced this kind of soul too, so that the lowest things[32] would be bound to the first by the indissoluble bindings[33] of an animating controller – it sometimes participates in the bad which is here.

Now the bodies here also seem to participate in a bad that appertains to them **334** when they are in the disposition contrary to their natures (i.e. disease and decay). But this, I think, is not actually bad, but rather good for bodies. For composite bodies, that is, bodies composed, as I've said,[34] of opposites which fight each other and have a hard time out of their natural places, are relieved of this burden when they are resolved into their elements; and it is even more of a liberation from conflict for the simple bodies to be returned for renewal to their own natural places and their own elemental masses. Even if they change into one another, this is nothing bad for them, since each one comes to be what it was before (e.g. water which changes to air comes to be water again). But the most significant thing is that both the dissolution of composite bodies and the changing into one another of simple bodies are good for the whole, given that the destruction of one is the generation of the other, and this is responsible for the cycle of generation remaining inexhaustible. We also see that both nature and art, as I've said before,[35] disdain parts on account of the whole: the former pushing away fluxes and discharges from the more important to the less important places, the latter often cutting, burning or chopping off the part on account of the preservation of the whole. Hence what happens to bodies should be 50 called good rather than bad, and their cause is the cause of something good and not something bad. For the elemental masses of the bodies under the moon have nothing bad, since they too are eternal, while what seems to be bad in their parts is predominantly good even in the parts themselves (i.e., as I've said, in simple and composite things),[36] 77,1 and is made perfectly good **335** when it is referred to the good of the whole. So for these reasons too the disposition of bodies contrary to their natures is not bad, since it has been made good in all respects.

But if someone contends – and I've said this before too[37] – that we shouldn't call this good, since it is a turning away from the natural state, don't immediately call it 'bad', either (to do so would reflect the unarticulated conception of the bad we have, as opposite to every 10 good). Rather, call it 'necessary', as something which is not *per se* choiceworthy, but introduces a large degree of what is required to make something *per se* choiceworthy. For if it were bad *simpliciter*, it wouldn't contribute to the good; whereas something 'necessary', even if it isn't choiceworthy *per se*, is itself made good by its straining towards the good, and is thus good itself in some respect, given that it is choiceworthy in some degree. After all, we choose cutting and burning, and pay money for them, and express our thanks to doctors, which would not be required if we believed them to be bad. And yet it's a low-level good, and in the second class of goods, since it is 20 something which is not primarily but only in a secondary way good. Hence its creator would be in no sense the cause of something bad, but rather of something either good or necessary – which is in turn a secondary good, and reasonably something flowing down in descent[38] from the fount of goods.

What I have said about the bad in bodies and its cause **336** should suffice for the present. But since the stumblings of the human soul seem to be particularly bad or erroneous, although I have already 30 spoken about them as well, nothing prevents us from tracing out their nature and cause again now.[39] What needs to be said is that the souls of our superiors – which are always above, and eternally situated in the good – never have anything bad. But the souls of irrational animals – which are intermediate between human souls and those rooted in plants – have a bad similar to the bad in bodies in virtue of their bodily aspect, while to the extent that they have a measure of desire and impulse, their badness is like the bad in human souls (and 40 hence it will be understood from what is going to be said about the latter). The human soul, however, came forward as something inter-mediate between the souls that always remain above on account of the excellence of their souls' essence and their participation in Intel-lect, and those always remaining below on account of the kinship between irrational life and the body – and it became the animating bond between things above and below. Hence, on account of its self-determining state, it is sometimes assimilated to the former, and sometimes to the latter. Yet when it remains above, it does not participate in the bad in any way, since it is situated in the good; but whenever it loses the intensity needed for that blessed life and those hidden and pure visions[40] owing to its being by nature able to incline to what is below when it wishes, it has that as the origin of whatever bad results (i.e. its self-willed descent to this mortal place). But, although it has an amphibolous nature, it is not constrained in its descent or ascent; rather, it subsists in such a way that it can descend and ascend when it wishes itself. And why should we be surprised at this feature of soul, which is self-moving by its essence, when amphibians (the irrational animals whose nature is to live in water and on land) also have such a nature, since they emigrate from one to the other according to their own desire, not constrained by anything, but when they want to? **337**

When the soul descends to its relation towards this mortal place, intending to embrace a mortal body and complete with it a single mortal animal, it projects irrational 'lives'. Some of these are cognitive (i.e. perceptions and impressions) and some are desiderative (i.e. spirit and appetite). It is through these that the mortal animal will have cognition (at least the cognition commensurate with it, which irrational animals have too), renew by food what is always flowing away,[41] preserve the eternity of its species by procreation of something alike, and ward off harmful things. A mortal animal would have none of these if it weren't completed by these irrational powers. After all, who, particularly of the purer sort, would endure to spend so much time eating and excreting like an irrational animal if he weren't provoked to it by irrational desire? Who would nurture a tiny embryo for so long, if the prick of that appetite (and that for the handing down of the species) didn't blaze up? But these points, which I have already made before,[42] suffice to make it clear that irrational desires were given on account of the good and for the constitution of the animal – and so far nothing bad has become apparent.

The rational soul is superior in essence to the body and irrational life, and its nature is to be a governing origin[43] with respect to them. So when it preserves its own rank with respect to them, transcending them, using them as a tool, and referring the good of their service to its own good, then everything is good and nowhere does any bad by-product arise. But when it forgets its similarity with what is superior, the soul throws away its governing sceptre and neglects its governing power, and it inclines as a whole towards the body and the irrational lives. (This happens to a soul especially when it prefers the intensity and kick of the **338** pleasure resulting from irrational desires to the pure and gentle pleasures resulting from rational desires.) If a soul does this, and abandons itself so wholly to irrationality as to think that *that* is itself, then, because the rational soul is acting irrationally, contrary to its nature and contrary to its own governing and masterly value (since it chooses to be enslaved and governed), then the bad does arise. The bad has no place among superior things, when they are existing by themselves, nor among worse things, when they remain among themselves; rather, it arises when something superior embraces something inferior in an immod- 50 erate way and takes on a similarity towards what is worse rather than a similarity towards what is better. And this happens to the soul without compulsion from something else, but when the soul itself chooses in accordance with its self-determination and what is up to us (since choice is up to us, given that it is our own internal motion).

Now pay attention to me here in case I have produced a fallacious 79,1 argument, and deceive you, the reader, too. That choice or prohaire-sis[44] is our own internal motion of the soul and compelled by no one from outside, is both evident, I think, and has been said and proven before.[45] And that in accordance with its choice or prohairesis the soul sometimes chooses the superior and sometimes the inferior instead of the superior is clearly shown, I think, by the fact that God, well-written laws, and sensible human beings judge good and bad human 10 actions not by the deeds but by the prohairesis.[46] For they honour and punish, praise and blame, looking only at the prohairesis on the ground that it is self-determined and up to us. Hence actions performed under force are thought worthy of forgiveness even if they are very harsh, and the fault is ascribed not to the agent but to the person who applied the force, because the latter applied force **339** by pro-hairesis, while the former acted against his prohairesis. So if prohairesis is the cause of badness, and it is a self-willed activity of the soul, and not shoved about by force, can we say that anything other than the soul is the cause of badness? And even this[47] is not a 20 cause of the bad *qua* bad – for nothing chooses the bad *qua* bad – but rather *qua* an apparent good which conceals within itself the bad which the soul necessarily takes along with the apparent good. (I have spoken about this before as well.[48])

So now that we have found the cause of the bad, let us cry out with a clear voice that 'God is not the cause'[49] of it, because it is the soul, not God, that enacts the bad; and the soul does so self-determinately. For if it were by force that the soul produced the bad in its actions, someone might hold God responsible for having allowed the soul to be subject to force without being itself the cause. And yet, if it had been 30 done by force, it wouldn't have been bad; while if it chose by prohaire-sis, the soul itself would rightly be said to be the cause. Whereas if someone claims that God should not even have allowed it to choose the bad, he means one of two things: either that, while its nature was such as to sometimes choose the good and sometimes choose the bad,

God should have compelled it never to choose the bad; or that it ought to have subsisted as something which was not even of such a nature as to ever choose the bad. But the first interpretation is self-evidently irrational: it would be pointless to have a choice which is by nature
40   between two options if it were never possible to opt for one of them.[50] Nor would it be choice if there was compulsion present, since choice and compulsion are related as opposites.

Proponents of the second interpretation should notice, first, that there never is any choice of the bad,[51] and next, that they seem to be recommending the eradication from the cosmos of that self-determined substance – the soul's – which self-willingly and without force sometimes **340** chooses the truly good, and sometimes the apparent good. Presumably they do so on the grounds that it is something extremely bad, without realizing that it is a greater and more honour-
50   able good than a great many of the things in the cosmos that are believed to be good. For it excels everything under the moon; and no one would choose to become a plant or any kind of irrational animal rather than a human being. So given that God was going to produce
80,1   the lesser goods, how could he not produce the goods that are greater than them? Next – a point which has already been made before[52] – if the inclination of souls in either direction is removed from existent things, the highly-honoured human virtues will necessarily be removed along with it, and the whole human form. Human temperance and justice no longer exist if the soul is not able to turn away by nature (since if it were unable to turn away, it would be an angelic or divine soul, and no longer a human soul). By this argument, then, the
10   soul's turning away and the badness ascribed to it are shown to be necessary, given that without it the human virtues, and quite generally the form of a human being, would not have come forward among existent things.

As a result, even if someone were to claim that that turning away was produced by God, in as much as it is necessary for the form of existence of the great good constituted by things naturally able to turn away, it would not be right to suppose that he has thereby said that God is a cause of badness. After all, when the doctor foments abscesses or cuts into the body, or cauterizes or chops off parts of it, no one says that he creates disease; rather, they take him to be
20   creating health, since it was impossible **341** for these people to be healed without these means. But divine justice also introduces the avenging aspect of punishment[53] – i.e. what exacerbates and increases the emotions of the soul – to a similar degree, since the soul cannot be healed until it has first acted (and sometimes, acted frequently) in accordance with its own insane desire. Hence it is also right for teachers not to oppose children's desires in every case, but frequently give in to them, and sometimes abet them, on the grounds that this soul can't completely vomit up that kind of emotion until

such a time as it has acted in accordance with it and is surfeited by   30
its activity. We don't say that either an educator like this or divine
justice is a cause of the bad; rather we take them to be causes of the
good because the means occur for the sake of the good. After all, we
call practices which tend towards temperance 'temperate', and those
tending towards health 'healthy', since every action takes its form
from the end for the sake of which it occurs. As a result, even if God
should be in some way the cause of the necessary turning away, it
wouldn't be right to claim that he is the cause of the bad.

Yet it's worth seeing in what way he is the cause of this necessary
turning away – i.e. that it isn't by his own activation of the turning   40
away (far from it!), but by giving to self-determined beings just this
power of the soul, so that this kind of species would have its place in
the universe, and great goods would subsist which couldn't subsist
without the turning away. What God is the cause of, to be precise, is
this self-determined substance, which is good and more honourable
than many of the goods in the cosmos.[54] The turning away is *its*
activity (albeit a passive one), and it acts willingly and under no
compulsion.

But that this self-determined substance is good, despite being
capable by nature of turning away, is clear, I think, even from what   50
is said by those who posit an origin of the bad so that God should be
revealed not to be the cause of the bad.[55] For even these people – who
claim not just that the soul is produced **342** by God, but even boast
that it is a part or limb of God – teach that it is by nature capable of   81,1
becoming bad. So whether they say that it becomes bad by its own
prohairesis (which is entailed by their saying that it is up to us to
conquer the bad or be defeated by it, and by their consequently
demanding justice from anyone defeated by it and considering anyone
who conquers it to deserve rewards – although the people who say this
nevertheless don't notice that it can't be consistent with these views
to say that the soul is shoved to the bad from the outside). – Well, to
put it simply, whether they say that it becomes bad by its own
prohairesis or because it is shoved from outside, it becomes bad   10
because it is something that is capable by nature of becoming bad
(since if that wasn't its nature it wouldn't have become bad). (It's for
this reason that they don't say that the first good becomes bad – since
its nature is such that it is not even able to become bad – or the other
goods which are contiguous to it – the Mother of life, as they call it,
and the Demiurge, and the Aeons up there.) Thus even these people,
who have God make the soul naturally able to become bad,[56] do not
say that God is the cause of badness, since a substance of this kind is
not bad but good.

But what we have said about the form of existence of bad things
should suffice for the moment. It remains necessary to examine   20
Epictetus' text, and see how he demonstrated in a short argument the

many things we have said about the bad. For since ethical well-being
deals with choice of the good and avoidance of the bad, it was
necessary to show that the nature of the bad is an oddity: it both is
(in a way) and is not, since it has a derivative subsistence, not a full
subsistence. Hence it is also something to be completely shunned,
because it doesn't have a primary form of existence.[57] And for this
30   reason it isn't choiceworthy for anybody either, nor is its derivative
existence a target for anyone, though if it arose primarily, it would
have to be a target for an agent. For when a builder is building a
house, the house is the target and goal on account of which he does
his building, and for a carpenter it's the door on account of which he
does his carpentry; and nothing is done for the sake of the bad.

Epictetus' argument **343** is, in brief, this.

[1] The bad is a failure to attain the target.
[2] What occurs in the cosmos primarily and[58] in accordance with
nature is a target for the agent, and its attainment is the goal (and
when that happens, the agent strikes the target).

So if [2] what occurs in the cosmos primarily and in accordance
40   with nature is not the failure to attain the target but rather its
attainment, and yet [1] the bad is a failure to attain the target, it's
clear that
[3] the bad does not occur in the cosmos primarily.[59]

That[60] [1] the bad is a failure to attain the target, is clear from what
has been said about it. For if someone sets up pleasure, *qua* something good, as his target, then he shoots at it *qua* something good (or
runs after it himself, faster than an arrow, in his thought or impression, at any rate). And if he doesn't attain the good, but misses it[61] and
turns aside from it, it's clear that by missing the target he's becoming
bad. What I said about the builder and the carpenter makes it clear
50   that [2] what occurs in the cosmos primarily is the target of the agent,
and its attainment is his goal. For everything which occurs is the
target of the agent, and by looking at this he directs his activities, like
82,1   arrows, towards it, and his goal is attaining the target. And, [3] when
Epictetus said 'there is no nature of the bad in the cosmos', he meant
by the term 'nature' what subsists in accordance with nature and
primarily. If you take the argument in this way, Epictetus set out the
minor premiss in 'A target is not set up to be missed' (this means [1]
that the bad is a failure to attain the target), then omitted the major
premiss (the one which says [2] 'what occurs primarily in the cosmos
10   is not the failure to attain the target, it is rather its attainment'), and
then explicitly drew the conclusion [3] that the bad does not occur
primarily and in accordance with nature in the cosmos.[62]

But it's also possible to read his assumption as the following
conditional: 'if a target is not set up to be missed, there is no nature

of the bad in the cosmos.' Then, when the antecedent is taken as the minor premiss, the consequent is secured. **344** It is plain that 'a target is not set up to be missed', and hence that 'there is no nature of the bad in the cosmos'. And the truth of the conditional is also clear – i.e. that 'if a target is not set up to be missed, there is no nature of the bad in the cosmos'. For if there were,[63] it would have been the target for the agent, which he looked at when he acted. But it would have been a target for avoiding, since the bad is something to shun; so it wasn't set up for attaining, but rather for missing. So if 'a target is not set up to be missed', then 'there is no nature of the bad in the cosmos'.

[*Encheiridion* Chapter 28 (= Lemma xxxvi): If someone handed your body over to the first comer, you would be annoyed. But when you hand your judgement over to any chance person you meet, so that if he insults you, it gets disturbed and confused – aren't you ashamed at that?

xxxvi: If someone handed your body over to the first comer, you would be annoyed.

[Commentary on Chapter 28, Lemma xxxvi]
The comparison between someone else and myself handing it over,   20
and between my body and my soul, is very vivid, because it's worse to be harmed by oneself than by someone else. After all, we are more disgusted at being harmed by our friends than by any chance person (owing to the impression we have of our friends' appropriateness to us, and the event's being contrary to our expectations), so it would be much more absurd to harm ourselves. And if we are disgusted when our body is harmed, we ought to be much more disgusted when our soul is harmed. Yet whereas someone else's **345** handing our body   30
over the first comer, or not handing it over, is not up to us, it is up to us whether we do or do not hand over our judgement to any chance person we meet so that, if that person insults it or abuses it, it gets disturbed and confused. Both of these are worthy of shame – being disgusted at what is neither up to us nor bad for us when it occurs, and voluntarily giving in to what is bad for us when it is up to us not to give in to it.

He was right not to say 'aren't you disgusted at that?', but instead, 'aren't you ashamed at that?' because we are disgusted and annoyed by bad things other people do to us, while we are ashamed by things   40
we do ourselves to other people. But we ought to be still more ashamed if we do them to ourselves, and still more if it's up to us not to do them. Someone is ashamed when he is aware of the shame of errors he has made in accordance with his own prohairesis. And what could be more shameful than not being able to see distinctions set out in this vivid comparison?

[*Encheiridion* Chapter 29 (no corresponding lemma):[64] With each work, consider the things that lead up to it, and the things that follow after it, and only then proceed with it. Otherwise, you will get to the first part eagerly enough, since you don't have the consequences in mind, but later when some difficulties turn up you will give it up shamefully. You want to be an Olympic athlete? Me too, by the gods – it's a dandy thing. But consider the things that lead up to it, and the things that follow after it, and only then come to grips with the work. You'll need discipline; you'll need to follow a diet, abstain from delicacies, do compulsory work-outs, on a fixed schedule, in the heat, in the cold. You can't drink cold water, or wine, except by orders – in general, you have to turn yourself over to your trainer as though following a doctor's orders. Then in the contest you'll need to dig in, and sometimes you'll sprain your wrist or twist an ankle. You'll swallow a lot of dust, and sometimes you'll get whipped. Oh, and after all that, you'll lose.

Take all this into consideration, and only then, if you still want to, proceed to be an athlete. Otherwise, you'll be behaving like children, who first play at being wrestlers, and then play gladiator, then play the trumpet, and then play in a tragedy. That's like you – now an athlete, now a gladiator, next a speech-writer, next a philosopher, but nothing with your whole soul. Whatever spectacle you see, you imitate, just like a monkey, and there's always something new to please you. You haven't proceeded to anything after due consideration or investigation, but randomly, and with a frigid desire.

Some people see a philosopher, or hear one speaking as Euphrates speaks (and no one can speak as well as he), and they want to be philosophers themselves. Friend, you should first consider what kind of thing it is. Next, get to know your own nature, to see if you can handle it. Do you want to be a pentathlete, or a wrestler? Take a look at your arms and thighs; get to know your back muscles. Different people are naturally good at different things. Do you think you can do it and still eat the same old way, still drink the same old way, still desire and get irritated? You've got to spend sleepless nights, you've got to do hard labour. You'll be away from your family; you'll be looked down on by the merest child, laughed at by everyone you meet. You'll get the worst of every situation – in reputation, political power, in law-suits, in every kind of business. Look it all over, and see if you are willing to trade it for imperturbability, for freedom, for tranquillity. And if not, then don't come near it. Don't act like children: first a philosopher, then a tax-collector, then a speech-writer, then a government official. These things don't go together. You've got to be one human being: either a good one, or a bad one. You've either got to work to develop your own mind, or external things; either devote your skill to what's inside, or to what's outside: in short, either maintain the rank of a philosopher, or of an ordinary person.]

[*Encheiridion* Chapter 30 (= Lemma xxxvii): The appropriate actions for us to do are usually measured out for us by our relations. He is your father: that indicates that you should take care of him, yield to him in everything, bear with him if he insults or strikes you. 'But he's a bad father.' I suppose your natural relationship was to a good father then? It wasn't, it was just to a father. 'My brother is unfair.' So keep up your position relative to him: don't look at what he does, but at what you can do while keeping your prohairesis in accord with nature. After all, no one else is going to harm you if you don't wish it – and you haven't been harmed until you suppose that you are harmed.

So that's how you'll find the appropriate actions for you to do towards your neighbour, your fellow-citizen, your general: by getting used to examining their relations to you.]

xxxvii: The appropriate actions for us to do are measured out for us by our relations.

[Commentary on Chapter 30, Lemma xxxvii]
Appropriate actions[65] are those which come about in accordance with what pertains to us, is incumbent on us, and fits the value of each individual;[66] and these are the works of justice – i.e. the kind of justice which includes the whole of virtue. For one kind of justice is defined in contradistinction to the other virtues, while the other kind of justice 'incorporates them all'[67] into itself' – since justice is rendering to each thing what accords with its value.[68] **346** Hence proper education, both in ethics and politics, turns on appropriate actions – since the first is the justice in the soul which determines what is appropriate for each part of the soul, and the other is the justice of the city which gives to each part of the city what corresponds to its value.[69]

So while he has educated the reader so far by using precepts (which themselves concerned appropriate actions), what Epictetus does now is to explain the technical method dealing with appropriate actions by showing how to find them and put them into practice. And what others have systematized in lengthy treatises – some of them writing treatises *On Appropriate Actions*, and others, like Nicolaus of Damascus, *On Fine Courses of Action*[70] – our philosopher explained in a few lines using effective illustrations and soul-stirring vividness.

There are three categories of appropriate action (if we divide them

50

83,1

10

into their organic parts): [a] those relating to human beings and generally to what is similar to oneself; [b] those relating to what is superior to oneself; [c] those relating to what is inferior to oneself. (There is perhaps a fourth category, [d], of those relating to our-
20   selves.) Each of these categories has many different forms, the most important of which he goes through here, beginning with appropriate actions relating to human beings ([a]).[71] He is right to teach us right from the beginning how to find appropriate actions, since it is not appropriate to give the same things to a father and a son, or to a fellow-citizen and a foreigner, or to a benefactor and someone who has harmed us. We should rather give different things to different people in accordance with the differences in the relations we have to them. After all, our relation to our fathers is distinct in as much as it is a relation to our cause (after God), the whole from which we came, and our benefactor; whereas our relation with our sons is quite different, in as much it is a relation to someone caused by us and in a way a part
30   of us.

But we should first grasp what a 'relation'[72] is, and then attend to its different kinds. Well, to put it generically, a relation is a coordina-tion[73] of things towards each other, and it is either *natural* or *prohairetic* and between things that are either *similar* or **347** *dissimi-lar*. And although one kind is *associative* and the other *disassociative*, the definition of the things in a relation remains the same.[74] For a relation is a mean between the things which have it, and they possess each other by the relation, or rather are maintained by each other, so that even when they are discriminated and become different from one another they are not completely torn apart, but remain each other's
40   relata. Hence things which have a relation are called (and are) 'correlatives'.[75]

An example of a *natural* coordination which is *associative* of *simi-lars* is that between brothers.[76] Hence they render what is appropriate to each other in the same degree – since a brother is the brother of a brother, an equal is the equal of an equal, someone's kin the kin of his kin, and a fellow-citizen the fellow-citizen of a fellow-citizen.

A *natural* coordination which is *disassociative* of *similars* is that between members of unrelated families. For this coordination is also natural and in virtue of similarity. (Hence they too are called correla-tive in virtue of similarity – since an unrelated person is unrelated to
50   someone unrelated.) But this coordination is disassociative because being unrelated separates families just as being akin unites them. And yet, owing to the similarity criterion, whether the coordination is associative or disassociative, each side owes the other side the same appropriate actions.

A *natural* coordination which is *associative* of *dissimilars* is that
84,1   between a father and son. For this is both natural and associative, but

between dissimilars, so what they render is no longer the same, as it was in the case of brothers. After all, we said there that a brother is the brother of a brother, whereas here the father is father of a son, and the son is son of a father. So this is a natural coordination which is associative of dissimilars, but the dissimilarity here is that between cause and caused. Another natural coordination which is associative of dissimilars is that between opposites, like that between left and right. These are also dissimilars, but while they are associated with each other, they are disassociated by their spatial opposition. **348** 10

A *natural* coordination which is *disassociative* of *dissimilars* is that between things that are disassociated in space, like that between what is above and below, or inside and outside. (There is a similar natural coordination which is disassociative of dissimilars between things divided by temporal intervals, like last year and this year, since that is also a disassociative relation, in time.)

A *prohairetic* coordination which is *associative* of *similars* is that between friends. A *prohairetic* coordination which is *disassociative* of *similars* is that between enemies (since enemies are also coordinated in a prohairetic relation, and are similar). Hence what they render is the same, since an enemy is the enemy of an enemy, just as a friend is the friend of a friend, although the coordination between enemies is disassociative where that between friends is unifying. 20

A *prohairetic* coordination which is *associative* of *dissimilars* is that between a teacher and a student, in as much as it holds between the cause and the caused (while that between a merchant and a customer is one which holds between opposed parties).

A *prohairetic* coordination which is *disassociative* by *dissimilarity* is that between a prosecutor and a defendant – since a prosecutor prosecutes a defendant. This kind coordinates dissimilars in a prohairetic relation, but the coordination is disassociative.

The relation between husband and wife, however, seems to be a sort of mean between the natural and prohairetic coordinations (since it participates in both), which renders appropriate actions in accord- 30 ance with the dissimilarity between them (since the husband is the husband of a wife, and the wife the wife of a husband). The relation of neighbours is also in a mean, although they render appropriate actions according to the similarity between them. The relation between ruler and ruled is partly natural (since it is always and everywhere natural for the superior to rule the inferior), and partly prohairetic (when the rich rule and the poor are ruled in virtue of this coordination), or partly mixed (when they choose the wiser people to rule by common consent[77]).

So that's how many relations there are (at least in outline). We should discover the appropriate action for us with respect to someone else from the kind of relation **349** we happen to have towards him. 40 And we should maintain it, whether or not he maintains the appropriate action; and especially in the case of naturally appropriate actions.[78] For either person can dissolve a prohairetic relation by using his prohairesis badly – or well – (using it badly dissolves friendship and using it well dissolves enmity). But while prohairesis created this relation, it wasn't prohairesis but nature that created a natural relation. Hence if one of our friends becomes an enemy owing

50 to his bad prohairesis, he dissolves our relation, and we no longer owe him the actions appropriate to friendship, since he no longer wants to be a friend, but rather an enemy. Whereas if a father uses his prohairesis for ill, his prohairesis doesn't dissolve the relation of the father to his son, since that is a natural rather than a prohairetic relation, and that kind of relation is to a father, rather

85,1 than to an absolutely good father. Even if the father happens to be bad, one still must render to him the actions appropriate towards a father.

So we must take care of our fathers in every way, both because they (after God) were the cause of our existence, and because we were brought up and have reached this point by their care and sympathy. We should act as though we had borrowed this care from our parents, and return it with interest, gratefully. We should also obey all their instructions enthusiastically, except for any that summon us to some-

10 thing bad for the soul; such instructions should be refused (without offending our parents if possible) as unpleasing to the Father of souls. But in the other cases we should yield to them in everything, irrespective of anything bad for the body or external things they entail. After all, if slaves submit their bodies and possessions to masters who own them by chance and bought them for money, shouldn't we submit ourselves far more to those who were the natural causes of our existence? So we should bear with them if they hit us more readily than slaves who are hit by their masters, and still more so if they

20 insult us or abuse us. (The ancient **350** laws of the Romans were attentive to both the superiority in nature of parents and the troubles they take over their children. Hence they tried to subordinate children to their parents in every respect, and, no doubt because they were reassured by the natural love of parents for their children, even permitted parents to sell their children or kill them without sanction. Indeed, yet more ancient peoples revered parents so much that they were even tempted to call them 'gods'. But because they were mindful of the superiority of the divine, they limited themselves to calling their mother's and father's brothers 'godparents' – thereby showing

30 the rank they thought parents had with respect to their own children.)[79] Further, while we must perform appropriate actions to our parents on account of the good and in order to preserve our prohairesis in accord with nature, in their case in particular we must also keep in mind even now divine justice, since it is likely that our own children will behave towards us as we have behaved to our parents.

So even if your brother is unfair, you must preserve the natural
coordination to a brother entailed by the relation, and you must
preserve the agreement you made with the universe when you chose
to come to these rather than to some other parents, brothers or   40
relatives.[80] Bear in mind as well that his dealings with you are not up
to you, while yours with him are up to you. Hence you shouldn't look
at how he deals with you, but rather at what you can do to him while
keeping in accord with nature. Strive to dispose what you are in
control of in accordance with what is fitting for you: that's where your
benefit and harm are. However he behaves, he isn't going harm you,
if you look for the benefit and harm in things which **351** are up to you.
But if you discern it in external events, you haven't been harmed by   50
your brother, but by yourself. Also bear in mind that if you make your
brother a friend as well by your own gentleness and love, the combination of the two relations produces a marvelous unity.   86,1

The appropriate actions towards teachers of good things are, in a
way, the same as those towards parents. But these actions are
perhaps charged with an additional intensity, because teachers are
nurturers and care-givers not of our bodies, but of ourselves, and they
act not by natural necessity (like parents among both irrational
animals and human beings), but by a good prohairesis that imitates
the divine Goodness in leading souls fallen into the realm of generation back up whence they came. Appropriate actions towards teachers   10
largely concern the requirement to follow their orders unhesitatingly,
as if god were giving commands. (A teacher of what is naturally fitting
for us will not order anything that does not tend to this aim.) But if
our parents happen to be teachers of good things as well, then since
the two relations have been combined, we should render to them the
appropriate actions according to both relations: we should revere
them as a model of the divine because, like God, they have become the
causes both of our being and of our well-being.

Next, I must address the appropriate actions towards friends, as   20
briefly as possible given their value and utility. The first of them is
selection of friends; second is the treatment of friends (as well as the
preservation of the friendship through the best **352** treatment); from
these points, the manifold goodness of friendship will become apparent. Well, one must make the selection first by looking at the
similarity of the two characters involved, since dissimilar characters
are unsuitable for friendship, even if both are of good repute (milder
and more stable characters don't fit with excitable and fiery ones).   30
The second thing we must determine is how the person we are
selecting for friendship treated his previous friends. And the third
thing, which is also the beginning, middle and end, is whether he is
ruled by his irrational emotions, or reason has control in him to any
extent. Following on this, one must examine his desires, to see
whether they are moved to fine and good things (or things praised by

good people) or to pleasant and shameful things (or things praised by
trashy people) – and still more, whether his desires and aversions are
40   well-controlled and easily persuaded by right reason, or intense and
unbridled, preferring what seems pleasing to themselves. Desires like
that, which force everything to do what they decide, are not suitable
for the unity of friendship. And desires that place their good in
external things – in possessions or bodies or political reputations –
these are also unfit for friendship.[81] For since such things are divisible, someone who desires them very intensely and takes the larger
share inevitably leaves the smaller share, so his friend can no longer
get an equal share.[82] This is obvious in the case of possessions and
50   bodies, but it's also true of those who thirst for reputation: they
inevitably want to be the only one with a reputation. The goods of the
soul, however, – the sciences and virtues –, are not diminished in one
person by another person's having them, since they are undividedly
present in the people who have them. In fact, they are actually
increased, since they are roused and blaze up together in the souls of
87,1 the people who have them, and **353** are multiplied by being shared
around, and a single light of truth and good life shines out (as it does
from sticks rubbed together).[83] Further, friends who direct themselves toward what is really good, and who regulate themselves by
right reason, use a single criterion for judging their advantage (since
their good is shared between them both, and there is only one right
reason). And when the criterion in their souls judging what is benefi-
10   cial and harmful and pleasant and painful for them is shared, they
are necessarily united with each other, and every division and disturbance is removed. But if they don't both use right reason as their
shared criterion, they are necessarily torn apart.

Such is the selection of friends. Their treatment [1] and preservation [2], however, will be correct by one set of rules: [1] [a] Treating
our friends as we want them to treat us. [b] Always minimizing in our
thoughts the goods they get from us, and magnifying the ones we get
20   from them. (And the opposite for oversights: minimizing their mistakes, and regretting ours as greater.) [c] Not supposing that we have
anything private which doesn't belong to our friends even more than
to ourselves. [d] Being first to yield with pleasure, as if you were
yielding to yourself, given that a friend is another self according to the
ancient saying.[84] But [2] since you are both human beings and will
necessarily err against each other at some time, [e] you ought first to
preserve the ethical disposition[85] of friendship with all your might,
and only then set about correcting oversights, gently, and in obedi-
30   ence to that genuinely golden precept which says: **354**

Don't make an enemy of your friend for a minor wrong
while you can avoid it.[86]

[f] It's a fine thing for the friend who is erred against to behave more gently than one who erred, and to offer him creditable forgiveness in word and deed. Otherwise the consciousness of error may put their friendship in doubt thereafter for the one who erred, because he won't believe that his friend preserves the same prohairesis.[87] [g] It's clear too that you must take sympathetic care over not just your friend but also his family, so you consider them to be no less properly related to   40
yourself than to him. And when he is away, it is no less, or even more, appropriate to take care of them (something I have experienced in the case of one of my friends). But, not to go on for too long, if the selection was correctly made and a good start established, the rational sympathy between friends will lead them thereafter to the required treatment of each other and easily teach them the appropriate actions for friends. It will then be automatic that the friend does everything he ought, because he will treat his friend as himself.

It would take a great deal of discussion to expound the value of   50
friendship and the number of goods it causes, but let us cover the following points now all the same. The first is that both friends will have two souls and two bodies (it's clear that their external possessions will be shared too). And if there are more such friends, each of   88,1
them is multiplied in souls and bodies and external possessions. Thus, in the investigation of existent things, a great light of truth reveals itself in souls united in this way; and in the practice of virtue, when the advantages of each individual are pooled in common and exercised together, a single complete virtue easily comes about, shared by them all, and in each of them individually – and one which is illuminated by our superiors[88] owing to its perfection. The counsels of many such friends will also be safe, and **355** their actions unstum-   10
bling, because they are performed through a wealth of both wisdom and power. Secondly,[89] when someone is away from his family, he is present to them through the presence of his friend; and he feels secure about them, not just while he is alive, but even when he dies, as if he were still living with them. Thirdly, what a pleasant thing it is! What could be more pleasant than a friend, and the very sight or sound of him, and the things he does? Fourthly, our trust and security cannot be as strong in either family or power or volume of possessions as it is in genuine friends. (Indeed, it is said that when Alexander was asked where he kept his treasury, he pointed to his friends.) Fifthly,   20
a friend is the best teacher. For someone who has made a mistake is corrected by no one else with as little offence as by a friend, and, in cases where we omit to do something fine, we are ashamed before no one else as we are before a friend. Sixthly, the presence of a friend increases joys and cheerfulness, and no one lightens or consoles us for our cares and sorrows as a friend does.[90] Seventhly, he is a safe training-ground for learning the best way to treat human-beings: people battle to yield to a friend with pleasure, and when something

30 goes wrong, they endure it without offence, and people say without
fabrication what they really think to a friend. Eighthly, a friend
strives enthusiastically to exchange benefactions and goodwill, and
the philanthropic and good part of the soul reaches out to no one with
as much joy as to a friend. Finally, no one could have a more unhesi-
tating ally, ready even to die, than a friend. If there could have been
an army constituted by friends, they would have easily prevailed
against far more numerous opponents, despite their fewer numbers.[91]

So if someone gets practice in these actions towards his friends

40 which is easy to bear, and becomes accustomed to them painlessly,
owing to the sympathy of friendship, he will apply **356** them quite
happily, when occasion calls, to other people as well, in accordance
with what is appropriate for each person. It's worth realising that
even in the case of natural relations friendship makes rendering the
appropriate actions welcome and sympathetic and worth enthusiasm.
For even if brothers, parents, children, and husbands and wives do
obey Epictetus and render what is appropriate to their natural relation, if they are not friends, they don't do it enthusiastically or with

50 joy, or even altogether voluntarily. Rather they do it as if they were
compelled in some way, taking themselves to be supplying a kind of
imposed service, and neither rejoicing in its results nor welcoming
them as primary goods, but treating them as necessary for the

89,1 completion of what is appropriate. The explanation for the great
power the relation of friendship has is that it is brought about by
prohairesis. For while things deprived of prohairesis are bound together by natural relations, prohairetic things have something
greater than a natural bond – prohairesis – because rational and
prohairetic substances are more elevated than natural substances,
and approach more closely to the One that unifies all things.

Now the goods of friendship I have mentioned are great and

10 amazing, although most of them are human goods. But the greatest
and most divine of its properties is ignored: that pure friendship,
because it leads the friends' souls to unity, is the finest practice for
unity with God. (It is impossible to achieve unity with something
superior prior to unity with souls of the same kind.) So the Pythagoreans rightly honoured friendship above the other virtues, and called it
the bond of all the virtues, because if any single virtue is neglected
357 friendship won't develop. How can anyone unjust, intemperate or

20 cowardly – or, even worse, thoughtless – receive the good of friendship? So anyone who wants to be a friend must purify himself to the
extent he can from the irrational emotions of his soul, and then seek
someone like himself, and embrace him once he's found him, believing
that he has found half of himself according to Aristophanes' story.[92]
Well, you can put this excursus down to my appetite for friendship,
which strives to see it even in small matters, owing to its nearly
complete withdrawal from the people of our times.

We must now go back to where we left off and add the remaining   30
relations Epictetus mentioned. After he has said that we must discover the various kinds of appropriate actions from the various kinds
of relations we are in, he adds that in the same way we must also
grasp the appropriate action concerning a fellow-citizen from the
relation of being a fellow-citizen.[93] This is, in a way, another kind of
kinship, since if the city is a shared mother (one's 'motherland and
fatherland'),[94] it's clear that in that sense the citizens are in some way
brothers. This is manifest in that some kinship between them, even
if a rather distant one, is found in practically all the genuine citizens
(who aren't resident aliens). But even kinship in nature is sufficient,   40
since there is a great deal of similarity in nature not just between
people of the same city, but even people of the same race.[95] So we must
deal with our fellow-citizens as though they were our kin, by taking
care as much as possible of their proper education – which will also
result in our living with good people. We must also take care that they
are not in need of necessities, and assist them in special circumstances; and we should seem like a father to the orphaned children
and widowed wives. Everyone can do this, one by his money, another
through political power (whether his own or his friends'), another by   50
good advice, another by physical service **358**, and another, even if in
no other way, at least by consoling his fellow-citizen by his sympathy.

But if a fellow-citizen is also a neighbour, he has a still greater
degree of appropriateness to us. For just as we aren't allotted the
same city and family for no reason, or by chance, so also are we   90,1
assigned the same place in the city in virtue of some shared worth.[96]
At any rate, we must display a greater sense of appropriateness
towards citizens who are our neighbours, by maintaining the appropriate actions towards fellow-citizens given above in their case too,
but with an additional intensity. So we must pass on to them the
goods we can, and share in their goods by joining in their pleasure,
and in their pains by joining in their mourning; and take care of them
when they are ill, as if they were our own relatives; and be declared
advocates of our neighbours in their disputes with other people by   10
helping them as much as we can when their case is just; and, to put
it simply, consider it shameworthy for our neighbour to be benefited
by anyone else in cases where he needs something we can help with.

There is also a relation towards strangers staying with us, a
relation bound together by the god who watches over strangers. So we
must render what is appropriate to them as well, both on account of
the god who watches over them, and to increase our philanthropy,
which should not only be attached to appropriateness, but also reach   20
out to the whole of humankind. Furthermore, we must render what
is appropriate to them so that we can pray sincerely for the assistance
of the god who watches over strangers, and so that, by divine justice,
we ourselves may receive what we have given to strangers. For we

must bear in mind that people invest their **359** good prohaireseis and actions with God, and he repays them more gratefully than any human being and with greater interest. So it is appropriate never to
30   be unjust to a stranger, but rather to help him as much as possible if he is injured by others (since the god who watches over strangers has more pity for someone who is bereft of human aid, and avenges him more). It is also necessary for anyone who can to assist the stranger in the purpose for which he came, and to provide him with what he needs as much as is in one's power, and, if he is ill, to help him as much as one can, and to aid him on his way back home as much as possible.

Epictetus also says that a soldier must find the appropriate action concerning his general from his relation to the general. It is appropri-
40   ate to obey his instructions quickly, given the speed of events in battle, and to fight courageously in obedience to the general, since the chance of the battle depends on him. It is also appropriate for the soldier to take risks on behalf of his general, because if one soldier dies it's not important that that part is harmed in the battle. Whereas if the general dies, even if the soldiers under him happen to win, their hearts sink, and, like sheep attacked by wolves when they are deprived of their shepherd, they all scatter in flight in every direction.
50   The result is that not just the army, but even their country is put in danger when the general dies in battle (as the events after the death of Cyrus make clear, which Xenophon recorded in the *Anabasis*).

It is also clear that there is a relation between the ruled and the
91,1   rulers in the city, and appropriate actions which fit the relation. It befits people ruled by genuine rulers to follow them in everything, to obey them enthusiastically, and to honour them as benefactors (after God). For genuine rulers begin with the soul, and continue taking care of every aspect of the person. So what Hippocrates said of doctors **360** is more readily applicable to rulers: 'they reap their own sorrows from others' mishaps'. Or rather, if they follow Epictetus, 'they reap their
10   own cares and troubles'.[97] Hence they neglect their own affairs and lack leisure, and are dragged away from caring for themselves and their superiors – which is another reason for honouring rulers. Those who are able to must also not just obey the rulers but work alongside them, and believe that the state is endangered when they are. But if they are only rulers in name, and don't perform the actions fitting for rulers, in that case we must condemn them as worthless, but still render to the state what befits it, yielding the
20   first ranks to them and obeying them in matters which do not harm our souls.[98]

But we must turn to the remaining chapters of Epictetus, lest I go on and on about appropriate actions, and forget that my purpose is to explain Epictetus' words.

[*Encheiridion* Chapter 31 (= Lemma xxxviii): You should realise that the most important aspect of piety towards the gods is this: having correct beliefs about them – i.e. believing that they exist and govern the universe well and justly – and positioning yourself to obey them and to yield to everything that happens and follow it willingly, in the belief that it is brought to completion by the best judgement. That way you will never blame the gods nor criticize them for not caring.

There is no way this can happen, unless you remove 'good' and 'bad' from what is not up to us and assign them only to what is up to us. If you believe that something not up to us is good or bad, then when you fail to attain what you want or encounter what you don't want, you will inevitably blame and hate its causes. For by nature every animal flees and shuns the things it thinks harmful and their causes, and seeks and reveres the things it thinks beneficial and their causes. So it is impossible for someone who thinks that he is being harmed to rejoice in what he thinks is harming him, just as it is impossible to rejoice in the harm itself.

Hence even a father is insulted by his son, when he does not give him a share of the things that the child thinks are good. That's what made Polynices and Eteocles enemies to one another: they thought that the possession of the tyranny was good. That's why the farmer insults the gods; that's why the sailor and the merchant, and people who lose their wives and children, insult the gods. For where there is benefit, there is reverence as well. So anyone who makes it his concern to desire and avoid as he should is also, in this very act, concerning himself with piety.

But as for pouring libations and sacrificing and making offerings at various times according to the customs of one's country, it is fitting to do so with purity, not in a slovenly way or without care, or in a stingy way or beyond one's means.]

xxxviii: You should realize that the most important aspect of piety towards the gods is this:

[Commentary on Chapter 31, Lemma xxxviii]
Since he has taught us the appropriate actions towards those of our own kind (i.e. towards human beings), he proceeds next to the appropriate actions towards our superiors. **361** (One should begin with the things contiguous to us, and mount up from there to those above us, in appropriate actions as well as elsewhere.) He discovers this class of appropriate actions through our relations, as well – for we are related to our superiors, as to primary and superior causes. (Though since that's what they are like they clearly don't need anything from

us).[99] Hence, the actions appropriate for us in relation to them are those that assimilate and subordinate us to them – which is what it means for what is caused to preserve its relation, i.e. its natural coordination,[100] towards the primary and transcendent causes.

Accordingly, we should honour them, and revere them, and obey the things which happen through their agency, and 'yield to them willingly' and contentedly, 'in the belief that they happen by the best
40   judgement' and by good forethought.[101] This will be the case when our judgement is true and our lives are disposed according to nature. Our judgement is true when it holds to correct beliefs and opinions about them – i.e. that they are the primary causes of the universe, they govern the things they produced, they exercise forethought over the universe, and they direct it well and justly. (For someone who believed that they do not exist, or that they exist but do not exercise forethought, or that they exist and exercise forethought but in a way that is not just or in accordance with the correct reason, would not honour and revere them, or yield to and obey the things that happen through their agency, as though they happened 'by the best judge-
50   ment'.)[102] And our life is disposed according to nature when it is contented with what happens, in the belief that the whole is governed by the best judgement, and doesn't 'blame' anything, or 'criticize' its causes.

But we can't achieve this unless we seek our good and bad in what
92,1 is up to us, so that we have our desires in that, and our aversions, and never fail to attain what we desire, or encounter what we avoid. For if we desire externals **362** as good things, and avoid externals as bad things, we will inevitably often fail to attain what we desire and encounter what we avoid; and when we fail to attain what we desire and encounter what we avoid, we will 'inevitably blame and hate its causes' or those who are able to stop it, but permit it. For, by nature, every animal (and perhaps everything that exists as well)[103] strives
10   for the good, and, by the same account, naturally avoids the bad. Hence it shuns as bad the things which either are or seem to it harmful, together with their causes, and it embraces and pursues things that either are or seem to it beneficial, together with their causes, and it reveres them as great things. 'So it is impossible[104] for someone who thinks that he is being harmed to rejoice in what he thinks is harming him, just as it is impossible to rejoice in the harm itself.' One is disposed towards the person harming one in the same
20   way as one is towards the harm; but the harm is bad, and hence shunned and hated (just as what is good is striven for and embraced).

As for the claim that one must necessarily hate and insult the person one believes to be the cause of what one takes to be bad, he supports it as follows. Even natural appropriation[105] is not enough to keep us from hating those who deprive us of apparent goods or afflict us with apparent bads. For this reason, 'even a father is insulted' and

hated by the son, 'when he does not give him a share of the things the child thinks are good', or leads him to things he thinks are bad, by striking him or habituating him to endurance. This is what brought   30
Polynices and Eteocles, the sons of Oedipus, to the point of fighting in single combat and destroying one another, although they were brothers: each believed he was being deprived by the other of the tyranny, which he took to be a good thing. The *farmer* also **363** insults the causes, when it does not rain after he has sowed, or rains too much later on, or one of the things that appear to harm or benefit happens or does not happen, sometimes actually blaspheming in words, or if not in words then at least in thought.[106] And *sailors* get upset when the favourable wind does not blow for them, even though one sailor often needs a south wind and another a north wind at the same time.   40
They don't consider that it is impossible for contrary winds to blow at the same time; they just become disgruntled at the one who causes the winds because they do not receive a favourable one, or are tested by the opposite one. And *merchants* want a great surplus of merchandise when they are buying, and a scarcity when they are selling, and no matter which one happens or doesn't happen, they get worked up about it and take those who govern the universe to be responsible. And *people who lose their wives and children* and in general the things that are dearest, blame those who govern because they failed to attain what they desire and encountered what they had avoided.   50

It is our nature to honour and revere those who provide the things that appear to be beneficial: the acquisition of something beneficial immediately arouses reverence in us towards those who furnished it, just as the acquisition of something unbeneficial arouses hatred and   93,1
rejection towards those who are the cause. 'So anyone who makes it his concern to desire and avoid as he should' and does not direct his desire and aversion towards external things, is, 'in this very act, concerning himself with piety'. Since he always attains what he desires and does not encounter what he avoids (because these things are up to us), he is content with what happens, and renders fitting reverence to its causes. But someone who desires and avoids external things may find that other people's judgements are not in agreement   10
with what he thinks best, and so too with his wealth and poverty, health and disease, life and death, victories and defeats, not to mention winds, storms, sleet and all meteorological phenomena, and the whole fated revolution. But since he has directed his desires and aversions towards these things, he will inevitably fail to attain many things he desires, **364** and encounter many things he avoids. Accordingly, he will get thoroughly upset and blame those who are the causes, and he will live a life that is not just full of distress and travail, but also impious towards the divine – and as a result, he will be unhappy in every respect.

He has taught us that the principal causes of reverence for the   20

divine are unerring knowledge about them, and obeying and yielding
to what happens through their agency willingly and contentedly in
the belief that they happen 'by the best judgement'; and he has shown
that this is impossible for those who do not locate 'good' and 'bad' in
what is up to us, but instead locate them in externals. Next, he adds
the honours that are offered to the divine through external things. All
the customary and lawful honours were revealed to human beings by
God (as historical research shows)[107] so that we could achieve assimi-
30   lation to him through them, and so that external things, which have
the benefit of divine illumination through our offerings, could become
bountiful and truly serviceable to us. For just as we dedicate and
sanctify our soul to God, its cause, by purifying it through a scientific
conception of him and a natural life, so we must dedicate and purify
our body, which was given by him, cleansing ourselves internally and
externally of our evident and non-evident blemishes. When the soul
has been purified in the manner described, it should also offer the
first fruits of the externals given to it by God, using a purified
40   instrument and garments as pure as possible. It is both holy and just
to make offerings to those who have given them to us, though not
because God needs these things (he doesn't even need our good life,
or our correct conceptions about him). Rather, it is we (those of us who
are worthy) who receive God through these external things, in the
measure that is fitting to them and when they have become suitable
for the divine illumination.[108] Thus even external things, if they are
offered and dedicated from a pure **365** life in the fitting manner, come
50   to have a share in divine goodness so as actually to display divine
activities. (Some people attest that they were cured of epilepsy
through taking hold of such things; and holy things of this sort have
often stopped hailstorms and violent seas.) And people who offer
94,1   these things in a holy manner share in the divine illumination of the
offerings through their relation to the things offered, in addition to
performing a deed that is both just and gracious (i.e. offering and
dedicating a portion to those who gave them).[109] And, as I said,
through the small portion that is offered, the entire species to which
it belongs is dedicated and sanctified to God, and obtains the assistance from God that is proper to it.

    'It is fitting' for each of us[110] to do these things 'according to the
customs of one's country'. For God is always simultaneously present
10   everywhere, with all of his divine powers. But we are limited to one
form among those many forms produced by God, the human form, and
within the human form are limited to one form of life for now and one
choice of life,[111] and are divided up into a little portion of the universe
and of the earth itself. So different people partake in a different
instances of divine goodness, and they do so in a different way at
different times and places. You can at least see that when it is day
with us, it is night for others, and when it is winter in one place, it is

summer in another, and that these sorts of flora and fauna prevail
here, and elsewhere other sorts: the earth and the things on it partake   20
of divine goodness in a divided way. So, just as the places and lives of
people differ, each person propitiates the divine through the rites
which God revealed and which they themselves became aware of
through experience, rites which differ in their occasions and methods,
and in the variation of the objects sacrificed and offered. And when
the affairs of God **366** are celebrated according to God, a particular
activity of divine illumination becomes evident on certain circum-
scribed days which is not at all evident on other days: the sick are
cured, and sometimes some beneficial events are foretold. A differ-   30
ence of time, or the consonance of place and method with what is
uttered, wrought and offered – all of these have a great effect on
divine assimilation.

He says that we must perform everything that pertains to divine
honour with purity, and not in a slovenly way. 'It is not permitted for
the impure to come into contact with the pure', since if anything
illegitimate is mixed into the pure and refined, it pollutes it.[112] So we
must not do anything in a slovenly way, since anything done in that
way participates in a sort of fundamental impurity. Nor should we do   40
any of these things without care, he says, so that we omit one of the
necessary parts, or confuse things, or change them, through negligence. If you delete the letters of a word, or rearrange them, the form
of the word does not occur; similarly in the case of divine words and
deeds, if anything is left out, or rearranged, or confused, divine
illumination does not occur – instead, the negligence of the one
performing the ritual waters down the power of the events. What is
most important is the concentrated eagerness of the agent, along with   50
his knowledge, as it is with the fulfilment and perfection of other
things. But how can someone who is patently careless and negligent
about things concerning God be in earnest about anything that is
necessary? Nor is it right for us to approach 'impiously', he says, – that
is, without **367** reverence.[113] For the more honourable and worthy of
reverence we consider the divine rituals to be, the more we participate   95,1
in them as such; and if we subordinate ourselves, in so far as we are
able, to the reverence of God, then we too are magnified.

When he said that one should not act 'without care', he was
worried, I suppose, that someone might think that he meant that we
must be competitive, making offerings and dedications beyond our
means, and so added that one shouldn't perform these rites 'beyond
one's means'. First, where can the best measure be found, if not in
divine things, which measure everything, and limit them in the best
limits? Secondly, nothing maintains divine rites as much as preserving their continuous and uninterrupted sameness both in word and   10
deed, and deviating, as far as possible, in no respect. Furthermore, it
is not possible to perform them 'beyond one's means' on a frequent

basis. Those who are excessively competitive with respect to divinity seem at one and the same time to convict it of accepting bribes and to be unaware of the purpose of providing these things for the honour of the divinity: they are meant to be the first fruits, i.e. merely a sampling, of the things given to us by God.

So far, I have been travelling in company with this marvellous man [sc. Epictetus] to the best of my ability, and explicating his sayings in their present form. But since at the beginning of the chapter, he gave
20   a concise exposition of three theses about the gods, there is nothing to prevent us from adding the proofs for these theses for the sake of the stubborn and 'horn-struck'[114] among human beings. Here are the three theses that must be agreed on prior to any legislation or proper ethical education: [1] that the gods exist, [2] that they exercise forethought, and [3] that they direct everything well and justly.[115]

By their nature not only human beings, but also irrational animals, plants, stones, and, in a word, all **368** existent things, are turned towards God, each in accordance with its power. In addition to this, human beings are habituated by their parents, from childhood on-
30   wards, to revere God; and they follow the common conceptions of human kind. For all human beings, whether Greek or barbarian, both now and throughout the infinite time before now, believe that God exists, even if some conceive of him in one way, others in other ways. The only exceptions are the Akrothoïtai (mentioned in Theophrastus' *Researches*),[116] who were swallowed up by the earth all of a sudden after they had become atheists, and perhaps one or two others re-corded throughout the entirety of the prior ages. But some people, because their belief is not based on demonstrative proof, and because they sometimes see people who seem to be good faring badly, and the
40   bad, on the contrary, undisturbed, end up belittling the conceptions they possess, and giving an opening for the tragedy to say:

> I am emboldened to declare that perhaps there are no gods;
> for the good fortune of the wicked astounds me.[117]

It will be well, then, if these people are persuaded by Epictetus[118] to assign 'good' and 'bad' not to the externals, but to what is up to us: in that way, a good person will never fare badly, and a bad person will never be undisturbed. But let us investigate to what degree we can confirm the undemonstrated conceptions of God through demonstra-tive proofs.
50   The first step in our investigation is to see what the name 'God' signifies. You should know that those who first established it[119] gave that name to the bodies that revolve **369** in the heavens, taking it
96,1 from 'to go', that is, to run and move swiftly.[120] But as time passed, they transferred the name to the incorporeal and intelligible causes of beings, and then to the one Origin and Cause of all things. So the

name signifies the origin of being, and the first and principal intelligible cause.

Now, either all the things that come to be come to be spontaneously
and by chance, or they have per se causes through which they come
to be.[121] But what comes to be spontaneously and haphazardly has
neither a determinate cause as its maker nor is it a determinate goal   10
for anything – otherwise it would have come into existence according
to a per se cause and goal, not just spontaneously and by chance. So
the continual generation of such chance things does not keep its order
and succession the same, whereas everything that comes to be by
nature and prohairesis is also a determinate goal for its maker. The
farmer sows and plants taking what is coming to be as his goal; and
the mating of animals has the production of offspring in view; and in
these cases the succession and order of generation are preserved from
beginning to end, because the things in the beginning, and the things
in the middle, and the things in the end all follow each other according   20
to the same concatenation.[122] For instance, in plants, the seed which
is planted and moistened by water, puts out roots and shoots, and
later grows a stalk or branches etc., until it has yielded a fruit and
ripened it. In animals, the seed is moistened by the menstrual fluid
and expands and is shaped into the embryo; once this has grown and
is completed, it is brought to birth at a suitable time. And the order
and succession of generation is always kept the same.

So things that come to be according to nature and prohairesis have   30
a determinate cause, are a determinate goal for the maker, and are
370 always brought to completion according to the same succession
and order, while things that come to be spontaneously don't have a
determinate cause, aren't a goal for anything, and aren't always
brought to completion according to the same succession and order. It
clearly follows that the things that come to be according to nature and
prohairesis, and in general all of the things that come to be per se[123]
in the cosmos, do not come to be spontaneously or haphazardly, but
rather according to per se causes. So there must be per se causes for
the things that come to be. And even if those causes are generated,
there must be other per se causes for them as well, until we come to
the ungenerated ones. These are no longer things that come to be, but   40
rather completely ungenerated things that are said to 'be' in a stricter
sense, since they have the cause of their being in themselves, and not
from outside. Hence the first and ungenerated causes must either be
self-subsisting, or superior to the self-subsisting causes, as the subsequent argument will show.

If we ascend in the same way from motion, we will again find that
the first causes of motion are either self-movers, or unmoved. For if a
thing is moved by something other than itself, then there must be
something else which moves it. And this second mover must either be
moved by itself or itself be moved by something else, and so to   50

infinity.[124] But the latter is impossible, since, without an origin of motion, nothing will be moved, nor will anything move anything else. So the first thing moved by something else must necessarily be moved either by a self-mover, or by something unmoved. But something unmoved in respect of every motion would instead have the effect of

97,1 stabilizing and fixing things, and would provide individual things with the property of always staying in the same state without changing. So it is necessarily a self-mover which initially moves the things moved by others.

The latter are the **371** things that come to be and perish, grow and are diminished, change in quality, and move from place to place. For what comes to be can't come to be through its own agency, since it would then have to exist before it came to be. Nor can what grows grow through its own agency, since what grows must grow by an

10 addition. Nor can what is altered be altered through its own agency, since what is altered is altered by an opposite quality. Nor indeed can something move from place to place through its own agency, for it will be shown that all of the things which move with these motions are bodies, and that bodies cannot be self-movers. So the causes contiguous[125] with the things that come to be and are moved by others must necessarily be self-movers. (For if one imagines everything at rest,[126] motion could take its beginning from no other source than from the self-moved, since the unmoved always remains the same, and some-

20 thing moved by others awaits the power of the mover.)

Origins must also be simple. For composite things are put together out of simples, and simples precede composites in nature. So, proceeding upwards and beginning our investigation from the contiguous causes, let us see whether it is possible for bodies to be included in the rank of origins – i.e. to be such as our argument has taken first origins to be – or whether it is impossible for these (i.e. bodies that are moved) to be self-subsistent or self-moving. A self-mover is said to be self-

30 moving either because it moves in one part and is moved in another, or because it moves itself as a whole, and is moved as a whole. But if it moves in one part and another is moved, we must ask the same questions again about the part that moves – i.e. whether it is a self-mover, or moves by being moved from an external source. And if this is the case, we shall either proceed to infinity, or we **372** must take the first mover to be a self-mover in the sense of moving as a whole and being moved as a whole. And we must say the same about the self-subsistent. For the first and properly self-subsistent must necessarily be something which subsists as a whole and is subsisted

40 as whole. But something like that must inevitably be partless and without extension. For if it is divisible and has extension, then it cannot as a whole fit itself to itself as a whole,[127] in such a way that the whole may be moving, and the same whole moved, and the whole subsisting, and the whole being subsisted. But bodies can't be simple,

since they are composed of a substrate and a form, and many other
things that fill it out, like magnitude, shape, colour, and the like. The
latter are not primordial forms, but rather participations of the
primordial forms which arise in a formless substrate participating in
them.[128] For where the forms are prototypical each thing is just what   50
it itself is, and there is no need for any formless participant; but where
there is participation in the prototypical forms, the thing that participates must always be something other than the form, and in itself
formless.

So if the origins are incorporeal, unextended, simple, primordial,   98,1
self-moving, and self-subsistent, or something superior to these, but
bodies are unable to be like this, it is clear that bodies can't be origins.
What is the self-mover, then, which, we say has the status of an origin
with respect to bodies because it is the mover of bodies (i.e. of things
moved by something else)? Is it what moves bodies from within rather
than externally? (For if what moves from within wasn't a self-mover,
but was itself moved by something else, we wouldn't say that bodies
are moved from within, but rather from without. After all, a mover is   10
strictly speaking the first mover – e.g. if I move a stone using my hand
and a stick, then it is I who am strictly speaking the mover.) What is
it that moves the bodies from within, then? What else, but the thing
we call 'the soul'? For **373** whatever is animate is moved from within,
and whatever is moved from within we call 'animate'.

If, then, the soul moves bodies from within, and what moves bodies
from within is a self-mover, the soul will be the self-mover which is
the origin and cause of things that come to be and are moved, and has
within itself their reasons,[129] in accordance with which things that   20
come to be come to be, and things that are moved are moved. For if
the forms in the bodies are not primordial, but get their subsistence
contiguously from a self-mover, it is clear that the primordial origin
of each of the forms in the bodies, and of generated things quite
generally, belongs to the soul, and that these forms in the soul are
more distinct and purer. (To base our argument on one example, let
us choose, e.g., beauty. The beauty in the bodies of, e.g., animals, is
in tissues, muscles, bones, and whatever else makes up their bodies.
It makes them beautiful, as much as possible, although it too participates in their shapelessness and is immersed in it. The beauty in the   30
soul, however, is a pure reason, since it is freed from all of these
material things; it is no longer an image of beauty but the beautiful
itself: not beautiful in one way, and not beautiful in another, but
wholly beautiful as a whole.[130] Hence, when the soul sees the beauty
in itself or in some other soul, it despises bodily beauty and spits on
it after comparing it to that beauty. We can make the same argument
for the rest of the forms: each of them is primordial and distinct in the
soul.)

It is clear that the souls that move bodies are distributed in the   40 same way as the bodies are – i.e. that some are the souls of celestial bodies, while others are the souls of sublunary bodies. (It would be absurd for the inferior bodies to be animate and **374** live while the superior bodies were inanimate corpses.) So souls have the same relation towards one another as bodies do, the souls in the heavens being the causes of the sublunary souls. And the soul is a genuinely august and honourable thing[131] (especially celestial soul), and suitable for the status of an origin. But not for the status of a first origin. For while the self-moving and self-subsistent pre-exists the things moved by others and given subsistence from without, it retains some

50 duality[132] as both mover and moved, and as subsister and subsisted; and the simple must come before the composite, and the one before the two. Furthermore, even if a self-mover is moved by itself, it is still

99,1 moved, i.e. it does change (though only in its activities; it doesn't change in its essence). Even though it does not move as bodies are moved – in that respect it is unmoved – still it does move as souls are moved. Its motions are named 'wishing', 'inquiring', 'planning', 'thinking', and 'judging'[133] – and by being moved with these motions it moves bodies in their bodily motions.

Further, before something changing in any way must come something perfectly unchanged so that the changing thing itself can remain a changing thing. Now motion and change belong to both

10 celestial and sublunary things because the first soul[134] moves. But what source[135] allows celestial things to remain always the same, and in the same state, and around the same things, and according to one account, and one arrangement? And what source allows sublunary things their eternal recycling of things from the same things, whether of the elements or the seasons or the animals and plants. (Even if these recycled things do not remain the same in number, like the celestial things, **375** things the same in species are still re-established. For out of fire comes air, out of air, water, and out of water,

20 earth, and then fire again. After spring come summer, autumn and winter, and then spring again. From the kernel of wheat comes the stalk, the flower, the sheaf, and then the kernel once again. From a human being comes the seed, the menstrual fluid, and a human being once again.) So what is the source of this sameness? Motion displaces things,[136] and makes them other. Hence, it is clear that the source is some cause which is unmoved and absolutely unchanged, which always holds itself the same and in the same state. For what at one time is thinking or doing one thing and at another time something else, and sometimes has temporal activities, must necessarily be preceded by what is always the same and in the same state, and

30 activates everything in a partless and unchanging eternity.[137] It is perfectly evident how superior the latter is to the self-moved, since it is unchanging not only in its essence, but also in its power and its

activity, and the superior necessarily exists in its essence prior to the more deficient.

If you are making an ascent to origins, you must investigate whether it is possible for there to be something superior to the origin you have posited, and if one is found, you must seek again above that one, and not stop the ascent until we come to the most elevated of our conceptions and we no longer have anything more august. And we don't need to worry that we will step into the void by conceiving something superior to and transcending the first origins: our concep- 40 tions are not capable of leaping a leap so great as even to equal the value of the first origins, not to speak of overleaping them. For the single kind of straining towards God which is best and the least likely to stumble is this: to attribute to God the most august, most holy and primordial names and actions of the good things we can conceive, and to know securely that in so doing we have attributed to him nothing that is worthy of him. That we do not have any conception higher than these will be enough to excuse us for doing so.

So our argument proceeds upwards from the self-moving cause to 50 the cause that is unmoving and unchangeable in every respect, is always the same and in the same state, both in its essence and in its powers and activities, **376** and is established in an eternity which makes time subsist for the things in motion. As we proceed we shall 100,1 see the more originative causes, that is, the causes of the many origins in self-movers, in the unmoving. These causes are unmoving, eternal, wholly complete, and unified in relation to one another, in such a way that through this unification each is all, even though the intellect discriminates them without confusion. (Where could the discrimination of the forms in the cosmos come from, unless the God who fabricated the cosmos produced the forms in accordance with causes that had already been discriminated in Him? We should not, however, conceive of the discrimination of the archetypal forms in the unmov- 10 ing as similar to the discrimination of their images here – after all, the discrimination of accounts in the soul isn't similar to the discrimination of bodily things, either.)[138]

So, for example, each of the eight heavens and the stars in them is both a part of the whole heaven, and yet a part complete in itself, since it has a complete essence, and its own proper powers and activities. (And this is true not just for the things in the heavens, but also for each of the sublunary species which are sempiternal – for instance, those of the human being, horse, fig or vine – since each of these is entire, if not as individuals, as the heavenly things are, still in their 20 forms, which fill out the cosmos by their own respective differences.) In the same way, each of the more simple genera that constitute the forms – for instance, being, motion, rest, sameness, difference,[139] beauty, truth, symmetry,[140] as well as all of the other properties in the bodily cosmos – is whole and perfect in its own form, even though it

has many differences within it.[141] And each one is more perfectly
complete as it pre-exists in the soul of the universe, the self-moving
origin and cause of bodily things here, which contains their differ-
30   ences compressed within itself; hence the things here are copied from
that, from something more perfect, more distinct, and more paradig-
matic. But the archetypal, intelligible and divine forms of those
genera are still more perfectly complete, because in them each one
377 has its completeness through a unification, which (as I said) is
not by contact or continuity or bodily mixture, but rather by the
coalescence of nonextended and partless forms into one, in which the
discrimination remains unconfused. And each one is an origin and
primordial cause for the form in accordance with it, down to the
lowest things.[142]
40   The many origins all have the rank of origin from one Origin: the
one must necessarily exist prior to the many, since each of the many
is also one. And yet these are not ones of the same sort as is the one
which is before the many, since a one from among the many is a part
of the many, and receives the simplicity of the one only in part. But
the one before the many, because it is the cause of the many, already
comprehended[143] the many things within itself, through its single
unification – that is, by being all things before all things, the Henad
of henads, the Cause of causes, Origin of origins, and God of gods (the
50   name of blessing by which all people address him, prompted by nature
itself). It is also the Goodness of all goodnesses, because that which is
the first cause in respect of every particularity is sought by all of the
things that are posterior to it, and that which all things seek is the
good. So the Origin of origins is the Goodness of goodnesses. In the
101,1   same way, it is also the Power of all powers, since each origin has the
highest power in the species that belongs to it, and the Origin of
origins has the highest power, above all of the powers of the origins.
Again, it necessarily has the highest cognition as well, since it can't
be in ignorance of any of the things produced by it, and every aspect
of everything was produced by it.
Therefore, just as a demonstrative argument proceeds from the
parts upwards to the whole (for we would not know the size or kind
of the whole if we had not previously seen the parts – indeed some-
10   times when we happen on a single part we take that to be the whole),
so here too **378** we must redirect the honour and reverence from the
parts up to the whole, given that each of the origins is an origin of
origins, and accordingly is the same in nature as the whole, just as it
is the same in name. For it is not the name alone that is common, but
also the rank of origin itself, and the superiority of an origin to the
origins descended from it (from a single and whole origin to the many
particular origins). But if someone is upset at our calling both the
whole and the particular origins by the same name, we should re-
20   spond, first, that his complaint is unreasonable given that what it is

to be an origin seems to be common as well. Secondly, he can call the particular origins 'origins', and the whole 'the origin of origins'. For even if each of the particular origins is also an origin of origins, since it contains still more particular origins subordinated to it – there is both an origin of the beauty of soul and a different origin of bodily beauty, and one that is common to both, the origin of beauty *qua* beauty – nevertheless the origin of origins strictly speaking is the origin to which no other origin is superior (and the same is true for the 'Cause of causes', 'God of Gods', and 'Goodness of goodnesses'). But it is even more important to understand that there is no name that is proper to the cause of all things which is above all things, since every   30
name is applied to a particular discriminated conception. Rather, we take the most honourable names of the things that come after him, and redirect them up to him. (Even the name 'God' itself was transferred, as I mentioned, from the heavens, because they move swiftly, i.e., 'go'.[144] And we are not ashamed to call him 'reverend', 'philanthropic', 'good', 'master' and 'powerful', although we think these names also apply to many human beings.)

But this should suffice concerning the first of the three theses – i.e. to show that the first origins of existent things, and God, the cause of   40
all things, exist – even if some further steps on the path upwards to its most perfect completion have been left out. For I know that some of what I have said **379** will seem unnecessary to some people, given that the primary aim of this work is to clarify Epictetus' *Handbook*.

The second thesis was that God exercises forethought and governs the universe. I take it that this has already been demonstrated in several of the arguments I have just given; but it would be no bad thing if it receives a specific examination as well. For there are people   50
who believe that divine beings exist, and are as our argument declared them to be (i.e. good, and possessed of the highest power and most perfect knowledge), but that they despise human affairs as small and trivial and unworthy of their divine care. These people feel   102,1
like this owing to what appears to them to be the anomaly of human affairs – i.e. when they see people whom they think bad in positions of political power, possessing wealth, enjoying health, and being happy[145] until their death at an old age (and sometimes handing on their happiness to their children), while good people are utterly ruined by such people, without (they believe) any just accounting in the end. As a result, as I said earlier, some people are emboldened to   10
deny even the existence of divine beings. Others, while they agree (owing to the common conceptions) that divine beings exist and are as we described them, do not believe that they take forethought for human affairs – especially when some personal trouble happens to themselves. An anomaly of this magnitude (the wicked going unpunished and the good unavenged) would not happen if divine forethought took care of human affairs.

So we should respond to this problem, too, more generally or universally. We can set up the argument by division as follows. If divinity exists, but does not exercise forethought, **380** then it fails to exercise it either [1] not knowing that it ought to exercise it, or [2] knowing. And if [2] it knows, then either it does not exercise forethought because [2A] it is not able to do so, or [2B] because it is not willing to. And if it does not exercise forethought because [2A] it is not able to, then this is either because [2Ai] affairs down here overwhelm the power of the divine owing to their magnitude, or because [2Aii] things down here escape divine foreknowledge owing to their smallness and triviality. But if [2B] it is able but unwilling, then either [2Bi] it is negligent owing to *indulgence* and *idleness*,[146] or [2Bii] it disdains to care for them owing to their smallness and triviality, even though it is capable of it.

Given a division of this sort, our first response, against all of its parts, should be that divinity really *is* the kind of thing we have assumed it to be – i.e. possessed of the most precise knowledge, the strongest power and the best will, and producing all beings from itself. Hence, [*contra* 1] it isn't ignorant of its duty to care for the things produced by it (an ignorance found not even in the least intelligent of the irrational animals, since even they care for their own offspring). Nor [*contra* 2A] is it likely that it lacks the power, either [*contra* 2Ai] because they are greater – how can what is produced be greater than what produces it? – , or [*contra* 2Aii] because they are too trivial to warrant receiving care – since if that was what they were like, why would it have produced them at all? Nor, again, [*contra* 2B] can its will be held responsible, either [*contra* 2Bi] because it is negligent owing to *indulgence* and *idleness* (these are faults[147] belonging to human beings, and wicked ones at that, since even irrational animals don't neglect their own offspring owing to *indulgence* and *idleness*). Nor, finally, [*contra* 2Bii] would it disdain as trivial the very things that it thought it right to produce. Accordingly, it is impossible on all these counts, for what has been produced by God not to receive his forethought as well. **381**

Next, we should make a more specific response to those who perceive, or seem to perceive, the superiority of the divine, but minimize human affairs, taking them to be unworthy of divine forethought: human beings, and human affairs, *are not* among the more trivial things in the universe. For human beings are animals and possess rational souls (the most honourable kind of soul); and *of all the* generated *animals* we are *the most god-fearing*. Hence human beings are no dishonourable or trivial *possession* of God's; and neither are human affairs, since they are performed by a rational soul. Further, even if someone does take human beings to be a small matter, he will agree that caring for them is all the easier. For although the senses grasp bigger things more easily, and smaller things with more difficulty (since smaller things are harder to grasp than bigger things for sight and hearing), powers bear smaller things more easily, and dominate them more than bigger things. It is easier 10 to carry a *mna* than a talent,[148] and to plough or dig up a half-acre than an acre. So if someone takes these things to be small, he must agree that the smaller they are, the easier they are to care for.

Moreover, if God cares for the whole cosmos, he necessarily exercises forethought for its parts as well, just as the crafts do. After all, a doctor who intends to care for the whole body isn't going to neglect its parts, since if the parts are neglected, the whole will necessarily be in a worse condition. (Likewise for a general, housekeeper, or politician.) So **382** God isn't going to turn out to be worse in his care 20 of his own affairs than are human beings, who care for the parts and the whole using one and the same craft, mostly for the sake of the whole, but also for the sake of the parts themselves. But we get upset at some events (as I said above),[149] because we are ignorant of the way in which even these contribute to the whole.

But someone might believe that God's forethought about human affairs will create a disturbance for God, and distract him from his 30 blessedness, since these affairs contain much that is anomalous, emotional, and confused.[150] Someone who thinks this clearly thinks that the superior caretakers are like human caretakers – that is, he doesn't understand the manner of their care, because he thinks that if God cares for someone, then (as is the case with us) He must be with him exclusively and care for each action performed by him, and thus be unable to have leisure for anything else. Someone like this fails to see that even a lawgiver in a city, once he has fixed the laws saying what must happen to someone who does or suffers such-and-such, and once he has appointed agents to take care of these things down to the smallest detail, remains *in the character that belongs to him*,[151] 40 and exercises forethought over the city through the laws, so long as they are preserved. He fails to see that far earlier than this and to a far greater degree God, who gave the universe subsistence, *recognized that our actions, which are animate, contain a lot of virtue and a lot of vice*. Therefore God *contrived what kind of person should* receive what kind of justice, and *be transferred to which places*[152] (whether worse **383** or better), and be stationed among what kind of souls (i.e. that people who become worse should be stationed amongst the bad, and people who become better amongst the good), and what we should 50 do to one another, and what we should suffer at one another's hands, according to our value. As for our becoming this kind of person or that, and our achieving this or that kind of value, however, God left *their causes up to the wishes of each one of us*. For we become the kind of person we wish to become, owing to the soul's self-determination – i.e. 104,1 because virtue and vice are up to us. And God has appointed for each person powers that make allotments according the individual's value, down to the smallest thing he does or has done to him.

God didn't contrive these laws once in the beginning of time, and then desist from forethought, like a human being satisfied with his legislation. For divine goodness, which makes everything good by always being good itself, has no beginning in time. Nor is God sometimes present and
10   sometimes absent (these properties pertain to bodies); rather he is himself always present to everything, although he transcends everything. And, because he is always everywhere, and is good, his forethought enfolds everything, according to the distribution of value that is appropriate to each thing. Everything is illuminated by the light of the sun, but some see and some are seen, some bloom and some breed, some are whitened and some are darkened, and some are solidified and some are melted, each one participating, according to its own suitability, in the single great goodness of the sun, without encumbering it, and without the sun's labouring at any of these effects in any way, or being distracted from its own blessedness. Similarly, though to a far greater
20   degree, everything participates in the goodness of God (who also gave the sun to the cosmos) without encumbering it, and everything is made good by his goodness, according to the degree of its suitability, without God's labouring at this in any way, or being distracted. For God doesn't undergo any reciprocal action **384** when he acts, as do things in nature, nor does he possess his goodness as something imported so as to grow weary at times through its expenditure. Nor is it his nature to be active in one respect at one time, and another at another, as our souls are, for
30   there is no point in time at which he could become incapable of forethought for the cosmos, or incapable of stretching upwards towards the good that completely transcends the cosmos. If the human soul is said *to walk the heavens* and *govern the whole cosmos*,[153] when it is perfected and has been drawn up to God, how much more will God, who gave subsistence to the soul, exercise undistracted forethought over the things he produces?

Further, even the things that happen to human beings who seem to be good or bad fail to provide worthy grounds for the objection
40   against forethought. Our belief that good people are sometimes ill-fortuned and fare badly, while bad people enjoy good fortune and are happy, is not true. At least, it's not true if what we said earlier is correct, and we weren't just rhapsodizing to no purpose when we demonstrated that the good man is someone who locates the human 'good' and 'bad' in what is up to us, and that someone like that neither fails to attain what they desire, nor encounters what they avoid. But if this is right, someone like that will never acquire anything bad (and note that the people who bring up this difficulty call these eventualities – failing to attain what you desire, and encountering what you
50   avoid – 'bad' too), and hence the good human being will never be ill-fortuned or fare badly *qua* human being. On the other hand,

everyone would agree that 'bad people' are those who live contrary to their nature as human beings. But such people, because they have forgotten their self-determination and what is up to us (i.e. what characterizes human nature), mistakenly locate 'good' and 'bad' in external things, locating 'good' in the health of the body, wealth, political power, birth, luxuries, and things of that sort, and 'bad' in their opposites. Hence **385** they desire things that seem to be goods among such things, and avoid others as bad. But since external things are not up to us, anyone who desires them will inevitably fail to attain them, and anyone who avoids them will inevitably encounter them. And these two eventualities are not good, even according to the people who raise this difficulty, but bad. So bad people will perceive, if they sober up even a little, that they are neither of good fortune nor happy, but the opposite, since what they encounter for the most part is bad. But even if someone imagines that these people are happy[154] with external things, whether for the most part or even always, they are still more unhappy. For since they desire and avoid contrary to human nature, they intensify their unnatural dispositions whenever they acquire these things, and what is contrary to its nature is the vice and unhappiness of each thing.

Yet, since we shouldn't just overpower our audience with demonstrative necessity, but also persuade them, if they are going to accept what we say about apparent goods and bads among external things, I will remind them of what I said before.[155] The things called 'bad' are not bad, even if they contain pains and unpleasantness; nor are the 'goods' strictly speaking good. Rather, the things called 'bad' are medical treatments for the diseased or gymnastic exercises for the healthy, and even the 'goods' are given in relation to the needs and the value of those who receive them or are deprived of them. Even in the case of wealth, it is given to someone able to use it well so that he can be at ease even about that with regard to himself, and so that his beneficent prohairesis in his good actions for others can be increased,[156] and it is given to wicked people for their retribution and correction. After all, money-lovers labour their whole lives through for the sake of money-making, and are often despondent and sleepless, and fear always hangs over them, so that they get no enjoyment from their money at all. And what justice could be more just or elegant than this? Again, people who live dissolutely are needy – they are more **386** penniless than beggars. Some of them are destroyed by their luxuries, owing to their wealth, or encounter many critical dangers; and, as befits their value, they fail to care for themselves owing to their wealth, failing to learn anything good or seek out and construct for themselves the natural life fitting for a human being. In the same way, health and political power are only a source of greater harm to the wicked: some 'goods' are given correctively, but some by way of retribution, so that by the exacerbation of their emotions they become satiated and eventually vomit out their emotional disorder,[157]

105,1

10

20

30

40

and thereafter become ready for correction and purification. For it is
not the concern of someone who exercises forethought over souls that
the souls should abstain from their emotional activities through fear
or some other emotion, but rather that they should grind away their
vicious state itself. I have spoken about these matters at greater
length above; anyone who needs to should refer back to those passages. These points are sufficient in response to people trying to deny
God's forethought by argument.

But the third libation is for the Saviour, as the ancient custom has
it, so let us proceed, accompanied by the Saviour, to the third atheistic
position.[158] This position accepts the existence of divine beings, and
their exercise of forethought over human affairs, but claims that they
are diverted by gifts and dedications and by donations of cash, as
people now believe. So people who are unjust, greedy, and thieving,
are permitted to carry on with these actions without paying the
penalty for their errors, by expending a small portion of their wealth
towards these ends, and giving it to people who pretend to pray for
them and persuade the gods. So some people today even think granting permission and forgiveness to those who err is worthy of divine
goodness, **387** although what they say and think is confused.[159] So
what shall we say in response to this position? Well, since it is twofold,
we should divide it into its claims about the doer of injustice and about
the sufferer of injustice, and inquire first what this alleged permission and forgiveness does to the people who are unjust, and then how
it affects the people who suffer injustice.

If being permitted to be unjust without paying the penalty is good
and beneficial for the unjust, the permission could perhaps come from
God, since everything good that reaches existent things comes from
there. But if being assisted in their injustice without paying the
penalty for their errors is the worst thing that can happen to them,
how could God be its cause when it has been demonstrated by many
arguments that God is *the cause of all goods*, but is not the cause of
anything bad?[160] Now, since injustice, greed, licentiousness and arro-
gance are unnatural dispositions of the soul (given that their
opposites are in accordance with nature), they are obviously diseases,
disgraces, and vices of the soul. So anyone who exacerbates these
conditions by permitting them, and leaves them uncured, obviously
intensifies their vice. But if he does this and takes bribes for it as well,
how could he avoid being manifestly worse than even middling human beings? For would anyone who has chosen to care for something
take a bribe to look on while it is made bad? Suppose a patient were
suffering harm from certain foods or beverages. Would a doctor (at
least a law-abiding doctor) allow the patient to indulge freely in the
harmful substances, and assist the patient's indulgence, because he
had been bribed or entreated to? Would he be persuaded by bribes to
neglect someone who was in need of surgery or cautery? Yet if God's

justice is *the art of healing* **388** *wickedness*, how can it be manifestly worse than the human art of healing?[161]

But God is said to exercise forethought over and care for people who suffer injustice as well; so let us also look at how he treats them, if he is won over by bribes to assist the unjust. And yet what moderate person would choose to betray people he is caring for by taking bribes? Would a general accept bribes from the enemy and betray the field of battle to them? Or a shepherd betray his flock to the wolves? And why mention the shepherd? Would the sheep dogs choose to receive from the wolves a portion of the sheep they have carried off, and allow them to carry away the remainder? How can this position fail to be impious, when it ascribes something to God that is not fitting even for dogs to do? And in general, how it does it make sense for God to be led astray by bribes from people who are unjust? After all, God often receives gifts from the pious, not because he needs them (the gifts, that is), but rather because the people offering them are stretching up to reach him in this way through external things, too, just as they do in their souls. If bad people offered gifts, begging to receive their just deserts and be cured, perhaps God would receive gifts even from them. But if they offer them so that they can become worse, how can it make sense for God to accept them? Even if they had been out of step in no other respect, their hoping to inveigle God with bribes would itself have sufficed to set them at still further remove from assimilation to him.

So why is this position that divinity is won over by gifts and dedications and prayers and benefactions and entreaties, and that it forgives **389** those who err, so popular? And what is its source? Perhaps there is something to the belief. Certainly when the matter is stated simply in this way, *it isn't true or pious* to accept it.[162] But when those who err genuinely repent, it contributes to their turning back to the divine, and becomes a token of their repentance and of their submission, not just in the soul but in the body as well, when they bend their knee and make obeisance, and dedicate external things and make expenditures for what is pleasing to God. For when we err, God doesn't turn away or become angry or separate himself from us; and when we repent, God doesn't turn back or approach us because he has become good.[163] These are all human attributes, and remote from divine blessedness, which is unchangeable in every respect. Rather it is we who tear ourselves away from there when we have become bad by our fall into an unnatural state, and have become unlike divine goodness by becoming unjust, impious, and devoid of wisdom. We do so not because we are ever able to flee from his forethought, which pervades everything, but to furnish a starting point for justice, the art of curing wickedness, within ourselves, (since it is through ourselves that we are then suffering the disease) and to render ourselves fit for that medical forethought and ministration from God. And as we recover our natural state, and become like him

50

107,1

10

20

30

40

(for *becoming just and pious along with wisdom is becoming like God*)[164] we approach him and are assimilated to him.

We describe our turning back towards him, as though it were his turning back towards us. Our experience in this **390** is similar to that of people who tie a rope around a rock at sea, and draw themselves and their vessel to the rock by pulling on it, but, owing to their inexperience of the event, think not that they are approaching the rock, but that the rock is little by little coming to them. Acts of repentance, entreaties, prayers, and the like correspond to the rope, since it is by them that people who have been pulled away achieve their turning back. But repentance does not come about by words, but by deeds: by our services to people who have been treated unjustly or arrogantly or in any way mistreated by us (services to them or to their offspring); and by our hating injustice, turning our back on unjust people and living with those who embrace justice, and by punishing ourselves. We must employ this repentance continuously and without exempting ourselves at intervals, becoming justice to ourselves, until we are completely purified.

It is a token and effect of genuine repentance that one no longer commits the same errors, or even lesser versions of them: when you're walking lopsidedly, like people on a boat, you must move over to the opposite side. It is clear that true repentance is sufficient for perfect purification, because God too sees this as the goal of our purification. For the goal of everything that happens to us, whether punitive or avenging, here or in Hades, is for the soul to repent of its errors, hate vice and the unnatural life, and willingly choose and embrace virtue and knowledge, which are the perfections of the rational **391** soul. So if somebody becomes justice to himself, he will perhaps be corrected more quickly as well, since his punishment is self-willed. For though people who err through luxury and pleasure need pain and distress, you must understand that people who are genuinely repentant punish themselves with the terribly sharp wounds of the conscience, wounds that are more excruciating than bodily punishment, and more withering, and harder to be consoled for.

Let this be our response to the third type of atheism, the worst of the three. It would be preferable for the gods not to exist or exercise forethought, than for them to exist and seem to exercise forethought, but conspire against the objects of their forethought. For that is what it is to be in a bad way, and we prefer not to exist than to be in a bad way. The reason for this is that the Good is beyond being, as well as being the origin of being. So the Good is also the goal of all things, and everything is for its sake. After all, even our existence is welcome to us only insofar as it's good: we prefer not to exist when we are in an bad way.

I have extended my discussion of these theses, perhaps beyond the declared aim of this Commentary, because the beginning and end of

50

108,1

10

20

30

40

every good life and perfection of the soul is stretching towards God, both by having the correct preconceptions about him (that he exists and exercises forethought well and directs everything justly), and by obeying and 'yielding willingly to the things that happen' through his agency, 'in the belief that they are brought about by the best judgement'. For even if the soul is self-moving and self-determining, and has in itself the origins of goods and bads, nevertheless it was God who made it a self-mover. This is why it is preserved and has its own 50 perfection (with which God brought it into subsistence) as long as it rooted in its cause. But when it has torn itself away and uprooted **392** itself from there (to the extent that it is up to it to do so), it withers and wastes away, becoming ugly and feeble, until it turns back again and is unified with its cause, and so takes back its own perfection. But 109,1 it is impossible for the soul genuinely to turn back unless these three theses have been thoroughly articulated, both in thought and in its life. Who would wish to stretch out to what does not exist? Or to what exists, but gives no thought to us? Or to what exists and gives thought to us, but directs its thought towards badness and harm?

[*Encheiridion* Chapter 32 (= Lemma xxxix): When you have recourse to divination, remember that you do not know *what* the outcome will be (that's the very thing you're there to learn from the diviner), but you already knew when you came what sort of thing it is, if you are a philosopher. For if it is one of the things that is not up to us, then there is every necessity that it will be neither good nor bad. So don't bring desire or aversion to the diviner, and don't approach him with trembling; instead approach him having already determined that every outcome is indifferent and nothing to you, and that whatever sort of thing it is, it will be possible to make use of it well, and in this no one will hinder you.

Go with confidence, then, and approach the gods as advisers. Thereafter, when the advice is given to you, you must remember whom you took as advisers, and whom you are disobeying if you disregard it.

Have recourse to divination in those cases in which Socrates thought it was right: where the whole enquiry has reference to the outcome, and when no starting points for understanding the subject are given either by reason or by some other art or craft. Thus, when you are required to share some danger with a friend or your country, do not ask of divination whether you should share the danger. For even if the diviner should announce to you that the sacrifices have come out badly (and it is clear that what is signified is death, or the maiming of some part of the body, or exile), still even at this cost, reason chooses to stand by your

friend and share the danger with your country. So pay attention
to that greater Diviner, the Pythian, who ejected from his temple
the man who did not come to the aid of his friend when he was
being killed.]

xxxix: When you have recourse to divination, remember that
you do not know *what* the outcome will be ...

[Commentary on Chapter 32, Lemma xxxix]
He has spoken about appropriate actions in relation to other human
beings and in relation to God, and he is about to speak about appropriate actions in relation to oneself. But he saw a sort of intermediate
10   form, which requires appropriate action both in relation to God and
to oneself: the case of divination. He divides the account into three
parts, telling us the subjects we should employ divination for, the
disposition we should have when we employ it, and how to make use
of its results.

But he starts with the second of these, perhaps judging that how
one should in general dispose oneself before proceeding to divination
is actually the first point. He says that one should project neither
'desire nor aversion', since then we would inevitably approach the
oracle with trembling, whether we desire (and are afraid the diviner
20   will say what we desire is impossible) or avoid (and are afraid he'll
predict it is going to happen).

How, then, will we be able to bring neither desire nor aversion to
bear? **393** If we keep in mind, he says, that the subjects we employ
divination for are externals. For there is no need of divination concerning things that are up to us. Who is going to employ divination to
decide whether they should desire what is in accordance with nature,
and avoid what is contrary to nature? So if the subjects for which we
employ divination are not up to us – whether we should sail, whether
we should marry, whether we should purchase the field – and we
should neither desire nor avoid what is not up to us, then it is clear
that we should 'bring with us to the diviner neither desire nor
30   aversion'. After all, we 'do not know what the outcome will be; indeed,
that's the very thing that we came to the diviner in order to learn'.
But, he says, you do know 'what sort of thing it is, if you are a
philosopher' – you know that none of the things that is not up to us is
either good or bad, and so none is either something to desire or avoid.
Further, those who are skilled in these matters also say that the signs
are confused by the desire of the people seeking divination. It will also
contribute towards your tranquillity when divining, if you know that
whatever sort of thing the results may be, it is up to you to be
benefited by them, and benefited all the more (if you use them well)
40   the more unpleasant they are. For these reasons, he says 'Go with

confidence, then', and proceed to your consultation with the divine, fearing nothing.

Next there remains the appropriate action towards God, that when you have been advised you must follow in every particular the advice given to you. For if someone does not obey when God gives him advice, who will he obey? And yet when people do disobey the results of divination, this only happens because they project their own desires or aversions. So if we come forward without desire and aversion, this   50
contributes not only to our coming forward with good courage and without trepidation, but also to our obeying the divine counsel.

Next, turning to the proper subjects for divination, he says that we should employ it only for those affairs whose end is unclear to us until the affair reaches its outcome because we are unable to envisage the   110,1
end either through wisdom or through the art or experience relevant to the affairs in question. For no one would turn to divination over the question of whether a human being should take food or sleep: **394** animals always need these things.[165] Nor over the question whether one should be a philosopher, or live according to nature: it is clear to anyone in their right mind that these things are highly beneficial. Nor, when a house is being built, over the question what type of house it will turn out to be: the craft grasped its form in advance. Nor will the farmer turn to divination over the question of whether he should sow, or plant: these things are necessary to the farmer. But as to when   10
or where, or what varieties he should sow or plant, if these things are not a matter of established custom or are in some other way not evident, then he might use divination about them. Likewise, whether he should sail, especially if the occasion is not without peril. However, he will not ask whether he should set off for the market, or go out into his fields, since, even though these things also sometimes have unpleasant ends, for the most part they reach their outcomes as envisaged. It seems plausible then that 'for the most part' is enough to make us not need to use divination. After all, even if 'starting points for understanding the subject are given either by reason or by some other art or craft', the outcome will not be entirely necessary since   20
neither nature nor art, nor prohairesis when it is directed towards external things, has necessary outcomes; but, 'in most cases' is enough to make us not need divination. Wanting to employ divination about everything makes people cowardly and inactive, and prepares them to believe that trivial things are important.

But it is worthwhile enquiring whether we should never use divination about things that are up to us. <For instance, about> what we should believe about the soul. Is it mortal or immortal? And should we take this person as our teacher? After all, many of the ancients are   30
known to have asked the oracles questions about the nature of existent things; and yet we say that believing this way or that is ours, and one of the things that is up to us.[166] So perhaps the answer is that

we should learn things that can be grasped by logical demonstration through demonstration, since this is how scientific cognition will come about, **395** namely if the demonstration comes about through the explanation. Whereas, while it is likely that hearing from God that the soul is immortal will produce conviction, indeed firm conviction, it still does not produce knowledge of the fact. (Someone might maintain that he learns the explanations and becomes possessed of
40　scientific knowledge from God. But that is a different form of goodness, not the divinatory one, which seems to reside in the prediction of the outcomes of practical affairs that are unclear to the human intellect.) This is why even if certain people did ask the oracles questions about the nature of existent things, they were few and far between, and not among the chief names of philosophy, but rather those who had been habituated to have unscientific and merely convincing convictions. Since the soul is self moving, God no doubt wishes it to see the truth through itself.

At any rate both Epictetus and Socrates seem to have forbidden us
50　to ask about things that the soul can know about in itself.[167] Hence he does not even admit into his presence[168] the man who asks whether he should incur some danger with a friend or with his country. Right reason commands that the danger be shared (and even if unpleasant things are foretold, one must none the less share the danger). So what
111,1　is the use of asking in such cases where it is clear what must be done? Likewise in the case of those who once asked whether they should surrender a supplicant – it is known that the God severely blamed them. For whatever right reason commands us to perform, this we must do, and not ask about it, even if there are unpleasant consequences for us in respect of our bodies or external things. We must prefer the good that is ours to the goods of our bodies or of external things, even if these do have some reference[169] to us.

He has shown that one should not use divination about such
10　things, on the ground that one must always share the danger, no matter what sort of omen may be given. He confirms it, by appeal to the fact that the God 'ejected the man who did not come to the aid of his friend when he was being killed'. For two men on their way to Delphi fell in with bandits, and while one of them was being killed by them, the other either **396** fled or did not come to his defence fearlessly.[170] When he reached the site of the oracle, the God ejected him, saying:

> Though present at the side of a friend who was dying, you did
> 　not defend him.
> You approach impure. Depart from our beauteous shrine.

20　Now it is clear that, even had he wanted to, he wouldn't necessarily have rescued his friend from death, but he still should have incurred

the danger along with his friend, and died along with him too, if this was a necessary consequence of assisting him. So it was on account of that prohairesis that the God judged him to be impure, because it was defiled by his betrayal of a friend through excessive sympathy with the body. Similarly, in the case of another man, even though a failure resulted, the God nevertheless approved of the decision. For again two other men fell in with bandits, and one of the two was seized by the bandits. The other hurled his spear at a bandit, but missed him and struck and killed his friend. And when he approached the site of   30
the oracle he did not dare to enter, believing himself to be impure because of the slaying of his friend. And the God addressed to him the following verses:

You killed your companion, defending him. The blood of slaying does not pollute you. You are more pure than you were before.

If after killing his friend he was not only not defiled, but was actually more pure than before because of his correct prohairesis, it is clear that right action and error do not depend on human beings' actions but on their prohairesis.

It should be noted that these remarks and those attached to them,   40
starting from the point I indicated,[171] are suited to the middle state, which has already made some progress and is engaged in philosophy. **397** (Here too he said 'if you are a philosopher'.[172]) The same thing is indicated at many points in what follows.

[*Encheiridion* Chapter 33 (= Lemmata xl-li): Set for yourself a particular character and type, which you will preserve both when you are on your own and when you encounter other people. And for the most part, keep silent, or else say what is necessary in a few words. Speak rarely, when the occasion demands it, and then not about the normal topics – gladiators, horse-races, athletes, food and drink, the commonplaces. Most of all, don't talk about other people, whether in blame or praise or comparison. Use your own conversation, if you can, to shift your companions' conversation to a suitable topic. But if you find yourself stranded among strangers, keep silent.

As for laughter, there shouldn't be much of it, or about many things; nor should it be unrestrained. Decline to take oaths altogether, if you can, and if not make them contingent on the circumstances. As for feasts, avoid those given in the outside world by ordinary people. But if an occasion does arise, then exercise the utmost attention not to lapse into the behaviour of ordinary people. Keep in mind that when a companion is sullied, anyone who keeps company with him must be sullied as well, even if he is pure in himself.

As for things related to the body, take them just to the extent of bare need, e.g. food, drink, clothing, housing and servants. Avoid altogether anything for show or indulgence. As for sex, before marriage you should keep pure of it to the extent possible; but anyone who does get involved should do only what is lawful and customary. On the other hand, don't make yourself obnoxious to those who are sexually active, don't be critical, and don't go on about the fact that you are not sexually active yourself.

If someone tells you that so and so is slandering you, don't defend yourself against the charges. Just reply, 'He must not know my other faults; otherwise he would have said more than that.'

As for the theatre, for the most part it is not necessary to attend it. But if the occasion should arise, show that you are no one's 'fan' except your own. That means, want just what happens to happen, and want just the winner to win – that way you won't be hindered. As for shouting or jeering at someone or getting carried away, you should completely abstain from it. And after the exit, don't talk a lot about what happened (whatever has no bearing on correcting yourself), because that shows that you were amazed at the spectacle.

As for public readings, don't go readily, or on a whim, but if you do go then guard your dignity and poise – at the same time, don't be obnoxious.

When you are about to meet someone, especially someone who is considered your social superior, imagine what Socrates or Zeno would have done in this case. That way you won't be at a loss for a suitable way to handle what befalls you. When you visit one of the very powerful, imagine that you won't find him home, that you will be locked out, the doors slammed shut in your face, that he won't care about you. If despite all this it is still the appropriate action for you to go, then bear with what happens when you go, and never say to yourself 'It was not worth it'. That's what an ordinary person would do, showing dissatisfaction with external things.

In conversation, refrain from reminiscing about your own deeds and adventures interminably – it may be pleasant for you to remember your own adventures, but it is not so pleasant for others to hear what happened to you.

Refrain from making other people laugh as well. It's a dangerous habit, that leads to the behaviour of ordinary people, and it is all that is needed to make those around you lower their respect for you. It is also risky to go so far as to use obscene language. When something like this does occur and someone goes too far, if the moment is opportune you should rebuke him; otherwise make your displeasure at what he says plain by falling silent, blushing, and frowning.]

xl: Set for yourself a particular character and type ...

[Commentary on Chapter 33, Lemma xl]
Starting here, he explains the actions that are appropriate in relation to oneself, addressing people already engaged in philosophy who have made some progress. He says we should 'set and determine a character' of conduct, the one that is appropriate to that sort of life, and make our individual actions conform to it. He goes through them in detail, and thus also presents the whole character of such a life, enjoining us to 'preserve it both when on our own and when we encounter other people'. By this he means, I think, that we should always persist in a state of constancy,[173] to the extent possible, always living out a single life of our own, and not rushing to and fro with the ever-shifting external incidents that befall us, like the tides in the Straits of Euripus.[174] At any rate, it is said that Socrates was always seen in the same demeanour, and never moved by things that seem pleasurable or painful, because he always lived out one and the same life, his own. Perhaps this is the one 'character that one should set' and determine, which he indicated concisely by saying that we should preserve the same one 'both when on our own and when we encounter other people'. **398**

The first and most important of the things that belong to such a character, he says, is to 'keep silent for the most part'. The whole purpose of his educational arguments is to turn the soul back to itself from the external things, from the irrational emotions in it, and from the body, so that it can live out its own life, always the same. Silence makes the greatest contribution to this purpose: that's why the Pythagoreans ordained a five-year period of silence as a most effective beginning to their way of life. The soul is distracted towards the outside by the senses when it acts in concert with them, as is shown by people closing their eyes when they want to collect themselves and turn inwards and rouse the attentive part of their soul. Uttered speech diffuses the soul towards the outside even more, since in that case it is not only acting in concert with the senses, but is acting itself. Silence is the cure for this diffusion. But Epictetus does not enjoin absolute silence; he advises a social form of silence, which is more commensurate with human beings, not the Pythagorean form of silence, which is completely withdrawn and god-like. At any rate what he says is 'either be silent, or say what you must in brief', i.e. when answering a question.

He gives a concise definition of the form of permissible subjects of speech, by saying they must concern what is necessary either for the

50

112,1

10

20

30

conduct of the soul in accordance with nature or for the needs of the animal. Because such things are few in number and more practical, rather than vacuous or indefinite, they do not have the same disturb-
40 ing effect, nor do they divert one's faculty of impression towards indefiniteness. He also defines the <correct> form of the speech, saying that it should be concise and brief.[175] Prolixity in speech is the result of having an impressionistic grasp of the things one is talking about, and not having a thorough mastery of their essence. When the intellect penetrates things straight as a shot and sees the epitome of each thing's essence (or its most important feature, in accordance with which it gets its form of existence), then the speech that it utters about things is also condensed down to their most important features.
399
But, he says, if the need for a longer speech should arise – i.e. not
50 merely for speaking in question and answer form, but for extending one's speech at one's own initiative – the form of the speech must necessarily be altered as well, since it is now longer rather than brief. But the subjects of speech should have the same form as before, i.e.
113,1 the speech should be about what is necessary: exhorting to virtue, teaching, offering counsel, consoling, making a common search for the truth about existent things, or piously proclaiming God's superiority and providence, and prayerfully beseeching his assistance in the life according to nature. But it should not be 'about normal topics' (i.e. those which any old people discuss), and so not be 'about gladiators or horse-races' and such things, or what so-and-so eats or drinks.
10 Speeches about such things rivet our thoughts onto them too, and sometimes they drag along desire in their wake and mould our lives on themselves.

'Most of all', he says, do not make conversation 'about other people, whether in blame or praise or comparison' (i.e. that A is better or worse than B in this or that respect). Now, it is clear enough that this form of speech also makes the soul stretch towards the outside and stand remote from itself and become involved with things alien to it and labour over futilities. But why does he say 'Most of all, etc. …'?
20 Why is this topic worse than the others? Perhaps the first reason is that the person whom Epictetus is addressing has made a start on philosophy, and so for the most part will steer clear of enthusiasm over gladiators and athletes and the like, but would be more likely to make conversation about other people. Thus it is just where the student has a leaning towards something that Epictetus reins him in most of all, as though he were saying 'You most of all should be on your guard about this.' Next, even if the same emotions are stirred in a similar manner in both kinds of speech – for both with the former and the latter topics, **400** conversation about them will stir up sym- pathies and antipathies – there is one particular emotion that is the
30 special consequence of speeches that are critical of people, namely

superciliousness and vanity. Anyone who judges people's lives makes his judgement as if he were superior to them; and a mistake in judgement about people's lives is more a matter for indignation than one concerning games.

It is not just saying such things that one ought to avoid, he says, but hearing them as well (for impressions and irrational emotions are set in motion in the audience by hearing, too). Still, people who say such things become even more shameless, and nurture in themselves   40
an unabashed and insolent licence in their speech, if no one they consider more dignified is present to keep them in check. Thus he says 'if you can, shift such conversations among your companions' to more virtuous topics. 'But if you find yourself stranded among' people who have been brought up and habituated in a different form of life, a corrupt one (he calls them 'strangers'), 'be silent', and purify yourself by turning back towards yourself in silence.

xli: As for laughter, there shouldn't be much of it, or about many things; nor should it be unrestrained.

[Commentary on Chapter 33, Lemma xli]
After he has given the general precept for philosophers that they should remain in the same character – and silence contributes a great   50
deal to this – he checks the very great diversion due to the excessive joy which comes about through laughter (perhaps indicating in these words the opposing diversion due to distress as well).[176] Laughter is like a sort of overflowing of excessive joy in the soul, which is why it happens when the breath is inflated, and produces a noise like   114,1
gurgling. **401** So it diverts the stable and gracious demeanour of the soul and body (just as crying and wailing do from the opposite side) and spoils the constancy that comes from commensurateness. So for these reasons we should guard against laughing – especially laughing 'about many things'. No doubt there is some need for occasional laughter so that we don't remain completely unsmiling and produce a peevish character in ourselves, and seem uncouth and lacking in the graces to those around us. But there are few things worth laughing   10
about. Someone who laughs about many things is clearly easily puffed up with excessive joy; hence you shouldn't feel this very often, or persist in laughing for a long time (that's what he means by 'much of it'); nor should you give yourself up to completely helpless laughter (I think that's what 'unrestrained' means here). Instead, your laughter should resemble a smile, producing a slight modification in the lips.

xlii: Decline to take oaths altogether, if you can, and if not make them contingent on the circumstances.

[Commentary on Chapter 33, Lemma xlii]

Here too, in this catalogue of appropriate actions in relation to
20   oneself, once he has checked the great throng of things that divert us
from remaining in the same character, he starts from reverence for
God. For an oath calls God as a witness, and sets him up as a referee
and guarantor for what one says. In any case, introducing God into
human affairs – which is to say, into small and trivial affairs –
encourages contempt for him. Hence we should absolutely 'decline to
take oaths, if possible', **402** choosing any possible pain or penalty in
preference to swearing an oath. But if it's necessary to employ an oath
at some point, either to rescue a friend from danger or to provide
30   assurances on behalf of one's parents or country, then it's better to
undergo anything than to transgress an agreement enacted through
the mediation of God.

xliii: As for feasts, avoid those given in the outside world by
ordinary people.

[Commentary on Chapter 33, Lemma xliii]

After this check on indifference to God, he checks 'many-headed'
desire[177] by instilling measure into it, beginning with the most necessary desire, for nourishment, and proceeding through the other bodily
desires to the desire for sexual intercourse. The feasts of illustrious
men relegate food and drinks and symposiastic amusements as inci-
40   dentals; they are in fact associations and occupations with words, as
is made clear in the *Symposia* recorded by Plato, Xenophon, Plutarch
and others. Most people's feasts, however, resemble the feeding of
irrational animals, in as much as they are directed towards indulgence and bodily enjoyment. (This is well expressed by the saying 'a
table without words is no different from a trough'.[178])

So the reasonable person should decline feasts for ordinary people
that are outside, i.e. of his own ethical disposition.[179] But 'if an
occasion for a feast does arise' **403** (e.g. when some communal festival
requires it, or when your father compels it, or in order to be accommo-
50   dating, or under some other pressing need), then he says you should
'exercise the utmost attention', i.e. let the attentive part of your soul
be fully awake, and let it be on guard to remain in itself. Otherwise
by alienating itself and manifesting the desires of ordinary people, it
115,1   may lapse into the rank of ordinary people, and 'be sullied in company
with' ordinary people through its irrational emotions. Anyone who
surrenders himself to people who are sullied, and manifests the
desires that are in them (that's what he means by 'keeping company')
becomes 'sullied through them, even if he was previously pure' and
had pure desires. That's what being sullied is: the mixing of the
impure with the pure.

xliv: As for things related to the body, take them just to the extent of bare need.

[Commentary on Chapter 33, Lemma xliv]
Things taken for the body's sake must first be acquired, and only then used, though Epictetus speaks about their use now, and will speak 10 about their acquisition later.[180]

Perhaps it would have been a good thing if human beings had no needs, being just rational souls; but since they also use a perishable body as an instrument, it is sufficient to supply what is necessary for it without sliding into excess. The carpenter who is designing an adze is content to provide it with a size and shape that are suitable to it, and a sharpened blade. He doesn't want to plate it with gold, or **404** set it with precious stones, since then he would be drawn into damaging expenditures, his concern with the instrument would be contrary to the rationale of his craft, and he would render it useless for the 20 craft. This is just the way that we should go through life in relation to our own instrument: we should supply only what it needs, and in our choice of foods and drinks we should select the most easily provided and most natural of the things that keep the human body nourished according to its nature. Such things will immediately be found to be purer, simpler, and healthier – for though the animal does need to be fed, it does not need this or that exotic food. Nature did not bring us into a natural relationship with the Thearions and Paxamoses of the world[181] with their wretched pseudo-craft of 'cookery'; rather, our natural relationship is to food that will weave up again 30 the part that flows off.[182] The truth of this is shown by people who are compelled through lack of resources to nourish themselves more naturally: they are much healthier than those who indulge themselves (compare country-folk to city-dwellers, or slaves to their masters, or the poor to the rich). Excessive and contrived things are burdensome to our nature, because they are treacherous and alien and in a way belong to the class of deleterious things; hence they generate destructive gases and fluxes. So we must measure the things supplied, both in quantity and in kind, in relation to the physical condition and needs of the instrument, so we aren't worn down by our 40 provision of excess expenditures, so our concern isn't contrary to the true rationale of the instrument, and so we don't make it less useful.[183] It is a fortunate thing to be raised **405** and habituated in this way from the beginning, since then a natural, simple, and non-excessive diet is easily tolerated by the body and is beneficial and pleasant.

The same holds good for clothing, as well. Socrates was said to use the same clothing both summer and winter; and, though it is indulgent by comparison to Socrates, it will be sufficient if we vary our 50 clothing for the extremes of the seasons, using both linen from the earth and the fleeces of familiar animals. But it is the height of indulgence and irrationality to search the rivers in the West to take pelts from the animals in them, or to importune the Seres in the East, and exchange gold and silver, the most enduring materials that are found among us, for the threads of worms that are found among them.[184]

116,1

We should have the same attitude to our houses, as well. Crates was satisfied with a tub for his housing, even though he had a wife, the lovely Hipparchia.[185] In our case, let us have a house, but one that satisfies need both in its size and ornamentation, with separate apartments for men and women – though perhaps even this is excessive – but not some establishment with thirty beds, covered with brightly colored mosaics throughout on the walls and floors, or different lodgings for each month of the year. Our needs do not demand such things, and it is an unfortunate fact that anyone who has grown accustomed to them is dissatisfied with everything else. And it goes without saying that people who have become attached to such things inevitably locate their happiness in them and completely forget themselves, so that if they fail to retain them (and many factors control this failure), they inevitably cry and mourn and believe that they are now wretched – whereas we were actually more wretched when we were immersed in such indulgences. **406**

10

20

We should use the same rationale for the number of our servants, looking to our needs and our other resources, both so that they can be adequately nourished, and so that they can perform their work attentively, without being oppressed by overwork. But the numerous servants in a retinue who lead the way and bring up the rear on excursions, and who have this as their sole function, turn out to be hateful guardians of their master without his noticing it, since he isn't able to go anywhere on his own, or to have a private conversation with anyone unobserved, or do anything that might please him but is forbidden to the servants. Furthermore, such servants are a hindrance to other people, stealing and grabbing things from the market-place, beating and assaulting people – and getting away with it, with the connivance of their fellow servants. And thus, because they are completely corrupted by such things, as well as by their idleness, most slaves are the complete enemies of their masters and at war with them. The masters meanwhile, because they have to provide for these indulgent, prettified libertines, are compelled to work endlessly, to stay awake endless nights, to flatter endless numbers of people, and even slave for them – and the crowning evil is that they completely miss out on the natural life that is fitting for human beings.

30

40

But as for a life of this sort, far removed from Epictetus' education, let it enjoy the punishment it deserves. Anyone who is already a philosopher will use the help of servants, as they use other things, in a way that is commensurate with non-excessive need. And this need will be slight (both because of the simplicity of their life and because of their being able to do most things for themselves), so that they might want a servant when they are sick, or as an assistant when need demands it, or because they are occupied with some finer task, as in the case of the admirable Epictetus himself. He lived alone for a long time, but late in life once he took on a woman as a nurse for a child.[186] The child was going to be exposed by a friend too poor to raise it, so Epictetus himself took the child and raised it. **407**

He has named each of the things we have need of, and now he draws the general conclusion, that in every case we must remove what is in excess. He divides the excessive into two forms, indulgence and external reputation – for in all the cases mentioned these are the two motives for overstepping need: there is no other. The following is an instance of the great zeal divine men had for doing away with everything excessive. They say that Diogenes always used to carry around a wooden cup in his knapsack for drawing water to drink. But one day when he was crossing a river he saw someone drawing water to drink with his hands, and he hurled his cup into the river, saying that he no longer needed it because his hands could fulfil the need.[187]

50

117,1

10

xlv: As for sex, before marriage you should keep pure of it to the extent possible ...

[Commentary on Chapter 33, Lemma xlv]
Self-control over any kind of bodily pleasure has good effects both on the rational soul and on the irrational desires. The rational soul is strengthened by it, and the experience makes it confident that it can master irrationality; and the irrational desires are checked in two ways, because they are abated through inactivity and are habituated to be defeated by reason. Self-control over the pleasure of sexual intercourse, in so far as it is more socially relevant[188] than the others, **408** is that much more useful to the soul and honourable.

Reason is not the only thing that is educable by good teaching and the best laws; even the most violent of the irrational desires may be educated to such an extent that the brute force of the bit is not the only way to curb them – i.e. so that they can also be controlled by obedience to the reins.[189] This is clear because even the desires for food and sex, if habituated in the right way, can be rendered quiescent without the use of force, even though they are natural and violent. People accustomed to fasts are not troubled by the desire for food; quite the opposite, they actually feel oppressed if they eat contrary to their habit of fasting. Among athletes, despite their being full-fleshed and in their prime, the desire for sex becomes quiescent once it has been habituated on account of the Olympic wreath of olive-branches. And, although it is law and custom that forbid intercourse with a

20

30

sister or brother, we see how it's as though it had been enjoined by nature itself: the desires simply cannot be moved in those directions (unless someone is struck with some kind of fury-driven madness).

As for 'keeping pure before marriage', this is quite generally a useful thing, and in particular it is a matter of justice that a wife should receive from her husband the same assurance of virginity that

40   the husband demands from his wife. But if it is necessary before marriage, he says, then 'do only what is lawful and customary'. For anything contrary to custom is generally impious as well (the law would not circumscribe it for no reason at all); it is also evidence of extreme lack of self-control. Furthermore, it accustoms you, and those who imitate you, to disregard other customs as well. **409**

But if you do abstain from such things, he says, 'don't make yourself obnoxious to those who are sexually active, don't be critical, and don't go on about the fact that you are not sexually active yourself.' Such criticisms and reproaches are hateful to the people

50   who hear them, given that we don't bear even our teachers' criticisms without feeling offended. The reason for our finding it hard to bear, I suspect, is that until we are criticized we think we are getting away with it unnoticed, and for that reason we think we haven't done anything wrong either. (The reason for this, in turn, is that we had

118,1 been making use of external reputation in judging ourselves, instead of using our own opinion or that of our superiors, which is to say, using the truth.) If the critic not only uncovers our own error, but also claims to be free of error himself, as though he were proclaiming himself victorious over us in a competition, then we think that we are worsted by the comparison as well, and we feel even more offended. And the fact that the speaker praises himself only adds to our offence, in that we are offended that our opponent has become the judge as well. But a criticism of this sort also harms the critic who goes on

10   about the comparison to himself. It directs his soul outwards, and makes it so that he doesn't abstain from such things or criticize them for the sake of the good, but so that he can gain a good reputation by criticizing others. And when he is seen in such a light by the person being criticized, it makes his criticism more offensive, and the comparison itself also provides a ready defense for the error: the person being criticized has only to say 'But *I* am not a philosopher,' and he has immediately granted himself forgiveness.

xlvi: If someone tells you that so and so is slandering you, don't defend yourself against the charges.

[Commentary on Chapter 33, Lemma xlvi]

20   **410** This seems to be directed to the spirit, since it is the spirit that is moved by such announcements, and it is our vanity and love of honour that are provoked (which are themselves movements of the spirit).

But why does he advise us 'not to defend ourselves against the charges', and to say that we are guilty of other faults as well? This might seem to be taking moderation to immoderate lengths. Perhaps even these comments are consonant with his established aim, i.e. to counsel the soul to rein in from the externals, and turn back to itself, so as to live by itself and not by the externals. Someone who defends himself and is not content with his own knowledge of himself and with the judgement of God (who knows all things), clearly wants to please 30 other human beings. As a result, if he can persuade them that he did not make an error, by lying if need be, then he comes to a stop as though he had made no error at all, contented with persuading the judges that he appointed for himself. But if he despises external things, and becomes his own judge, immune from bribery, then he is convicted of error by the testimony of the perpetrator himself. And actually accusing oneself of other faults strikes at the very roots of the love of honour. For the love of honour is a terribly clever affliction, that clings to the soul and gets rooted in it and turns the soul towards 40 itself. We suppose that we are not the least bit affected by the love of honour, **411** because we want to be honoured for the sake of the good; we do not notice that it is an ugly affliction of the soul that we often seem to want to be honoured for good things.[190] We do not realize that this defiles the good and does not permit it to be good or to be desirable per se, if we choose it not for itself but for the reputation that accompanies it. For then reputation becomes our aim and our good, and the virtue of justice (for example) is merely taken alongside of it under compulsion, i.e. so that we can gain a good reputation by being just.

In the case of those who have other emotions, love of honour seems 50 useful. For we control many other intense emotions by means of the love of honour, and we often choose the most arduous things for its sake, things that are not a whit more moderate than intense punishments. It's for this reason that the love of honour is called 'the last tunic' of the emotions: because when we have used it to strip off the 119,1 other emotions, it clings to the soul even more.[191] But in reality, the love of honour does not relieve us of the other emotions; it simply checks their visible activity. It keeps some people from active fornication, but they don't stop being shameless in their thoughts; hence it does not stop the other emotions, and is itself intensified and made more difficult through its suppression of the activities of the other emotions. So for a young man it seems to be useful in the beginning 10 for bringing youthful emotions to heel; but if it persists as one advances in age, then it is a real menace. It does not permit the soul to turn towards itself, since it must always gape at external reputation, and it never permits the soul to choose a good per se but only for the reputation that results from it – which is to say, it never chooses the good as the good.[192] **412**

There is another ridiculous thing that happens to people with this
sort of character: as a rule, they despise and spit on the multitude of
20   humanity, and consider them unworthy of mention, but all the while
they are dependent on their opinion, as if they were of great importance, so they are hanging from it as if by a thread.

Since the love of honour is that sort of thing, there is nothing else
so effective for its eradication as moderation in character, and the
declaration of one's own faults. But we must be careful not to do even
this in a vain way; if it's to be done genuinely, there must no longer
remain even the hope of a good reputation. If it could be made
necessary that our excellences were never known to any other human
being, while our deficiencies were known to all, this would eradicate
our love of honour, and our doing what we do for the sake of a good
30   reputation, because we could no longer hope for one.

xlvii: As for the theatre, for the most part it is not necessary to
attend it ...

[Commentary on Chapter 33, Lemma xlvii]
It is not only desires for food and sex that are irrational, but desires
for visual and auditory displays as well. So he teaches us the attitude
we ought to have towards them, when he says 'as for the theatre, it is
not necessary to attend it' all the time. Or rather, it is necessary not
to attend it all the time; for people who devote themselves to the
theatres have a histrionic life. 'But if the occasion should arise' (e.g.
because of a traditional festival celebrated by theatrical contests; or
in order to be accommodating to the masses – for they take offence at
40   people who seem to be evading the usual way of life – ; or for a sort of
trial or examination, to compare how we reacted to such things last
year and how we react now; or for some other **413** reasonable need) –
'if an occasion should arise' for going to the theatre, then here too[193]
we should 'exercise the utmost attention' so as to remain in ourselves
rather than surrender ourselves to the things that happen there. We
should 'want just the winner to win and want just what happens to
happen', i.e. we should not import our desires and aversions into these
things, since they are the most external of all externals. And we
50   should be cautious not to make our demeanour so dignified that it
strikes our companions as offensive. Rather, it should be calm and
deliberate, yet with a certain urbanity, so that we don't 'shout' out
loud and 'get carried away' with the winners, or abandon ourselves to
laughter at people who say witty things; instead, we should praise the
winners in a discriminating way, and acknowledge the wits with a
smile.
120,1   'And after the exit from the spectacle', he says, 'don't talk a lot
about the things that happened' that have 'no bearing on correcting
yourself.' They are not educational enough that one should think

them worthy of further discussion. So we can understand the words 'whatever has no bearing on correcting yourself' in two ways: either as referring to everything we say about the events in the spectacle; or, if the 'whatever' is used to distinguish some specific portion of what we say, then I suppose he would be advising us to say only what does have some bearing on correcting ourselves. (An instance of the latter would be critical remarks about badly conducted motions of our own during the spectacle.)[194] But excessive discussion of the events in the spectacle is clear evidence that one considers the spectacle to be something great and worthy of amazement, which would not be the case in the absence of vulgar sympathies.

xlviii: As for public readings, don't go readily, or on a whim.

[Commentary on Chapter 33, Lemma xlviii]
414 After spectacles, he speaks about public readings given by people who are devoted to poetry and rhetoric in order to display their verbal facility. Sometimes they deliver encomia of people in power, and sometimes they narrate the ancestry of cities, or give vivid descriptions of locales, or practise forensic topics, or things of that sort. Since they are meant for display and are focussed on the external, he says that we should not go 'readily' or without some reason that permits our attendance (e.g. friendship with the speaker, or the power of the person being praised, or for the sake of some accommodation – since that is everywhere much in demand, in order to mollify people who are jealous of anyone who makes a retreat from vulgar habits). 'But if you do go to a public reading', he says, 'then guard your dignity and poise – at the same time, don't be obnoxious.' 'Dignity' consists in commensurate praise, delivered at the right time; 'poise' consists in not being moved in a disorderly fashion, or shouting, or saying something at the wrong time, but instead keeping one's character and body orderly and constant. 'Not being obnoxious' consists in not seeming too preoccupied, as though you were pondering something else, and not keeping silent more than you have to (one may praise whatever is moderately said), and not judging the speeches harshly and criticizing them as false or badly versified or ill-phrased. And in general **415** the policy that is least obnoxious and most agreeable, as well as just, is to show yourself pleased with the speaker when he speaks well, and to be pleased with the subject of praise when he is truly and justly honoured.

xlix: When you are about to meet someone, especially someone who is considered your social superior …

[Commentary on Chapter 33, Lemma xlix]
People who are turning back towards themselves and want to live by

themselves are for the most part unaccustomed to encounters with
the powerful; that is why Epictetus sets out for them the examples of
Socrates and Zeno, so that by looking at them they may find a manner
of encountering the powerful that will be appropriate for themselves.

50   So we should keep in mind how Socrates and Zeno used to encounter
such people; bearing themselves with a sober greatness of spirit that
is the result neither of artifice nor pretence, but is of a piece with their
121,1   own lives, and is purified of any superciliousness or bravado; neither
humbled by the weight of power, nor arrogantly disdainful of it. It is
a function of the same character to engage in neither flattery nor
aggressive criticism, but to give commensurate praise for things that
are done well, and to begin one's conversation with this (as doctors
are wont to smear honey on harsh-tasting drugs). Then one does not
seem to be a harsh inquisitor of whatever is not done well, but a
partner in its correction, who is solicitous and sympathetic, and
10   shares the person's dismay when their fine deeds are occasionally
besmirched by a few oversights. **416**

The followers of Socrates and Zeno, I believe, generally demonstrated to such people how many unchoiceworthy things are involved
in positions of power and apparent superiority over human beings,
and that the sole choiceworthy thing about such positions is doing
good, so that anyone disregarding that reaps what's bad about it and
is deprived of its goods. Now, while it is clear that one should set
Socrates and Zeno before oneself as a pattern, one should also guard
the measure of one's own life and naturally employ things commen-
20   surate with it. For how could someone with a life that is still in
progress and still in need of the teaching of Epictetus make use of the
words of Socrates or Zeno or Diogenes? He would inevitably seem
ridiculous. Antigonos, who became the great king of Syria after
Alexander, is reported to have said that he felt he had never really
been put to the test except when he encountered Zeno; and yet he had
encountered many other philosophers.[195]

From here on, Epictetus relates the appropriate actions for a
student regarding encounters, beginning with encounters with those
in positions of power and superiority.

1: When you visit one of the very powerful …

[Commentary on Chapter 33, Lemma 1]
30   He said roughly the same thing earlier in the chapter beginning **417**
'When you are intending to take on an action, remind yourself etc.'[196]
But in that passage he advances his argument using the case of
bathing, whereas in this passage he uses a more important example,
that of visiting someone in power. The point he developed there was
disdaining events and preserving our prohairesis in a natural state,
whereas here it is that we should make our advance deliberations

secure, and not make frivolous suppositions about the unpleasant
things that will happen, but ones as close as possible to the truth. For   40
we chose to visit the powerful even if the things he mentions follow;
but when they happen we often feel regret and say that it was not
worth incurring the consequences, either because we did not choose
well at the start, or because we are more disturbed than we should be
by what happens. Both of these belong to ordinary people and involve
a use of externals that is neither good nor according to their nature,
but rather takes them to be important.

He has already spoken about encounters with people who are in a
position of superiority, but are not too difficult to encounter, and told
us how we should conduct ourselves, i.e. on the model of Socrates and   50
Zeno. Now he sets out to speak about people whom it is harder work
to meet, and tells us how we should prepare ourselves for encounters
with these people. If no necessity demands it, then you should decline
the visit; but if it is necessary, and if it seems right to choose it even
along with its unchoiceworthy aspects, then you should bear what   122,1
befalls you without regret.

li: In conversation, refrain from reminiscing about your own
deeds and adventures interminably ...

[Commentary on Chapter 33, Lemma li]
418 After encounters with those in positions of superiority, he talks
about encounters with the masses and how we should act there too.
We should not render ourselves obnoxious or disdainful of the people
we encounter – rather, we should be beneficial to them, to the extent
possible. 'Not reminiscing about your own deeds and adventures
interminably' removes the obnoxiousness from this procedure (for   10
people are offended by those who praise themselves, thinking that
they are themselves thereby accused by them and reproached by the
comparison). It also checks the soul's tendency to look outward and
love honour, and indicates greatness of spirit.

Earlier he said that we should not laugh at 'many things' ourselves,
or indulge in frequent or 'unrestrained' laughter; now he says that we
should also not provoke laughter in others. He supplies the explanation for this when he says 'It's a dangerous habit, that leads to the
behaviour of ordinary people.' For to say the kind of thing that
provokes laughter in ordinary people means that what we say is   20
completely acceptable to them and belongs to the condition of ordinary people. Thus they think that the person who provokes laughter
is as much an ordinary person as they are, if not more, and even if
they happened to hold him in respect before, 'this is all that is needed
to make those around him slacken their respect for him.' (Even some
people who seem to be sensible make jokes, because they want to look
clever.) **419**

As for 'obscene language', it is clear that anyone who seems to have made any degree of progress will never tolerate using it themselves. But Epictetus advises that, so far as possible, we should not tolerate
30   others' using it, either. Instead, 'if the moment is opportune', i.e. if the person who introduced it is young, and not beyond shame or filled with conceit at their wealth or stature, he says 'you should rebuke him', since in that case you will not seem ill-bred, either to the person who used the obscenity or to the company. But if he happens to be older and haughty in character and elevated in wealth or stature, then it is offensive to rebuke him, and your frankness of speech will actually seem ridiculous, as well as being ineffective and obnoxious and likely to gain you an enemy. So what should one do in that case? 'Make your displeasure plain by falling silent.'
40   Note how he preserves a measure that is suitable to the different cases. In the case of those who talk about 'gladiators, horse-races, food and drink, or other people, whether in praise or blame', he says, 'if you can, you should shift the conversation'. But in this case, 'if the moment is opportune', he bids you to 'rebuke him as well'. In the former case, if it is not possible to 'make the shift', he says 'keep silent'; whereas here he says 'make your displeasure plain'.

[*Encheiridion* Chapter 34 (= Lemma lii): When you get an impression of pleasure, guard yourself, just as you do in other cases, so you don't get grabbed by it. Instead, let the thing wait for you, and give yourself a bit of a break. Then remember both times: the time in which you enjoy the pleasure, and the time after the enjoyment, in which you will feel regret and revile yourself. And contrast with these how much you will rejoice and praise yourself, if you abstain.

But if it should seem to you that it is the opportune moment to engage in the act, then be careful that its seductiveness, sweetness and enticement don't get the better of you. Instead, contrast with this how much better it is to be aware that you have won this victory.]

lii: When you get an impression of pleasure, guard yourself, just as you do in other cases, so you don't get grabbed by it. **420**

[Commentary on Chapter 34, Lemma lii]
Bodily pleasure is the most harmful for the soul: each one, like a nail, nails the soul to the body; and it is for this reason that God made them
50   of brief duration.[197] In the case of food and drink, the pleasure is only there so long as we feel them in our mouths; once they are swallowed down, it completely disappears. Likewise in the case of sexual intercourse, the feeling of pleasure is present only through the actual time
123,1   of the activity; once it has past, the experience[198] is as though it had

never happened. It is clear, then, that the pleasure consists in its being perceived, since what is not perceived does not give any pleasure. But pleasures concerning external things, like clothing, ornament, money or possessions, are also of brief duration. Although we are pleased when we acquire them, once we are accustomed to them we no longer feel any pleasure in them. When they are taken away, however, they are succeeded by a violent distress, which is much more long-lasting than the pleasure. So in this way, although pleasure,   10
especially bodily pleasure, lasts for a very brief time, it leaves in its wake harm to the soul always and in every case, and often to the body as well (when the enjoyment is incommensurate).[199] Whereas self-control with respect to pleasure produces a lasting benefit for the body and the **421** soul, and a pleasure of a different kind, which by nature accompanies self-control, and is unharmful and non-violent.

Now that we have made these preliminary points, then, let us see what Epictetus says.[200] 'When you get an impression of pleasure', he says, 'just as you do in other cases' – for instance, wealth or political power or any of the other external things – so, but even more so in the   20
case of pleasure, 'guard yourself' immediately, so the impression 'does not grab you', rushing you into the act. Rather, let it wait a little, and once you have secured yourself 'a bit of a break' by collecting yourself in this way, consider the two times: the time of enjoyment, which is very brief, and the long one that follows, which is full of harm and regret, in which you rebuke yourself for having been worsted. And contrast with these the longer time in which by exercising self-control you will be seen[201] to have a benefit and a pure pleasure when you praise and approve yourself. For if you get completely clear about this   30
comparison, then the desire will readily be tamed in its shame at the obviousness of its inferiority. And if you do this again and again, then it will be humbled and no longer bother you.

If the pleasure ends immediately after the act, and afterwards there is no difference between the person who has enjoyed the pleasure and someone who didn't enjoy it, except his impression of having enjoyed it, then isn't the latter in the same state as the one who did already enjoy and reap the pleasure, except he didn't share in the harm? For the mere impression of having enjoyed a pleasure has no value on any account – our memory of enjoying things in dreams makes that clear (it retains only an obscure trace of pleasure).

But since there are times when we also partake of certain pleasures according to right reason (for instance, begetting children or   40
bathing for a fever), whenever 'it should seem to you that it is the opportune moment to engage in the act', he says, 'be careful that its seductiveness and enticement don't get the better of you' – i.e. not to lose yourself and give yourself wholly over to the pleasure. Instead, compare at that moment how much finer it is **422** to control pleasure than to be worsted by it. For it is clear that mastering one's irrational

emotions is better than being their slave to the same degree that being a human being is better than being a beast.

[*Encheiridion* Chapter 35 (= Lemma liii): When you have determined that something should be done, and you do it, never shun being seen to do it, even if most people are going to believe something rather odd about it. If you are not right to do it, then it is the deed itself that you should shun; but if you are right, then why fear those who are wrong to rebuke you?]

liii: When you have determined that something should be done, and you do it, never shun being seen to do it, even if most people are going to believe something rather odd about it.[202]

[Commentary on Chapter 35, Lemma liii]

50   He is very eager that the good should be chosen on account of the good itself, rather than on account of the opinion of the many, so that it may be really good. For anyone who chooses something for the sake of reputation, posits that as the good instead of the good itself. Hence if your decision that it was good to do this thing was incorrect, then

124,1   you must shun the action for the reason that it's not good. But if you have correctly realized that it should be done, and you do it, then you ought not to shun being seen to do it because of those who will incorrectly find fault with the outcome. Otherwise the consequence is that in the place of what is genuinely good (i.e. what is correctly recognized as being good), you will prefer what is not good but rather bad, because it is false (i.e. the incorrect belief of the many concerning the action performed). Another consequence is that you believe that the very thing judged good by right reason is bad, since you shun it

10   (and one only shuns the bad). And a further consequence for someone like this who stands apart from himself and from the facts, is that he is carried off to the opinions of the many, and seeks the good and the bad there, as well as the true and the false.

[*Encheiridion* Chapter 36 (= Lemma liv): Just as 'it is day' and 'it is night' have great value for a disjunction, but disvalue for a conjunction, so too selecting the larger portion may have value for the body, but it has disvalue for preserving the communal aspect of banqueting as it should be. So whenever you eat in company with someone, remember to consider not only the value of the things set before you for the body, but also to preserve your respect for your fellow banqueter.]

liv: Just as 'Either it is day or it is night' has great value for a disjunction, but disvalue for a conjunction ... [203]

[Commentary on Chapter 36, Lemma liv]

423 Some hypothetical syllogisms (a field whose technical treatment the Stoics refined) are disjunctive and some are conditional or conjunctive.[204] Disjunctive syllogisms are those in which, when one <proposition>[205] is the case, the other never is, and when one is not the case, the other always is. Thus, when I say:

'*Either it is day or it is night*;

but it is night;

therefore it is not day';

when one <proposition> is posited, the other is always denied. But when I say:

'but it is not day;

therefore it is night',

or,

'but it is not night;

therefore it is day',

then by the denial of one <proposition> the other is posited. That's what a *disjunction*[206] is like; it's where '*Either it is day or it is night*' is assumed as an axiom, i.e. as something evidently true and in accordance with the common conceptions. (The Stoics called these 'axioms'.)[207] A *conjunction*,[208] on the other hand, is whenever two <propositions> have been conjoined with one another in such a way that one is the antecedent and the other the consequent, and then by the positing of the antecedent the consequent follows, but by the denial of the consequent the antecedent is denied. E.g. 'it is not night' is truly conjoined with 'if it is day'. For 'it is not night' follows truly on the antecedent 'if it is day'.[209] **424** After all, in this conjunction, the consequent is posited by the positing of the antecedent: '... but it is day; therefore it is not night.'[210] And by the denial of the consequent, the antecedent is simultaneously denied: '... but it is not the case that it is not night' (or rather, '... but it is night' obviously, because the two denials make one assent) 'therefore it is not day'. That's what a *conjunction* or conditional is like.

But let us now consider what Epictetus said. '*Either it is day or it is night*' is accepted as an indisputable axiom for a disjunctive syllogism, but not for a conditional syllogism, where the axiom you need to assume as premiss is the conjunction 'if it is day, it is not night'. So, he says, just as '*Either it is day or it is night*' *has great value for a disjunction* (for on this fact depends the whole disjunctive syllogism[211]), *but disvalue for a conjunction* (for it tears apart the combination in 'if it is day then it is not night'), so too in a dinner-party, *selecting the greater part* is useful for the body, and beneficial and choiceworthy, but has disvalue for *preserving the communal aspect of banqueting*. For taking the greater portion tears apart the communal aspect, just as the disjunction '*Either it is day or it is night*'

20

30

40

50

125,1

tore apart the conjunction. *So whenever you eat in company* with other people, *remember to consider not only the value of the things set before you for your own body*, and to choose from among them, *but also* the value for the communal aspect of your soul, which you ought to *preserve* in an unimpeachable condition.

10 Even though he constructed his argument for the case of banqueting, it is clear that we should extend it generally to every communal association and interaction. For taking advantage severs every community, just as each person's getting their share holds it together and makes it grow and endure. Even a community of bandits, despite being composed of such men, **425** is safeguarded so long as it preserves the injunction not to take advantage of one another, because even an unjust association like that is held together by this trace of justice.[212] He has previously exhorted the reader to freedom in many

20 places, and elsewhere to bravery and magnanimity, to wisdom and to temperance; in this chapter he encourages him to justice, by proposing the removal of what impedes it – i.e., taking advantage of others.

[*Encheiridion* Chapter 37 (= Lemma lv): If you take on a role that is beyond your ability, you cut a poor figure in this role and neglect the role that you could have fulfilled.]

lv: If you take on a role that is beyond your ability, you cut a poor figure in this role and neglect the role that you could have fulfilled.

[Commentary on Chapter 37, Lemma lv]
We shouldn't practise the best thing simpliciter, but rather the best of the practices that fit our measure. For nothing comes to be in incommensurate receptacles.[213] Hence we shouldn't take on the larger roles rashly (those of a teacher or philosopher or pilot in a ship or ruler

30 of a city). It is better to act creditably in a role of lower degree, fully mastering this role, even surpassing it, than to 'cut a poor figure' in a superior one, falling short of its value. And its better to be the best au pair than a cheap professor,[214] or a worthy household-manager than a wretched ruler. For, in addition to cutting a poor figure in the greater role (and 'cutting a poor figure' I mean not as matter of reputation, **426** but rather according to the very nature of the business) we also lose the right action of the role we could have performed, if we had practised in a measure that fits. After all, someone who acts the part of the slave well is the better actor[215] in a tragedy or comedy

40 than someone who fails to perform well in the role of a despot or king.

This chapter also seems to look to justice, by advising us to select the role in life that is of the appropriate value,[216] and not to take advantage.[217]

[*Encheiridion* Chapter 38 (= Lemma lvi): When you walk you're careful not to step on a nail, or to twist your foot. In the same way, you should be careful not to injure your commanding-faculty. If we protect this in each endeavour, then we will handle the endeavor more securely.]

lvi: When you walk you're careful not to step on a nail, or to twist your foot.

[Commentary on Chapter 38, Lemma lvi]
The human soul is harmed in two ways. First, when the soul impales itself on the irrational emotions, and glues itself to the body through them, it grumbles and complains to itself to some degree, but is worsted by the emotions because once they have become muscular it is tyrannized by them.[218] Secondly, when it is distorted in its own judgement, it does not even distinguish itself as something different from the irrational emotions. So the teacher instructs us to guard ourselves against both of these in the conduct of our lives, which he compares to walking. Otherwise the soul is impaled on the irrational emotions, which being bodily, like nails[219] nail it (once it has been glued to them) onto the body. Is there any nail that can so transfix the soul as these irrational emotions, which make the soul believe that itself and them and the body are one? As for the distortion **427** of the believing or pedestrian[220] part of the soul, by which the soul associates with the body and with the bodily lives,[221] he quite properly likened this to twisting one's foot. And just as we guard our bodies when we are walking, so too in the progress of the endeavours of life, he advises us to guard our rational soul, which by nature is the thing that rules in a human animal, and which actually characterizes this animal. Otherwise it will forget itself, whether it is impaled by the emotions through gluttony,[222] or distorted in its judgement and opinion through laziness. For 'if we protect ourselves' in each case, like walkers, 'we will handle each endeavour more securely'. Even if some minor slip occurs, we can more readily correct it if we are protecting ourselves (since even if we stumble a little and step on the nail or tread awkwardly, still because we are paying attention we can easily take our foot off the nail before it is impaled, and easily correct the awkwardness of our tread).

50

126,1

10

20

[*Encheiridion* Chapter 39 (= Lemma lvii): The body is the measure of an individual's possessions, as the foot is for his shoes. So if you take a stand on this, you will preserve the measure. But if you overstep it, from then on you will inevitably get carried away (as though over a cliff). Just like with shoes: if you overstep your foot, you get a golden shoe, then a purple one, then an embroidered one. Once you exceed the measure there is no limit.]

lvii: The body is the measure of an individual's possessions, as the foot is for his shoes ...

[Commentary on Chapter 39, Lemma lvii]
In the things that concern the body – clothing, food, possessions, property – **428** there are two things: possession and use. He spoke earlier about the use of these things,[223] telling us that we should employ them for the bare needs of the body, stripping away every excess that tends towards vanity or indulgence. Now he teaches us about their possession, by telling us that its measure is also the body.
30 For if the measure of possession is use (we acquire possessions in order to use them), and the measure of use is the body and its needs, then it is clear that the body and its needs must also be 'the measure of possession', as the foot and its needs are the measure for shoes. Hence if someone looked to this need, he would be satisfied with bare skins (with the upper to warm and protect the foot, and the sole not to step directly on harmful things). But if someone oversteps the needs of the foot with an eye to adornment and indulgence, then 'you get a golden shoe, then a purple one, then an embroidered one', as he
40 says. (Purple and embroidered shoes were apparently so elaborate among the Romans that they were preferred even to golden ones.)
Likewise in the case of possession and the things that serve the needs of the body. If someone oversteps the measure of need and the limit it imposes, 'from then on he gets carried away' into limitlessness, piling up things on things, until he has been carried away into the deepest depths of indulgence and empty vanity (the sources of his wrong turn), and of the needy indigence (which follows the wrong turn), **429** and of pinching oppression (which follows that).
50 If we acquire ten possessions, we want twenty; and if we get twenty, we want forty, and so on; and there is no end of this propulsion into the chasm of insatiability. It is clear that for anything accepted for the needs of the body, possession that steps beyond the
127,1 limits falls into limitlessness. And in the end we actually forget the goal and forget the need to which it contributes: the need of the body. That is why we often even betray our bodies owing to the insatiability of our acquisition of possessions.[224]
Perhaps the illustration of the shoe, if we interpret it as exceeding the measure with reference to size, and not with reference to adornment [... [225]] as we make our way in it, often stumbling as well, and sometimes one falls headlong over a cliff? But we must distinguish what he says about possession from what has been said about use.
10 These chapters can also[226] be seen to be directing us towards

justice, by teaching us to preserve the fit measure in our possession and use of externals.

[*Encheiridion* Chapter 40 (= Lemma lviii): As soon as they are fourteen, women are addressed by men as 'Ladies'. That's why when they see that there is nothing else for them to do except sleep with men, they begin to beautify themselves and put all of their hopes in this. So it is worth being careful that they feel that they are honoured only for appearing orderly and modest.]

lviii: As soon as they are fourteen, women are addressed by men as 'Ladies'.

[Commentary on Chapter 40, Lemma lviii]
He has permitted even marriage to those who choose the natural life. Now he goes on to indicate in a few words the appropriate way for them to care for their wives.[227] **430** He compares it with the usage of most people, and guides the former on the basis of the bad results of the latter.

For most people, he says, flatter women right from a young age, and honour them, addressing them as 'Ladies', with no other end in   20
view than sleeping with them. Hence the women quite reasonably make themselves ready for this: they 'beautify themselves and put all of their hopes in this'. Nor should they be held responsible so much as the men, who honour them on this account. Hence it is necessary to provide them right from the start with the awareness that among us they would be honoured for no other reason than that their characters have become orderly, and that they have subordinated themselves to their husbands through respect. For the woman who has these qualities will then easily be habituated to housework, child-rearing and caring for her husband, and the frugal life, all of which befit women   30
who are going to be beautiful.[228]

[*Encheiridion* Chapter 41 (= Lemma lix): It is a sign of a bad nature to busy oneself with the affairs of the body – for instance exercising a lot, eating and drinking a lot, excreting and fornicating a lot. All this should be done only incidentally; all your attention should be directed back towards your own judgement.]

lix: It is a sign of a bad nature to busy oneself with the affairs of the body ...

[Commentary on Chapter 41, Lemma lix]
Just as those who have a good nature are zealous about the highest and most perfect and precise aspects of their proper nature and busy themselves with these things, so too those who have a bad nature

busy themselves with its trivial aspects, the lowest and most diffuse and accessible to the many. So for human beings, who get their essence from the rational soul that uses the body as an instrument, to abandon the activities that are natural to the soul, and to busy
40 themselves with the body, 'is a sign of a bad nature', just as its cause is a bad nature. For what craftsman worth mentioning **431** wastes his time on the maintenance of his instruments,[229] while neglecting the craft that makes use of them? 'To busy oneself with the affairs of the body' is a sign not only of a bad nature, but also of excessive sympathy. (We busy ourselves with the things we rejoice in and feel sympathy with.) So we must consider business about the body to be *incidental*, he says, and instead channel our eagerness principally towards that which uses the body. This is the just distribution of our appropriate actions in these spheres.

> [*Encheiridion* Chapter 42 (= Lemma lx): Whenever someone treats you badly, or speaks badly of you, remember that he did or said it because he took it to be the appropriate thing for him. It isn't possible for him to follow how things appear to you, only how they appear to him. So if they appear to him wrongly, then he's the one who is harmed, since he's the one who was deceived. After all, if someone believes a true conjunction is false, it isn't the conjunction that is harmed, but the person who has been deceived. Taking your impulse from these points, you will be disposed gently towards the person insulting you: you should repeat in each case 'That's what he thought'.]

lx: Whenever someone treats you badly, or speaks badly of you ...

[Commentary on Chapter 42, Lemma lx]
50 This injunction too exhorts us to mildness and the endurance of bad things, and goes about it in two different ways. In one way, because each person follows his own impression (or 'appearance') of what's right, and it is not possible for someone else to follow what we think is right unless it appears to him in the same light. So you should not
128,1 get annoyed if he follows what appears right to him, since you follow this yourself as well, and so do all human beings. So who in their right mind would get annoyed at our common nature?

Secondly, if you get annoyed because he thought something was right that was neither right nor just, then your annoyance is also absurd, because he is the one who has been harmed, not you. For someone who believes that what is not right is right has been deceived; and anyone who has been deceived is harmed. **432** So the
10 person who 'treats you badly, or speaks badly of you' is the one who has been harmed, not you. Anyhow, you wouldn't have the strength to harm him (nor would even a really powerful person with their

greater strength), given that the external things thought to be harmful happen to the body and to externals, so they are not even harmful to *him* strictly speaking, while deceit belongs to the soul, in virtue of which he subsists.

Further, the person who has been deceived is himself the one who has been harmed, and not the person concerning whom he is deceived, as Epictetus demonstrates plainly with the case of the conjunction.[230] For instance, if someone believes that 'If it is day, then the sun is over the earth' is false, it isn't the conjunction that has been harmed (it has its own truth), but rather the person who is deceived about it. So too, 20 the person who insults or mistreats you contrary to what is right is himself the one who is harmed. But you have not been harmed at all, nor have you suffered anything bad, especially if the essence of the good and bad is in what is up to us.

Keeping in mind, then, both that each person inevitably follows how things appear to himself, and that he is the one who is harmed, not you, you will be disposed gently and magnanimously towards someone who insults you, if in addition[231] you habituate yourself to say on each occasion of this sort 'That's what he thought; following what one thinks is inevitable.' 30

[*Encheiridion* Chapter 43 (= Lemma lxi): Every object has two handles, one of them bearable, the other unbearable.[232] If your brother acts unjustly, then don't take it from that side, namely that he is unjust (for that's not its bearable handle) but rather take it from the other side, namely that he is your brother, and reared with you. Then you will take it in the way in which it is bearable.]

lxi: Every object has two handles, one of them bearable, the other unbearable.

[Commentary on Chapter 43, Lemma lxi]
Because generated things are composed of contraries, in one respect they all agree with and correspond to one another and are mutually bearable; **433** but in another respect they disagree and are unbearable. Fire, for instance, because it is hot and dry, agrees with air in respect of being hot, and is bearable to it; but in respect of its dryness it is opposed and in conflict. In the same way, a brother who is unjust also has two handles. One handle is bearable, the handle of 'brother'. The other is unbearable, the handle of 'being unjust'. It is clear that 40 we are at ease, mild and contented with things that are bearable, but we get upset, become harsh and are discontented with unbearable things. So if we want always to be in good spirits and contented and mild in every respect, then, since all things have these 'two handles,

one bearable and the other unbearable', we must grab hold of them by the bearable one.

For everything really is like this: wealth, poverty, health, disease, marriage, being single, children, childlessness, and everything else in life. Wealth has a bearable aspect, namely abundance of means, and
50 an unbearable aspect, namely preoccupation and distractedness. And what is bearable in poverty is the peace and freedom from entanglements, but what is unbearable is the want of means. In health the bearable part is the physical ease and its utility, the unbearable part its audacity and empathy. What is bearable in illness is the moderation of the emotions in the soul, what is unbearable is the suffering.
129,1 In marriage what is bearable is having children and looking after people, while what is unbearable is its plurality of needs and irrational sympathy. And lack of children brings freedom, and for the finer sort a life of scholarship, without having to give thought to providing means after one's death, and, greatest of all in my view, not being compelled to have sympathy for one's children even if they are sometimes bad (which means one has sympathy for something bad). Being mistreated and insulted have bearable aspects: sometimes we
10 learn something about ourselves which we had not known before, but always it challenges our ability to endure evils. Bodily punishment, the thing we shun most of all, has a bearable aspect in the training and purification of the soul. **434** And everything of that kind offers the great good of enduring it courageously. For passing through things nobly when you have encountered them is more beneficial for a human being even than not encountering them to begin with, given that not encountering them is a good for the body and external things, while passing through them nobly is a good for the soul. Indeed, even our enemies have two handles, and it is possible to benefit from them
20 as well, since they put our emotions to very bitter trials, and make us become more secure. (In fact, Plutarch of Chaeronea wrote a whole book *On Benefiting from One's Enemies*.)

[*Encheiridion* Chapter 44 (= Lemma lxii): The following arguments are invalid: 'I am wealthier than you; therefore, I am greater than you;' 'I am more eloquent than you; therefore, I am greater than you.' Rather, it is the following that are valid: 'I am wealthier than you; therefore, my possessions are greater than yours;' 'I am more eloquent than you; therefore, my style is greater than yours.' But you are neither your possessions nor your style.]

lxii: The following arguments are invalid: 'I am wealthier than you; therefore, I am greater than you.'

[Commentary on Chapter 44, Lemma lxii]
People who are zealous about speeches are also for the most part equally zealous about style and composition. This does not befit the philosopher, unless he has this sort of verbal felicity naturally and without training, owing to his having been carefully brought up from childhood with the liberal studies. And even should he have this, Epictetus does not want the philosopher to think it any great thing, since he does not have this as his end, and does not have his essence in accordance with it.   30

When style is beautiful, then it has its own proper good; and someone who makes beautiful style their end is a poet or a writer. But it wouldn't be right for someone who has his essence in accordance with the rational form of existence and takes as his end the way of life natural to it, to say that he is greater than someone else when he is more verbally felicitous. **435** For the style is not the person himself, nor does he posit the style as his end in such a way as to have his specific form in accordance with it (as every craftsman is specified by his craft). Rather, the right thing for him would be to say, 'My style is more beautiful than yours.'

Since he is addressing philosophers, the principal thing that needs   40
repressing is their excitement over style; he uses 'being wealthier' as an example, and also in order to moderate his rebuke.

[*Encheiridion* Chapter 45 (= Lemma lxiii): Someone washes quickly. Don't say they wash 'badly', just 'quickly'. Someone drinks a lot of wine. Don't say they drink 'badly', just 'a lot'. Before you have determined their belief, how do you know if they do it badly? That way, you won't be getting cataleptic impressions of one set of things, and assenting to another.]

lxiii: Someone washes quickly. Don't say they wash 'badly', just 'quickly'.

[Commentary on Chapter 45, Lemma lxiii]
He wants us to have a more precise judgement about things, so that we don't blame or praise anyone for what he does unless we know the target he is looking at when he does it, since it is the target that gives the specific form to the event. Hence someone can benefit when he hits out, but harm giving nourishment; and sometimes one performs a just act by stealing and an unjust act by providing something.   50

So we must judge events in themselves, he says, and if someone washes quickly, say that they wash quickly, but not add the qualification that they do it well or badly until we learn their target. What if they are unwell and happen to suffer insomnia some night, and   130,1
need a bath for therapy? It is the target that adds the quality of doing⸱ it well or badly, and we must wait for this before adding 'badly' or

'well' to the 'bathing quickly'. (Even drinking a lot of wine is permitted on account of bodily idiosyncrasy, **436** or the condition of the air – e.g. before or during the Dog-Star – , or a type of disease, or a plague-ridden place.)

But if we do not act in this way (judging the actions themselves as they stand and saying that it is done 'quickly' or 'a lot', but not adding
10   the qualification until we learn the target) the result is that we perceive one thing (that's what 'getting cataleptic impressions' means), that is, we grasp how one set of things appears, such as its speed, or its quantity, but we 'assent' (that is, we bring our judgement to bear) to another by saying that what appeared was either badly or well done. But it is absurd that we should see one thing and say something else about it.

I take it that he wants us not praise or blame at random, but especially to reject unjust blame. Hence this chapter is constructed
20   around the latter sort of case, and so it too will tend towards justice.

[*Encheiridion* Chapter 46 (= Lemma lxiv): Never claim to be a philosopher when you are with ordinary people, or even talk about doctrines very much. Instead, do what follows from the doctrines. For instance, when at a dinner-party, don't talk about the right way to eat; instead, eat the right way.

Remember that Socrates had so thoroughly got rid of any showiness that people would come to him looking to have him put them together with philosophers – and he would do it. That's how patient he was when he was slighted.

When you are among ordinary people, if the conversation should come round to some bit of doctrine, then for the most part you should keep silent; otherwise, there's a great danger that you will immediately vomit up material that you have not digested. And when someone tells you that you don't know anything, and you remain unbitten, you will know that you have started the work. After all, even sheep don't show their shepherds how much they have eaten by bringing the fodder to them; instead, they digest the grass inside, and produce wool and milk on the outside.

The same goes for you, then: don't make a show of the doctrines to ordinary people, but rather show them the works that stem from the doctrines once they've been fully digested.]

lxiv: Never claim to be a philosopher, or even talk about doctrines very much, when you are with ordinary people …

[Commentary on Chapter 46, Lemma lxiv]
He addresses these comments to the person still making progress (not to the complete philosopher, who would no longer need such advice;

nor would he say to a complete philosopher 'there's a great danger that you will immediately vomit up material that you have not digested') because people still making progress are troubled by the emotion of love of honour or showiness. So he set out to eradicate this emotion using a variety of approaches, for this reason. **437** Now it would be false to say that the molten bronze is a statue, or that the embryo is a human being; similarly it is false to say that someone still making progress is a philosopher. (Indeed, if one considers the great-   30
ness of the life[233] of a genuine philosopher, as well as their superiority to other people, it will seem not only false but actually impious to say that.) But someone who does not claim to be a philosopher, and does not arrogate to himself the teaching status of a philosopher, wouldn't try to teach either. Someone may object: 'How can the progressor get training, if Epictetus forbids him to talk to ordinary people, where words are not for the sake of training, but for show? How will he fit in with them then?' By perfecting the works that are taught by the   40
words, and not spouting empty words. For the goal is not to talk, but to do what you are talking about.

So if you find yourself 'at a dinner party, don't talk about the right way to eat; instead, eat the right way'. That way, if an occasion for teaching does arise, your words will proceed from your life, and their appearance will be more effective. For what a sorry thing it is to teach the right way to eat, or how to deal with situations, and then not to stick with the laws that you yourself have laid down! And don't just abstain from starting such conversations, he says, but even if other   50
ordinary people are discussing such things, don't wish to appear to be a teacher among ordinary people, since you are in danger of 'vomiting up material that you have not digested'. For just as food, once di-gested, nourishes the condition of the body, so too words, once digested, nourish the condition of the soul; and this will later give   131,1
forth fruitful words, like an enduring root-stock. But if someone regurgitates words he has heard before this condition has been per-fected, he is in real danger of 'vomiting up what he has not yet digested'. (Regurgitating the very same words one has heard **438** instead of producing them from one's internal condition, really does resemble vomiting up food.)

After the soul has inclined towards the outside, it benefits from good examples, and for that reason he introduces Socrates, who, despite being a complete philosopher – to the extent of having been declared by the god to be the wisest of all human beings – had thoroughly got rid of any showiness in his own life. When he was   10
approached by some people who foolishly looked down on him, but 'looked to have him put them together' with other people for their education, he took them enthusiastically and introduced them to sophists. For instance, when Hippocrates the son of Apollodorus asked him, he put him together with Protagoras; and in the

Theaetetus he says 'I've matched up a lot of people with Prodicus, and a lot with other wise and divinely-favoured men.'[234]

But, he says, don't just 'get rid of showiness' and desire for reputa-
20   tion to the extent of not talking about doctrine among ordinary people, or being silent when they speak: rather, even if someone 'tells you that you don't know anything, you should remain unbitten'. For that is good evidence that you disdain external opinion – even better evidence than not chatting about doctrines, since it was not yet clear from that that you were considered by outsiders 'not to know any-thing'.

But if, even when you hear that, 'you remain unbitten', though you had been bitten by it in the past, then 'you will know that you have started the work'. That's why you took on all these words and all this eagerness for philosophy yourself – so that you could do the work that
30   is in accordance with nature, not to talk and hear about it. 'Remaining unbitten when you hear that you don't know anything' is already work: it is disregarding external reputation, whether good or bad. **439** And even if it is sometimes necessary to display your progress to a teacher examining it, what you should display are not the words, but the works that stem from the words when they have been digested and have nourished your condition. After all, 'even sheep don't show their shepherds how much they have eaten by vomiting up the fodder. Instead, they digest the grass, and produce wool and milk on the outside.'

[*Encheiridion* Chapter 47 (= Lemma lxv): Once you have got used to accommodating your body on the cheap, don't get fancy about it! If you drink water, don't take every opportunity to say 'I drink water'. And if you want some practice at hard work some time, practise by yourself, not for an external audience. Don't embrace statues; instead, some time when you are really thirsty, suck in some cool water, and then spit it out – and don't tell anyone.]

lxv: Once you have got used to accommodating your body on the cheap, don't get fancy about it!

[Commentary on Chapter 47, Lemma lxv]
40   There are many grounds on which we want to base a good reputation among people. Some of us seek a good reputation by narrating our actions; others seek to base it on their eloquence; others present themselves as instructors of correct behaviour; and finally, some people base it on their simplicity and endurance.

Epictetus has already given the former cases some medical treat-ment, and now he directs his argument at the last type, advising them not to get fancy about their simplicity and practices (the argument is directed at both) – i.e. not to vaunt and boast, or think one has something great. Instead, one should consider, first, how much simpler than us beggars are, and how much more they endure.[235] Next, even if we are in noteworthy shape in that respect, we should consider 50 how many other goods we do not have, that other people do have. Again, boasting about having an advantage in some respect is harmful in two ways: both because we think the thing is already great and so do not purify it, and also because we do not strive after anything else out of complacency with that. But, he says, don't do these things for show. E.g., if you are a water drinker, don't drag the topic of 132,1 conversation around at any cost **440** to a discussion of this, in order to make it seem quite natural for you to mention that you drink water.

'And if you want some practice in hard work' and self-control, and training in endurance, then do it by yourself, and don't make it obvious to outsiders, or seek to be observed by a lot of people, like the victim violently attacked by a more powerful group of people, trying to call out to the crowd for help, who climbs up on a statue and denounces their violence, collecting a crowd around himself.[236] So 10 don't do your training for show; rather do it by yourself. For instance, 'when you are really thirsty, suck in a mouthful of cool water, and then spit it out – and don't tell any one' that you did it afterwards. In the first place, someone who does this for show has gaped wide open towards the outside, and become completely beside himself, given over to externals. And then he has lost the goods of simplicity and endurance, once he takes their goal to be the opinion of the many.

Nevertheless, practice and endurance are in themselves beneficial, inasmuch as they habituate the body and the irrational emotions in it not to revolt from reason, but rather to obey it, even when it is 20 commanding rather difficult things. Conversely, someone who is used to bearing pains will not be compelled to abandon their freedom at a critical moment because of their inability to bear hard work.

[*Encheiridion* Chapter 48 (= Lemma lxvi): Here is the stance and character of an ordinary person: never to expect benefit or harm from oneself, but only from external things. Here is the stance and character of a philosopher: to expect every kind of help and harm from oneself. Here are signs of someone making progress: not to criticize anyone, not to praise anyone, not to blame anyone, not to accuse anyone, not to say anything about himself as though he were someone or knew something.

When the progressor is hindered or impeded, he accuses himself. And if someone praises him, he laughs at his admirer – but on his own and by himself. And if someone criticizes him, he doesn't defend himself. He goes about like an invalid, being careful not to disturb anything that is being restored, before it has achieved stability. He has kept every kind of desire at bay, and transferred his aversion to what is contrary to nature among the things that are up to us. His impulses towards anything are relaxed. He doesn't care if he appears foolish or ignorant. And in a word, he is on guard against himself, as though against an enemy plotting against him.]

lxvi: Here is the stance and character of an ordinary person: never to expect benefit or harm from oneself, but only from external things.

[Commentary on Chapter 48, Lemma lxvi]
He has already arrived at the end of his advice, and is about to draw the conclusion **441** that one should not remain at the level of spoken words, but should put into practice the works they describe, and that one should posit as the goal not speaking and hearing, but acting. But first he gives us the three states that cover all human beings: some
30 are ordinary people, others, diametrically opposed to them, are philosophers, and a third group, standing apart from the ordinary people and approaching the philosophers, are the people he refers to as 'making progress', to whom the earlier passages were addressed. (In his comments he further divided this group into those who are only beginning to be educated, and those who have already made some degree of progress.)

He gives an outline account of each of the three states mentioned, saying first that 'the stance and character of an ordinary person is never to expect benefit or harm from oneself, but only from external things.' There are two things that are up to us: reason, in accordance with which we get our essence, and the irrational emotions, in virtue
40 of which we have something in common with irrational animals. And of these two, reason is the 'Hermes common to all', as the proverb has it.[237] For even if the reason internal to each of us differs numerically from that in others, still it is one in form, inasmuch as everyone is drawn to the same goods, and avoids the same bads, and takes the same things to be true through reason, and conversely takes the same things to be false, with the result that the reason that is in each person is a criterion for judging[238] the good and the bad and the true and the false. The reason in each of us strives for forms that are incorporeal and undivided and always are in the same state and
50 condition[239] – for instance temperance, justice, and wisdom. Each person partakes of each of them as a whole, **442** without the forms being diminished by the participation; hence judgements in accordance with right reason do not conflict, but harmonize, because they are the same for everyone.

In the case of irrational emotions, however, like anger and passionate desire and their sub-species, even if the anger in you is one in form

with the anger in me, still my anger is aroused at some things, 133,1
whereas yours is aroused at others. Our irrational desires are also
different, as are their objects; and likewise our aversions are different
and peculiar to each of us. Even if we do desire things that are the
same in number, these things are corporeal and individual, divisible
and diminished by one person's participation in them – for instance,
possessions or bodies or land.[240] Again, if you mention honour or rule
or power, since these too are individuals it is impossible for each of us
to partake of each of them as a whole, because they are diminished by 10
the participation. Hence these are the subjects on which our judgements differ and are peculiar to each of us, and 'here are the fights,
and factions, and wars'.[241]

The 'ordinary person', then, is someone who has abandoned the
common criterion and the common object we strive for, by marking off
for their own peculiar judgement and object of desire some individual
bodily thing; and such things are found in the externals. And wher-
ever one's desire and avoidance are directed, whether according to
nature or contrary to it, there one's good and bad appear to lie. (An
object of desire is thought to be good, and an object of aversion bad.)
But the philosopher stands aloof from the pull of the externals and
takes them to be alien, because he has already been completely 20
purified from the **443** simulacra and shadows of existent beings;[242] he
turns back to himself and to the genuine being and the common forms
of reason that are inside him, and finds the good inside himself. For
badness has no place within him.

So when Epictetus has characterized the two diametrically opposed groups in this way, he goes on to introduce the signs of 'someone
making progress', to whom the whole of the foregoing account has
been addressed. After all, it wasn't addressed to the philosopher,
since he isn't regarded as someone to be educated and taught, but
rather as someone already educating and teaching others. (Nor is it a 30
peculiar quality of the philosopher 'not to criticize anyone' and 'not to
praise anyone', since it is occasionally fitting for a teacher and rector
both to criticize and to praise.) But then neither does what has been
said suit an ordinary person, unless he is going to renounce his
ordinary status and entrust himself to a philosophical educator and
accept the beginning of progress. So it's to someone making progress
that all this pertains, and what he says now is like a brief summary
of what he said before, for the most part in the same words, both
reminding us of it, and also providing for its memorization though its 40
brevity.

(By 'being on guard against oneself, as though against an enemy'
he means us to be suspicious of our still unstable state, and to be eager
to judge rather harshly our own motions as we judge those of our
enemies, not granting any concession out of sympathy – which is what

most of us usually do in our own cases and with our friends. A 'slippery knave'[243] is a dissolute person, who is like a softened hide.)

[*Encheiridion* Chapter 49 (= Lemma lxvii): When someone prides himself on his ability to understand and interpret the books of Chrysippus, say to yourself, 'If Chrysippus had not written unclearly, this person would have had nothing to be proud about.'

But what do I want? To learn nature, and to follow it. So I look for someone who can interpret it. And when I hear that Chrysippus can, I go to him. But then I can't understand his writings. So I look for someone who can interpret them. And so far there's nothing to be proud about. When I find someone who can interpret them, the remaining step is to apply the precepts. Only here is there something to be proud about.

But if I am amazed at the interpretation itself, then instead of a philosopher, I've become nothing more than a grammarian, the only difference being that instead of Homer I interpret Chrysippus. So when someone says to me 'Read me Chrysippus!', what should make me blush is <not my inability to interpret the words>, but my inability to show works that are similar to and in harmony with the words.]

lxvii: 444 When someone prides himself on his ability to understand and interpret Chrysippus, say to yourself 'If Chrysippus had not written unclearly, this person would have had nothing to be proud about.'[244]

[Commentary on Chapter 49, Lemma lxvii:]
He has distinguished the three states that arise among human be-
50   ings, i.e. the ordinary person, the philosopher, and the progressor, and given a brief reminder of the things he has said to the latter. Finally, in this and the following passages, he draws the conclusion: we must put into practice the works that are described by these words. For the works are the point of the words, and it was for their
134,1 sake that the words were spoken. (What the Orator said is especially true in cases of this sort: 'Every word,' i.e. every educational word, 'appears futile and empty in the absence of the work'.)[245]

So he says that we must keep in mind from the beginning what a human being who is seeking his own good would want: he wants to discover what his own nature is, and what it befits that nature to do and suffer (e.g., that it is a rational life, using the body as an instrument, and that he must adapt his own desire and aversion to its perfection). **445** So in my search for this, I hear that Chrysippus
10   has written about these matters. I get the book, and find that on my own I am not able to understand what is written. Then, in my search

for 'someone who can interpret it', I come to realize what Chrysippus means. And 'there's nothing to be proud about', either for the interpreter or for the person who understands. After all, Chrysippus himself didn't write with the intention that what he wrote would be interpreted and understood, but rather that it would be applied. So if I do apply it, then I partake of the good in it. But 'if I am amazed' at the interpreter because he can interpret it well and understands it, and because I myself can interpret it, and indeed if I get absolutely everything else from it except that one thing, namely applying it, then 'instead of a philosopher, I've become nothing more than a grammarian', since interpretation is a part of the art of grammar, and I differ from the grammarian only in that I interpret Chrysippus rather than Homer.   20

Nor is merely reading Chrysippus' writings, or expounding them to someone else when they ask for it, without applying them, irreproachable. After all, a sick person who found remedies for his disease in writing and could read them clearly and articulately, and interpret them to others should need arise, and yet did not apply the remedies to his own disease, would be justifiably ashamed.   30

[*Encheiridion* Chapter 50 (= Lemma lxviii): Stand by everything set before you as though they are laws, as though you would be committing impiety if you were to transgress them. But pay no attention to whatever someone may say about you; for this is no longer up to you.]

lxviii: Stand by everything you set before yourself as though they are laws, as though you would be committing impiety if you were to transgress them.[246]

[Commentary on Chapter 50, Lemma lxviii]
A single swallow, as the proverb says, does not make spring.[247] In the same way, **446** applying the precepts of Chrysippus on one or two occasions does not create a state of character. Rather, he says, one must firmly stand by what has been set up as good and beneficial, and consider transgressing it to be impiety. For if the transgression of ordinary agreements seems outrageous and impious, on the grounds that we are rendering invalid, so far as it is up to us,[248] the truth and trust through which everything takes its subsistence and persists, then how can it not be impious to transgress the agreement concerning philosophy and the good life? Someone who first agrees that what is said and written is noble and true, but later, sometimes even when he has actually begun to apply them, does not stand by them, does transgress them. So, he says, 'stand firm', and 'pay no attention to whatever someone may say about you'. (He is indicating the point made before,[249] that there will be many people who will say 'He has   40

suddenly come back to us a philosopher' and 'Where did this weighty brow appear from?' and the like.) For it is not up to us whether they do or do not say anything. A person like this is in a state resembling the point indicated by the symbolic saying of the Pythagoreans.[250] They used to say 'Having set off for the temple, pay no attention',[251] thereby indicating that someone who has an impulse towards God must not be in two minds about it in any respect, and must not cling to human things.

50

> [*Encheiridion* Chapter 51 (= Lemma lxix): To what further date are you postponing the time to judge yourself worthy of the best things and never to transgress critical reason?[252] You have received the doctrines you were supposed to accept, and you have accepted them. So to what further teacher are you looking, to hand over to him the job of straightening you out? You are no longer a youth, but already a perfect adult. If you are negligent and lazy now, and turn one excuse into another and set one day after another as the time for attending to yourself, then without noticing it you won't make progress, and you'll end up an ordinary person both living and dying. So you should already be judging yourself worthy to live as someone perfect and making progress. Further, take whatever appears best to be an inviolable law for you. Whatever is brought to bear upon you, whether it is burdensome or pleasant, reputable or disreputable, remember that the contest is now, the Olympic games are already here, and it is not possible to postpone any longer: it is a matter of a single day, and of a single action, whether progress is destroyed or preserved. That's how Socrates became himself; no matter what was brought to bear on him, he paid no attention to anything but reason. As for you, even if you are not yet Socrates, you should live like someone who wants to be Socrates.]

lxix: So to what date are you postponing the time to judge yourself worthy of the best things ... [253]

[Commentary on Chapter 51, Lemma lxix]

135,1   This too is appropriate reading for those who have been receiving his advice for some time: **447** they should no longer delay or postpone. 'The man who delays ever wrestles with catastrophes.'[254] Delay is a pretext for laziness. So, he says, 'to what further date are you postponing the time to judge yourself worthy' of applying the sayings in detail (that is what he means by 'the best things', in that they are the most perfect and are the target and goal of his words) 'and never to transgress' right reason, but instead to do everything in accordance with it, both in desiring and in avoiding? Someone else might be able

10

to say that they were waiting to hear the logical and ethical theorems; but you have already made some degree of progress in philosophy, and as for the theorems that one should first receive, and then assent to as well-said, and then put into practice – you have assented to them. 'So to what further teacher are you looking, to hand over to him the job of straightening you out?' Someone else might be as young in judgement as they are in years; but 'you are no longer a youth, but already a perfect adult' (and thus not a superannuated old man, either). 'So if you are negligent' and through laziness set one appoint-   20
ment after another and 'set one day after another as the time for attending to yourself', then you are nourishing within yourself an empty hope. You have your mind on today and tomorrow, without noticing that you have made no upward progress, but are rather bent to stooping from the gradual habituation into negligence, and have ended up 'an ordinary person both living and dying'. For just as things up there are the origin of things here, and the preconditioning we receive from there is a great help, so too things here **448** are the origin and predisposition for things up there. All of life is one, and the life   30
you live is one, alternating between here and there.[255]

'So,' he says, 'you should already be judging yourself worthy to live as someone perfect' – not in the sense of 'having attained one's end'[256] (someone like that would have no need of these words), but perfect so far as making progress goes, i.e. making constant and uninterrupted progress. Further, 'take whatever appears right' to be a law that enjoins on you its own accomplishment. It is possible to find a good use for everything that happens to you, and their opposites as well, if you use them according to right reason. Even if something 'burden-some or pleasant, reputable or disreputable, is brought to bear upon you', you must embrace what is brought to bear, not disdaining it if it   40
is small or losing heart if it is large, and letting it run out of control. Instead, in each case you must believe that the contest for virtue is already set, so that it is necessary either to carry off the wreath, or to be publicly declared out. There is no further postponement once the contest has been started; and we must not neglect 'a single day, or a single action', in the belief that we won't be harmed in any way by our disdain for them.

Why does he say that 'it is a matter of a single day and of a single action, whether your progress is destroyed or preserved'? Presumably   50
because when someone neglects a single day or a single action, he becomes lazier and more negligent, so that when the next thing happens to him he is less intent than before and is worsted by it to a   136,1
greater degree than before, and even more so the next time; and in this way his lack of intensity is increased little by little, and the progress **449** of right reason is completely destroyed. But progress is preserved and increased in the opposite way. For from 'a single day and a single action' there arises some sign, some sort of progress, so

that when the next thing happens he meets it in a better state of
progress, and still more so for the next time. 'That's how Socrates
10 became' the wisest of all men,[257] as he says; because he always
accustomed himself not to postpone his own benefit, but instead
always 'to obey nothing other than the reason' that appeared best to
him as he reasoned about it.[258] 'As for you, even if you are not yet
Socrates', nevertheless 'you should live like someone who wants to be
Socrates.' For someone who keeps an example in view and wants to
emulate it does not give in, because he is always comparing himself
to the imitation of it.[259]

[*Encheiridion* Chapter 52 (= Lemma lxx): The first and most
necessary topic in philosophy is the one that concerns applying
the theorems, e.g. not lying. The second topic concerns proofs,
e.g. why is it that one must not lie? The third is the one that
makes the proofs secure and explicit, e.g. why does that constitute a proof? After all, what is a proof? What is consequence?
What is incompatibility? What is the true and the false?

So the third topic is necessary on account of the second, and
the second on account of the first. But the one that is most
necessary is the first one, and that is the one we should dwell
on. Yet we do the opposite; we spend our time on the third one
and direct our entire effort towards it, and completely fail to
attend to the first one. That's why we lie, though we have ready
to hand a theory showing how to construct a proof that we should
not lie.]

lxx: The first and most necessary topic in philosophy is the one
that concerns applying the theorems ...

[Commentary on Chapter 52, Lemma lxx]
For someone engaged in philosophy, who wishes to attain their
20 natural perfection both of life and of cognition, it is necessary to have
a scientific knowledge of what the true is; otherwise one comes to
believe what people say without learning it, encountering it through
mere opinion and irrationally, **450** and thus both makes mistakes and
is compelled to change positions later. Scientific knowledge comes
through proof, and it belongs to the study of logic to teach what a proof
is (i.e. an argument that reaches a conclusion from evident premises
that have been technically arranged) and which premises are evident and how many figures of arrangement there are.
30   So in light of this, there are three most necessary topics of philosophy: the first is 'the one that concerns applying the theorems',
which is temperance in action, e.g. not lying. The second 'concerns
proof', which proves (via the cause) that one should do these things.
And the third uses the methods of logic to 'secure and make explicit'

the fact that this is a proof and that we are not being deceived, and teaches what a proof is, what consequence is, what incompatibility is – i.e. that the more universal things are consequent on the more particular things (for if this is a human being, then it is also an   40 animal), and that opposites are incompatible (e.g. 'someone' with 'no one', and 'every' with 'not every'), and that it is impossible for these to be simultaneously true or simultaneously false. It also shows what sort of argument is true and what sort false, and from what sort of premisses with what sort of arrangement.

Now, it is clear that this third topic, which teaches the method of logic, is 'necessary on account of the second', so that we may have scientific knowledge of the things that are good for us; and that 'the second is necessary on account of the first', so that once we have learned the things that are good for us and what we must do to secure them, we will secure them by the works themselves. And this is the   50 most necessary topic and the goal that 'we should dwell on', since it is on account of and for the sake of this that we take on the other parts. Yet we do the converse; 'we spend our time on the third one' most of all, and only a little on the second, and 'fail to attend to the first one', which is the point of the others. **451**   137,1

'That's why we lie, though we have ready to hand a theory showing how to construct a proof', and through what methods of logic, 'that we should not lie'. But what should have happened was that, once we learned how to prove that we should not lie, we then had demonstrative and scientific knowledge that we should not lie, and once we knew that, we proceeded put it into practice thereafter, since it was also for the sake of this that the previous topics were transmitted.

So in this chapter too Epictetus has given guidance for us to put his exhortations into practice in a way that is very methodical as well as   10 very emphatic.

[*Encheiridion* Chapter 53 (= Lemma lxxi): On every occasion you should have the following ready to hand:
  (1) 'Lead me, O Zeus, and you, Destiny,
     to whichever place I have been stationed by you.
     I shall follow without hesitation. Should I not wish to,
     because I have become bad, I shall follow nonetheless.'
  (2) 'Whoever has rightly conceded to Necessity,
     is wise, in our judgement, and understands divine things.'
  (3) 'But, Crito, if that is the way that it is pleasing to the gods,
     then let it happen in that way.'
  (4) 'Anytus and Meletus can kill me, but they can't harm me.'[260]

lxxi: On every occasion you should have the following ready to hand:

[Commentary on Chapter 53, Lemma lxxi]

Since the educational accounts we have imparted through detailed exposition have also been imparted by some of the ancients in a concise form, Epictetus counsels us to have the latter 'ready to hand' at all times, both because they are easily memorized, and because the testimony of illustrious men who expressed themselves appositely strengthens our credence in the advice.

So the first quotation is from Cleanthes of Assos, the Stoic, who
20 was a student of Zeno's and the teacher of Chrysippus. (I saw an extraordinary statue of him in Assos itself, **452** erected in his honour by a decree of the Roman Senate). In these iambic lines he prays that he should be led by God, and by the efficient and moving cause that comes from God and permeates all things in order, which Cleanthes called 'Destiny' or 'Fate'. And he promises that he will follow 'without hesitation' and willingly. 'For if I resist,' he says, 'the only result will be that I will be bad, and that I will wail and groan as I follow.' The weaker necessarily follows the stronger, and what is caused its cause.
30 Epictetus himself indicated this in the chapter in which he says 'Do not seek to have the things that happen happen as you wish, but rather wish that the things that happen happen; and you will be happy.'[261] The essence of all well-being is to coordinate oneself with the wholes and wish to be wholly with them, rather than to resist the wholes by detaching oneself from the whole and narrowing oneself down to little or nothing, and to want the wholes to follow such a trivial part.
40 The second quotation is from Euripides the tragedian, and it has the same meaning. 'Necessity' is what leads all things, willing or unwilling, to the things that are above and the divine cause. Someone who is consonant with this, and follows, and does not resist, but follows without hesitation, is genuinely wise, because he rightly understands the nature of existent things and the difference between the wholes and the parts, and gives the appropriate honour to all aspects of the divine power. **453**

The third quotation ('Crito, if that is the way that it is pleasing to
50 the gods, then let it happen in that way') is from Plato's *Crito*, and Socrates is the speaker. This too has the same meaning, in a more concise form. Anyone who doesn't just say this, but actually lives it, heals his division from the wholes and exile from God, and keeps clear
138,1 of everything inferior, by surrendering himself to the wholes and yielding himself to God. In my view, by adding on these testimonies at the end of his work, Epictetus indicates that the entire perfection of the human soul culminates in turning back to God and coordination with him.

The quotation added at the end ('Anytus and Meletus can kill me, but they can't harm me') comes from Plato's *Apology of Socrates*, and
10 refers to Anytus and Meletus, Socrates' prosecutors. This quotation

binds the end to the beginning, by reminding us of what was said at the beginning: that the person who locates their good and bad in what is up to us, not in external things, can never be compelled by anyone, or hindered, or harmed.

[Epilogue]

454 That concludes what I had to contribute, to the best of my ability, to the elucidation of the sayings of Epictetus for anyone undertaking to study them. I myself am grateful for the opportunity to devote my time to such studies, which came at a fitting time for me, in these tyrannical circumstances. I shall end my treatise by finishing it with a prayer that is appropriate to the people present.[262]

I beseech you, Lord, father and guide of the reason in us, remind us of our noble origin, which we were deemed worthy to receive from you. Act with us (as we are self-movers) for our purification from the body and its irrational emotions, that we may be superior to them and rule them, and that we may use them as instruments in the fitting way. Act with us also for the precise correction of the reason in us and its unification with the genuinely existent things through the light of the truth. And the third request to the Saviour:[263] I beseech you, completely remove the mist from the eyes of our souls, 'so that we may clearly know', as Homer says, 'both God and man'.[264]

Notes

1. *tithetai*; there is probably a pun here on the sense of literally setting something up (as e.g. a physical target) and the sense of theoretically positing something, which in philosophical contexts is by far the more common sense. E.g., a student may have asked Epictetus whether the presence of bad things gives us reason to posit a nature or origin of badness in the world, and he responds by saying that there is no need to posit or set up such a thing. In preparing an archery contest, one does not set up two targets, one for hitting and one for missing; all that we need to posit is one positive target (sc. the good), and the endless variety of ways of missing it will come along with it.

1a. Numbers in bold indicate pagination in Hadot's edition (editio maior Brill 1996); numbers in the margin refer to pages and lines in Dübner's edition. References to Epictetus' text are abbreviated 'cap. X §Y.Z' where X is the number of the *Encheiridion* chapter in question, Y the number of a paragraph within that chapter, Z the number of the line in the paragraph. References to Simplicius' commentary are by Hadot page and Dübner page and line (H / D); more general references to Simplicius are abbreviated 'in cap. X', i.e. Simplicius' comments on *Encheiridion* ch. X.

2. 'Form of existence' renders *hupostasis*, elsewhere translated as 'subsistence'. The point of this chapter is to argue that people tend to misunderstand the bad so profoundly that they do not even understand its ontological category – they think it is a per se existent, like a substance, when in fact it is an accident, having only a sort of derivative status. Thus *hupostasis* here ranges over all the various ways that a thing can exist, i.e. all of the forms of existence it might have, e.g. genuine being (*ousia*), mere subsistence (*hupostasis*), or an attenuated derivative subsistence (*parupostasis*) as is in fact the case with the bad. Simplicius uses the latter term in e.g. his *in DC* 429,34, and *in Ph.* 1262,8; his use of it here follows Proclus' lead, e.g. in *de Malorum Subsistentia* IV.50, *in Rem.* 1.37.20-38.40, and *in Tim.* 1.373.22-376.15.

3. cf. Aristotle *Cat.* 6a17; cf. Plotinus *Enn.* 1.8.6.40-54, Proclus *de Malorum Subsistentia* II 37.

4. *huphesis*; cf. H200 / D5,31. The argument for a single origin or principle is also given by Proclus, *de Malorum Subsistentia* II.31.

5. The Manichees, as we are about to learn. Simplicius' argument in H324-6 / D70,28-71,43 is an elaboration of the anti-Manichean dilemma proposed by Nebridius in Augustine, *Confessions* 7.2.3: either the onslaught of the Bad could harm God, in which case he is corruptible, or it could not, in which case there was no need to send a portion of himself – i.e. what became our souls, cf. Augustine, *Contra Fortunatum* 6 – into the Bad.

6. *Iliad* 9.537.

7. Simplicius resumes the question raised in the second sentence of this paragraph, after a glance at the details of the cosmogony. Similar, but far more detailed, criticisms of the Manichean pre-cosmic cosmic geography are given in Augustine, *Contra Epistulam Fundamenti* 12.15-13.16, 20.22-22.24, and 24.26-29.32.

8. This is the sending of the Logos, after the primal 'fall'; cf. Augustine, *Contra Fortunatum* 3.

9. *Odyssey* 1.53. In *Confessions* 5.3.3-5.9, Augustine reports that he lost his faith in Manichaeism when he realized the unscientific nature of their astronomical claims.

10. The Manichees' commitment to the literal interpretation of their sacred texts is criticized in very similar terms by both Augustine *Contra Epistulam Fundamenti* 23.25 and Alexander of Lycopolis *Contra Manichaei Opiniones* 25. Sallustius *peri Theôn kai Kosmou* §3-4 explains the proper philosophical uses of mythical accounts for a Platonist audience.

11. cf. H329 / D73,45, H331 / D75,25.

12. *Paroemiographi Graeci*, 1839, p. 314.

13. If the Bad is an origin on par with the Good, sc. God, then it is equal to God in power. If so, then we are incapable of resisting its compulsion. If so, then none of our wrong actions are culpable, and thus they are not properly speaking *bad* actions at all. But if so, then there are no individual bad actions, and thus 'nothing is bad at all'. But to be an origin, a thing must be an origin of something, sc. the individual instances it produces; so if there are no individual bad actions, then there is no origin of the bad, either. Simplicius' psychological argument is elaborated at length in Augustine – cf. *de Duabus Animabus* 10.12-14.23, *Contra Fortunatum* 21, and *Confessions* 8.10.22-4.

14. A *proêgoumenon* form of existence or substance is 'primary' because it exists or subsists *per se*. The axiom that 'it's impossible for anything to be generated without a cause' applies only to per se existents, esp. substances; it does not apply to things which have a merely derivative or accidental existence (*parupostasis*). Thus the key to seeing why it is misguided to look for a cause of the bad lies in seeing that the bad is not the sort of thing that has a determinate cause, i.e. it is an accidental or derivative thing rather than a per se thing. (It is notable that while Simplicius follows the theory of evil set out by Proclus in *de Malorum Subsistentia*, most clearly in IV.50, his insistence that one must first articulate what it is before inquiring where it comes from is contrary to Proclus' procedure, and in harmony with Augustine's at *Contra Epistulam Fundamenti* 36.41 – which itself corrects his original misguided efforts, recorded in *Confessions* 7.5.7.)

15. cf. n. 11.

16. cf. Porphyry *Isagoge* 12.24 Busse. For the appplication of this doctrine to the case of badness, cf. Augustine *Contra Epistulam Fundamenti* 33.36-35.39.

17. *hupostasis*.

18. cf. H332 / D72,25-30.

19. One word, *kakia*, means both 'vice', and more generally 'badness' (i.e. is the abstract noun from *kakon*, 'bad').

20. *episumbainein*: one might almost say it 'supervenes'. The point is that if there were no such thing as normal healthy walking, there would be no such thing as limping.

21. Again, one could translate 'failure supervenes on the target of attainment'. A separate point: one might have expected 'failure happens instead of / supervenes on the attainment of the target' rather than 'the target of attainment'. But the manuscript clearly says *episumbainei tôi skopôi tês epitukhias*, and no palaeographical story would support rewriting to *tou skopou têi epitukhiai*, nor is their any vacillation in the mss. Furthermore, Simplicius has just told us that for the archer, the *telos* is the *epitukhia*, and from there it is an easy step to thinking of the *epitukhia* as the *skopos*.

22. 'But what involuntarily supervenes on the primary / per se goal could rightly be said to derive its existence from the goal, not the primary / per se goal from what involuntarily supervenes on it.'

23. cf. *EN* 1.1 1094 a3.

24. 'the bad sometimes supervenes on the activity'.

25. This may be a reference to Stoic characterization of *pathos* as *ptoia*. Cf. *SVF* 1.51, 3.127.

26. cf. n. 11.

27. in cap. 1, H201-18 / D5,54-15,25.

28. in cap. 8, H256-73 / D35,5-44,35.

29. A difficult passage which has attracted scholarly controversy. The sentence aims to vindicate God's creation of souls capable of turning towards the bad, i.e. sublunary souls, by showing the unacceptable consequences of omitting their creation. Had they been omitted, there would still be the first goods (the One, the goods-in-themselves, etc.), and the intermediate goods, i.e. the class of souls, but now restricted to celestial, divine and angelic souls that are always good and are incapable of turning downward – this is the point of saying that these two classes would then be 'uniformly good'. The omission of sublunary souls, however, also implies the absence of sublunary material bodies (i.e. the things that are generated and perish), which are produced by the celestial souls (H258 / D36,27). But in any sequence of production, the last member must be unproductive (else it would not be last); thus on this hypothesis the intermediate goods are rendered unproductive (impotent), which is inconsistent with their exalted status. See the close parallel at H212 / D12,01.

In the next sentence (our [4]), the identity of the third class has been disputed, but that it must consist of sublunary bodies, rather than human souls, is clear from three things. First, a comparison with H258 / D36,37 and H270 / D43,12 shows that it is the sublunary bodies that get their subsistence and their generation and destruction from the 'turning of the celestial bodies' (= moving causes; and compare *peritropê* here with *trepontai* and *sumperitrepetai* in those passages); this is further supported by the vehement denial at H212 / D12,17 that human souls get their subsistence from the celestial movers. (H374 / D98,44 says that celestial souls (not bodies) are in some sense causes for sublunary souls, but not causes of their subsistence, much less causes of their generation and destruction). Second, the middle member of the current triad is not, as before, the class of divine and angelic souls that always remain good, but rather the class of celestial bodies that are governed by these souls – only those, not the celestial souls, change in location. This makes it more plausible that the third member should be bodies, too, rather than souls. Finally, we are about to be told, in the next paragraph (H333 / D76,21) that the soul is unchangeable in its essence; H374 / D98,54 repeats the point that self-movers, i.e. souls, do not change in respect to essence. The potential for confusion between a triad whose lowest member is human souls, and one whose lowest member is perishable bodies, is in part due to Simplicius' desire to draw a parallel between psychic and bodily diseases, and his alternation between the two cases.

30. Hadot suggests there may be a reminiscence of *Theaetetus* 176a5-8.

31. *skhesis* – cf. H209 / D10,10.

32. Note that these are the absolutely lowest things – i.e. physical things – which are distinct from the lowest goods (apparently) which are human (etc.) souls (i.e. animating controllers of bodies).

33. cf. *Timaeus* 43a2.

34. H259 / D36,50-37,10. And cf. for what follows Aristotle *GC* 2.4 331a13-16.

35. H260 / D37,15-25.

36. H260-1 / D37,5-15.

37. H267-8 / D41,2-45, and cf. Proclus, *in Rem.* 1.37.20-38.40. At the end of this line we read *pantelôs* with the majority of the manuscripts instead of Hadot's *panti*, which appears only in B. The mistake Simplicius warns us from is the thought that turning away counts as the kind of opposition to the good that renders something a bad.

38. *huphesis*; cf. H200 / D5,31.

39. H260-3 / D37,10-38.45; H270 / D43,15.

40. cf. *Phaedrus* 248c5ff.

41. cf. *Phaedo* 87d.

42. H262 / D38,15-25, H199 / D4,40-5. On the rational soul's projection of these irrational 'lives', and their functions, cf. Proclus *de Providentia* IV.10 and *in Rem* 1.37.20-38.40.

43. *arkhikos*, cf. H201 / D5,50. There it sufficed merely to translate 'origin'; here, the imagery of governance (sceptres etc.) right below requires some mention of the other common sense of *arkhe*, namely 'political rule'.

44. *hairesis kai prohairesis*, here and a few lines below, followed by singular verbs. Presumably Simplicius thinks of his topic as something which is most naturally called *hairesis* ('choice'), in Peripatetic as it were, but which he glosses for this occasion with what he takes to be the Epictetan equivalent *prohairesis*. See §5.3 of our introduction.

45. H197 / D4,1-10; H204 / D7,30-5.

46. Similarly at H204 / D7,40.

47. Earlier (H327 / D73,5-10), Simplicius had emphasized that God is not a cause of the bad qua bad; thereafter, he continues to argue that God is not a cause of the bad in any way. Here, he concedes that the soul is in some sense the cause of the bad. But even it – like God – is not a cause of the bad qua bad, i.e. does not set out with the express intention of causing badness.

48. H330-1 / D74,45-75,15.

49. *Timaeus* 42d3-4, *Rep.* X.617e5.

50. It is not clear whether we are being told something about the nature of all choice (*hairesis*) here, i.e. about the concept of choice, or about the particular choice that is being envisioned in the hypothetical. Simplicius might be saying that since it is simply in the nature of choice to be set over multiple options, then it would be pointless to have a choice that was compelled to adopt only one – a claim about all *hairesis*. Or he might be elaborating on the suggestion that he is rejecting, that God could have given souls a particular choice, i.e. a nature such as to choose between good and bad, and that it would be pointless to give them *that* kind of (faculty of) choice and yet compel them to adopt only one. This bears on whether he thinks that choice requires two-way possibilities, and also on whether he thinks that the higher souls and intelligences, which never do turn downwards towards the bad, have any kind of choice. See H202 / D6,30, where it is said that the first souls 'have their choice uniformly intent on [the good], never declining towards the worse'; this is then followed with an unresolved worry about whether this counts as prohairesis or not.

51. i.e., that the bad is never chosen qua bad; it is always chosen *sub specie boni*. And thus, the argument proceeds, God could not forbid the souls to choose the bad, for in order to do so he should have to forbid them to choose goods, too.

52. H216 / D14,15-25.

53. cf. *Laws* 716a2, 872e2.

54. The sequence of thought would be clearer with a middle step supplied: what God is responsible for is the *substance*, [not the turning]; it's the soul that's responsible for the *turning*.

55. The Manichees, as the rest of the paragraph makes clear. Simplicius is taking them as allies against one particular objection: the claim that if God produced something naturally able to become bad, then God produced something bad. The Manichees are witnesses for Simplicius, because they agree that the soul is naturally able to become bad (however the details go), but they emphatically deny that the soul is bad, 'even boasting that it is a part or limb of God' etc.

56. Oddly, the Greek has the Manichees as the subject of the verb which usually is used of God's production of the soul (i.e. 'they produce the soul etc.') and the only strictly correct way to construe the clause 'by God' is with the verb 'to become bad'. I.e., the natural way to read this is 'who produce a soul of such a nature as to be made bad by God'. Since that sense is presumably wrong, one must either rest content with a loose construction, or take recourse in emendation, e.g. changing *paragontes* to *para<gesthai le>gontes* would produce a sentence meaning 'who say that the soul is produced by God with such a nature as to become bad'.

57. Again, 'primary' probably means 'per se'. It seems ill-advised for Simplicius to make the lack of primary existence a reason to shun it, since there will presumably be many things in the world that have a derivative sort of existence (e.g. the magnitude by which the darkness of one silhouette exceeds another) but are not especially evil. It would be less implausible to say, as the next sentence does, that its derivative form of existence means that it is never a per se target – but even that should not entail that it is an object of avoidance.

58. The 'and' is supplied from its appearances below. Without it, it seems that 'primarily' somehow modifies 'in accordance with nature'; but that is clearly not intended. The two qualifiers are on a level, and, if anything, seem to be nearly synonymous here.

59. Simplicius makes no attempt to put this into Peripatetic normal form, but it could be regimented into something like Camestres:

every per se subsistent is an attainment

no bad is an attainment

so, no bad is a per se subsistent.

Interestingly, Simplicius seems more careful to approximate normal form when he is giving the Stoic MPP version.

60. Here Simplicius annotates each of the two premises and conclusion, first offering further support for the premises, then offering reason to think that the conclusion that he gave is equivalent to the conclusion in the lemma from Epictetus.

61. cf. *Theaetetus* 194a3-4.

62. In this sentence Simplicius shows how to relate the text of Epictetus to the quasi-peripatetic argument he has constructed in the previous passage.

63. sc. if there were a nature of the bad in the cosmos, which, given Simplicius' gloss on 'nature', means 'if the bad were a primary subsistent in the cosmos'. Simplicius here attempts to justify the suppressed conditional major premiss that he finds in the second (quasi-Stoic) construction of the argument:

(1) There is a nature of bad in the cosmos. [assume for purpose of reductio]

(2) if there is a nature of bad in the cosmos, then the bad is a primary subsistent. [gloss on 'nature' in 82,2-3]

(3) if the bad is a primary subsistent, then the bad is a target for an agent to act with reference to. ['what occurs in the cosmos primarily is the target of the agent' 81,50]

(4) if the bad is a target for an agent to act with reference to, then the agent shuns it. ['since the bad is something to shun']

(5) if the agent shuns something, then he sets it up as a target for missing. ['so it wasn't set up for attaining, but rather for missing']

(6) so, a target is set up for missing.

(7) so, if a target is *not* set up for missing, then there is *not* a nature of bad in the cosmos.

Unfortunately, premisses 4 and 5 seem to be supported by reference to the actual behaviour of avoidance, and this seems to show that people really do set up bad things as targets for avoidance. This in turn undercuts our ability to assert the minor premiss.

64. Simplicius does not comment on cap. 29, and editors may be right to think that it was not in the original edition of the *Encheiridion* assembled by Arrian (it also very nearly resembles *Dissertations* 3.15). We include the translation of cap. 29 for the reader's convenience.

65. *kathêkonta.*

66. This definition includes both Zeno's original etymology for the term 'appropriate action' or *kathêkon* (what is pertaining to, i.e. *hêkon*, someone, D.L. VII.108), and a version of the Stoic definition of justice (see below). The Stoics did not associate 'appropriate actions' exclusively with justice, or with actions which relate to other people (although these were, of course, a significant part of what they thought it appropriate for us to do).

67. This phrase is a rearranged quotation of an archaic verse, sometimes attributed to Phocylides, which Aristotle quotes at *EN* 1129b29: 'in justice, every virtue is incorporated'.

68. Simplicius offers us an Aristotelian theory about the two senses of the word 'justice' (cf. *EN* V.1), i.e. the one in which it is a synonym of 'virtue' in general (or at any rate other-regarding virtue) and the one in which it is the name only of the particular and partial virtue that excludes wisdom, temperance, and courage. He also offers a rationale for the ambiguity, or a way for reducing the one sense to the other: since justice in the narrow sense is rendering to each *person* what is due, it is natural to extend this idea to cover the rendering of what is due to other *things* in the whole array of special contexts that cover the other virtues, e.g. rendering what is due in fearful situations (courage), rendering what is due with respect to physical pleasures (temperance) and so on – thus all virtue is in this sense a matter of acting 'justly', or as we might say, 'doing justice to' the situation.

69. Once again, Simplicius tries to show how every kind of virtue can be analyzed as a sort of justice – ethical well-being of all sorts (e.g. temperance, wisdom, courage, etc.) is a matter of the different parts of the soul treating each other justly; and political well-being of all sorts (political harmony, good government, etc.) is a matter of the different parts of the city treating each other justly. (The view is obviously inspired by the psycho-political theories of the *Republic*.) In this sentence, however, Simplicius adds a further equivalence: since justice is a matter of rendering to each thing the 'appropriate actions' (*kathêkonta*), one can also say that ethical and political well-being are reducible to a matter of appropriate actions.

70. Nicolaus of Damascus was a universal historian, and a Peripatetic historian of philosophy or philosopher, of the late first century BC. Simplicius elsewhere refers to Nicolaus as an authority on Aristotle's physics and on the Presocratics (*in A. de Caelo*, vol. 7, pp. 3, 398-9, citing works 'On the universe' and 'On Aristotle's philosophy', and *in Phys.* vol. 9, pp. 23, 28, 149, 151, citing a work 'On the Gods', also used by Porphyry).

Simplicius presumably cites Nicolaus' work on practical ethics to emphasize that it was not just Stoics – the writers of treatises 'On Appropriate Actions' (a title attested for Zeno, Cleanthes, Sphaerus and Chrysippus; cf. Antipater, *SVF* iii: Antipater 62-3) – but adherents of all the late Hellenistic 'schools' who wrote technical books on these subjects. Other examples from the same period are Brutus, an Antiochian, (Seneca *Ep.* 95.45), and the Academics Philo of Larissa (cf. Stobaeus, *Ec.* 2.7, p. 41 Wachsmuth), Cicero (in the *de Officiis*), and Plutarch (e.g. in his *Marital Precepts*).

One might think that Epictetus' *Diss.* and Simplicius *Commentary* itself were examples of the genre criticized here for unnecessary prolixity.

71. Simplicius thinks that [b] is taken up in the next chapter of the *Encheiridion*; see his commentary on cap. 31 below.

72. 'Relation' = *skhesis*.

73. 'Coordination' = *suntaxis*.

74. It is not clear what this means. If instead of *menousês tês perigaphês tôn en skhesi ontôn* we were to write *enousês tês perigaphês*, then this would mean 'A relation is a coordination between things etc, and the definition of 'relata' is present in it.' For a parallel see Sextus Empiricus *PH* I.11.

75. 'Correlative': *prosallêla*, which is not etymologically related to *skhesis* as 'correlative' is to its translation, 'relative' .

76. Having given us three contrasting pairs, Simplicius now turns in an extraordinarily efficient and precise way to giving us examples for all eight kinds. His arrangement is reminiscent of a truth-table:

natural	similars	associative	brother / brother
natural	similars	disassociative	stranger / stranger
natural	dissimilars	associative	father / son
natural	dissimilars	disassociative	up / down
prohairetic	similars	associative	friend / friend
prohairetic	similars	disassociative	enemy / enemy
prohairetic	dissimilars	associative	teacher / student
prohairetic	dissimilars	disassociative	prosecutor / defendant

For both the natural and the prohairetic classes, he offers two sub-classes of the class 'associative of dissimilars', i.e. those related as cause-and-caused (father / son, teacher / student), and those related as opposites (right / left, buyer / seller).

77. i.e. what is natural about this is the outcome, namely that the wise rule, whereas what is prohairetic is the method, namely their election by common consent.

78. One should probably delete 'appropriate actions' here (sc. *kathêkontôn*) as a mistaken gloss, and then translate 'especially in the case of natural relations'. We have not heard 'natural' used as a label for *kathêkonta* yet, and what Simplicius goes on to say in the next sentences bears more directly on relations than *kathêkonta*.

79. 'Godparents': Simplicius literally says 'uncles', but the Greek term *theios* is ambiguous, being both the normal classical Greek word for 'uncle', and the adjective meaning 'divine' or 'godlike'. Our use of 'godparents' is an attempt to suggest Simplicius' point. Philologists deny any relation between *theios* = uncle and *theios* = divine, but it is typical of philosophical anthropology to claim that ancient wisdom is handed down in the etymologies of words.

80. On the choice of lives that the soul makes before its incarnation, cf. H214 / D13,10, H382-3 / D103,43-104,4, and Proclus *de Decem Dubitationibus* IX.59

and Hierocles *de Providentia*, at Photius *Bibl.* cod. 251 466a 21 (echoed at H358 / D89,53-90,3). The line between natural and prohairetic relations gets a bit unclear if after all we chose our relatives. Just above, he had argued that our greater obligation to our parents is the result of parenthood being a natural relationship instead of a prohairetic one; it now looks as though what was driving the earlier ranking of obligation was not the natural / prohairetic split, but rather the reversible / irreversible split (or revocable / irrevocable). If your friend neglects his *kathêkonta* towards you, he will in time cease to be your friend, thus freeing you of friendly obligations towards him. But one cannot cease to be a parent merely by being a neglectful parent, so your obligations to your parent remain in force regardless of his treatment of you (cf. *Ench.* 30: you were not related to a good father, but to a father).

Accordingly, between the natural and irrevocable and the voluntary and alterable there will be a *tertium quid*, namely the non-natural and irrevocable. E.g., if someone voluntarily puts my eye out, he cannot thereafter cease to stand in the relation of blinder to blindee.

81. This phrase shows that a second group of desires must be being introduced, distinct from the unbridled and forcing ones – it would be redundant to say of the same desires both that they 'are not suitable for the unity of friendship', *ouk eisi pros philikên henôsin epitêdeioi*, and that 'these are also unfit for friendship', *kai hautai pros philian anarmostoi*, and the 'also' shows the distinctness of the second group. But if this is so, the clause 'and desires that place their good in external things', *alla kai to agathon en tois ektos tithemenai*, must be introducing a new subject, not predicating something of the unbridled desires. If so, one might emend *alla kai <hai> tithemenai*, which would give the subject an article, and be palaeographically trivial.

82. cf. H442 / D133,1-10.

83. cf. *Rep.* 435a; *Ep.* VII.341cd.

84. See Porphyry *Vita Pythag.* §33; Cicero *de Amic.* 21.80.

85. *enstasis*.

86. ll. 7-8 of the *Carmen Aureum* (i.e. 'Golden Verses', hence 'genuinely golden').

87. It is not clear what his prohairesis is the same as. Presumably the one who erred may suspect that the erred-against forgave him only verbally, or only temporarily, and that the erred-against no longer preserves the same friendly attitude (as before the contretemps) or forgiving attitude (as when the forgiveness was offered). But possibly there is a reference to the earlier idea that each genuine friend has the same sort of prohairesis as the other friend's.

88. i.e. God, gods, daimons, etc.

89. The numbering is added by the translators.

90. This entire passage contains many reminiscences of Agathon's speech from *Symposium* 195-7.

91. cf. *Symposium* 178e-179a.

92. cf. *Symposium* 191a6.

93. Citizens are listed after neighbours in our text of cap. 30; Simplicius discusses them in reverse order. It may be that his text of cap. 30 reordered them.

94. *Rep* IX.575d.

95. 'Race': *ethnos*, i.e. cultural group (e.g. Hellenes).

96. See *Laws* X.904b6-e6; 903d6ff.; 903e1 (and *Rep.* 620e4; cf. d8) for lots, and *Phaedrus* 249b2-4 for assignments. Cf. also in cap. 1, H214 / D12,50, where Simplicius mentions our pre-incarnation selections of lives, which also seem to extend to our selection of neighborhoods.

97. Hippocrates *de Flatibus* 1.2. The point being that cares and troubles are not irrational emotions, whereas sorrows are. In the next sentence, we do not follow Hadot in taking *epistrophês* from the corrector of A instead of *epimeleias* with all of the mss. (With her text, read 'dragged away from their turning back to themselves and to their superiors.') Either makes sense, but Simplicius may well have thought that 'genuine rulers' are already 'turned round', as Plato does in *Rep.* V-VII.

98. This seems to be the treatment appropriate to a natural relation, i.e. that we should still render our appropriate actions even if the other party does not render theirs.

99. Throughout his commentary on cap. 30, Simplicius had said that appropriate actions are to be discovered by considering our relations to others. In the last several paragraphs of that chapter, he had stressed that many of our appropriate actions consist in attending to the needs of those to whom we are related – see the comments on needy orphans (H357 / D89,45), needy fellow citizens (H358 / D90,12), and needy strangers (H359 / D90,34). It is because of that pattern that Simplicius here takes pains to deny that all relations are needy relations.

100. In the previous chapter, Simplicius defines a 'relation' (*skhesis*) as a sort of coordination (*suntaxis*), and then proceeds to use the words as near synonyms. Thus the *kai* here in *skhesis kai suntaxis* is epexegetic.

101. In Epictetus the object of the verb *peithesthai* in this passage is 'the gods' (and hence it means 'obey'), but Simplicius takes it to govern 'everything that happens' (and hence to mean 'to follow' or 'to go along with' – i.e. as a synonym of 'yield'). The misconstrual may be doctrinally motivated, i.e. Simplicius may feel that obeying the gods exactly consists in yielding to what happens.

102. cf. *Laws* 885b4-9, 888c4-7.

103. cf. H367 / D95,20; and cf. *EN* 1094a2.

104. *amêkhanon* in Epictetus' original, *adunaton* here. This is probably a gloss by Simplicius rather than a textual variant.

105. *oikeiôsis.*

106. *ennoia* should mean 'conception', and could mean that here, since what is at fault in the farmer is at least in part his conception of god.

107. Soon (H368 / D95,35) Simplicius will refer to a lost work of Theophrastus, probably called *Researches into the Divine*. It may be that Simplicius already has this in mind in this very compressed and elliptical reference.

108. The point of this qualification is that externals, when sanctified and offered to God, can play some role in uniting us to God and assimilating us to him. However, the role they play will never be more than subordinate and secondary; it will always be the quality of our knowledge and life that makes the real difference.

109. This sentence details a third way in which the divine illumination is brought down to lower things: theurgy. First, of course, we share in the divine by living and thinking correctly, and by performing the external rituals that are customary in our land. Secondly, the external things used in the rites themselves come to share in the divine – they are not merely empty counters in a game of exchange between the gods and us, they come to have divinity of their own by being sanctified. But then this permits a third pathway of illumination, for now we are illuminated from this second vantage, as it were, because of our relation to the external ritual objects which have themselves become illuminated.

110. *hekastois.* This seems to us strong evidence that Simplicius' text of the *Encheiridion* differed from our own by reading *hekastois prosêkei* where ours reads *hekastote prosêkei.*

111. *biou hairesis*, the phrase used in the *Phaedrus* 249b and *Rep.* 619b to describe the soul's antenatal selection of its lot in life.

112. cf. *Phaedo* 67b2-3.

113. This is clear evidence of another deviation in Simplicius' text of the *Encheiridion*; in our text there is nothing about 'impiety'. Instead we find a word *gliskhros*, i.e. in a stingy way, which Simplicius seems to ignore.

114. *kerasbolos*. This very rare word again shows that Simplicius has his mind on the *Laws*. It appears there at 853d, as a metaphor for those future citizens of the Kallipolis who will somehow resist its good education and training and so need to be punished. The Athenian stranger says that, if it were not for the 'horn-struck' among men, he would not need to enact any provisions for punishment among his laws; here Simplicius says that it is because of them that it is worth his while to provide proofs of the nature of the gods. The meaning and provenance of this curious word are the subject of the second of Plutarch's *Platonic Questions* (700b-d).

115. Simplicius has in mind the discussion of theology and theodicy in the beginning of *Laws* 10 (885ff.). His commentary echoes Plato's phrasing perhaps to a greater extent than Epictetus' own; for instance, the suggestion that the crucial beliefs are three in number is explicit in the *Laws*, and not terribly obvious in Epictetus (Simplicius must treat the clause in Epictetus 'they govern the whole well and justly' as though it has the structure 'they (2) govern; and (3) do it well and justly'). These three points will occupy the rest of the chapter, so that the chapter has the following contents: H360-367 / D91-5, exegesis proper of *Ench.* 31; H367-378 / D95-101, proofs of the first point; H378-386 / D101-6, proofs of the second point; H386-392 / D106-9, proofs of the third point.

116. Alas, the charming story no longer survives in detail. Schweighäuser supposes, plausibly enough, that it was contained in the six books of *Researches (Historiai) into the Divine* that Diogenes lists among his works (D.L. 5.48). This would also explain Simplicius' choice of the verb *historei*.

117. Sometimes attributed to Euripides, now expelled from his fragments and made anonymous (Nauck fr. adesp. 465). The same couplet is quoted by Olympiodorus at *in Gorgiam* 17.2.38.

118. Why *kai tôi Epiktêtôi*? Perhaps the thought is that these people would naturally be persuaded by their own common conceptions, were they not dissuaded by the appearance that bad things happen to good people. But this dissuasion arises only because they falsely place their good and evil in externals. So if they listen to their common conceptions, and listen to Epictetus as well, then they will be uniformly persuaded.

119. cf. *Phaedrus* 244b7.

120. Simplicius connects *theos* with the somewhat archaic verb *theein*, which means 'to run'. Someone might with equal accuracy connect 'God' with 'go'. This etymology is found at *Cratylus* 397c-d.

121. The following arguments are indebted to Plato *Laws*, esp. 888eff.; 894-5.

122. cf. *SVF* 2.284; Hierocles *in CA* II.442.

123. *ta proêgoumenôs ginomena*. As often in Simplicius, the adverb does not mean 'principally' or 'antecedently', but rather 'intrinsically' or 'per se'. Hence the contrast here is between things that come to be per se – i.e., in accordance with a (determinate) 'preceding' cause – and those that come to be incidentally (or derivatively) and by chance (or automatically). The latter class includes deprivations and negations (so that there is no per se cause of the bad), as well as chance occurrences, and also certain Cambridge changes: there may be a per se cause of Socrates' death, without there being a per se cause of Xanthippe's being widowed.

124. There is some confusion in the textual tradition here. The translation follows Hadot's supplements for the most part (without much confidence in her specific proposals for emendation). The sense remains clear.

125. The contiguity is not spatial here, as of one billiard ball adjacent to another, nor is this a claim about any causal relation between things that touch. Rather, the image depends on the vertical chain of dependence stretching from the highest immaterial origins, down to the lowest material particulars. The rank of being that is contiguous with, i.e. next higher than, the realm of material generation is the rank of souls, which are self-movers. Thus there is no contradiction between this and H258 / D36,30.

126. Simplicius is echoing *Laws* 895a-b.

127. cf. H201 / D6,7-13.

128. cf. Damascius *de Princ.* p. 425, where LSJ gives 'without specific difference'.

129. *logoi.*

130. cf. *Symposium* 211d-e.

131. Hadot suggests this is a loose echo of Plotinus *Enn.* 4.2.1.68.

132. *diploe* means both 'doubling' and 'flaw, weak spot'. A favourite Platonists' word, cf. *Sophist* 267e.

133. *Laws* X.896e.

134. Following Hadot's supplement. (The point being that we can explain all physical change in terms of the motion of the world-soul; the question, as Simplicius goes on to explain, is how to explain the constancy through change that physical things exhibit.)

135. The word 'source' does not represent any particular Greek, e.g. *arkhê*; merely the interrogative *pothen*, here and in the next sentence.

136. cf. Plotinus *Enn.* 6.3.21.

137. Hadot prints Schweighäuser's suggested supplementation *pote de tade* ('and at another time something else'); this helps clarify the earlier contrast (with 'thinking or doing one thing ') but leaves the connection of the next clause ('and sometimes has temporal activities') still obscure.

138. Two objections to the thesis that noetic discrimination recognizes the forms in *nous* as both distinct and unified, without confusion are answered here: [1] why should we suppose the forms are in any way separate, and not simply unified in the unmoving? [2] isn't it absurd to say that a properly functioning discrimination sees them both as separate and unified? Simplicius responds to [1] that we must conclude that the forms are distinct, even in the unmoving, since otherwise they could never become distinct in the cosmos. The forms in the cosmos are like copies of the forms in the unmoving, and fashioned in accordance with them; if the originals were not in some way distinct, the copies could not be. He replies to [2] that what would be absurd for common-or-garden discrimination need not be absurd for noetic discrimination; it can see things as both separate and unified without being confused. 'Discrimination' is anyhow ambiguous, since conceptual discrimination is different from physical discrimination (e.g. physical discrimination entails difference of place, where conceptual discrimination need not).

139. *Sophist* 254-5.

140. *Philebus* 65a2.

141. Simplicius is still illustrating how something can be unified and discriminated at once: motion, for instance, is a single form, even though it contains within itself growth, diminution, alteration, locomotion, and the other species of change.

142. *akhri tôn eskhatôn* could mean either 'up to and including sensible physical particulars', or 'up to and including the most specific forms, prior to sensible particulars'.

143. cf. Proclus *ET* theorems 65, 79, 103 and 118.

144. cf. H368 / D95,50ff.

145. *eurhoein.*

146. Italicized words here, and throughout Simplicius' proof of divine providence, mark allusions to or quotations of Plato's *Laws*. (Simplicius works in citations progressively from *Laws* X.901-4).

147. *pathê*, also the Stoic term for emotions and emotional dispositions.

148. Ancient names for moderate and heavy weights, respectively.

149. Referring to his entire commentary in cap. 8.

150. The thesis that divine occupations (e.g. paying attention to human affairs, or causing the heavens to rotate) make their lives laborious and so conflict with our preconception of divine happiness is frequently stressed by Epicurus (e.g. *KD* 1), but occurs as far back as Mimnermus fr. 12 West.

151. Here citing *Timaeus* 42 e 5-6 (rather than *Laws* X).

152. This paragraph is a loose paraphrase of *Laws* X.904 a-d (with some additional points made by Simplicius). The post-mortem places have been described in the section on fate, H213 / D12,40ff.

153. *Phaedrus* 246c, cited by Proclus, *de Malorum Subsistentia* II.23.

154. *eurhoein*, contrasted immediately with *kakodaimones*, 'unhappy'.

155. cf. H264-8 / D39,25-41,45; H274 / D45,5.

156. Our translation of this complicated sentence is not very secure.

157. 'Emotional disorder' here, and 'emotion' above, might also be rendered 'disease' or 'affection' – Simplicius literalizes the play on medical / emotional vocabulary only at the end of this passage.

158. cf. H454 / D138,30.

159. Presumably more anti-Christian polemic.

160. cf. *Rep.* II.379b, *Epinomis* 976e5, and Simplicius in caps 1, 8 and 27.

161. cf. *Gorgias* 478d6-7.

162. cf. *Laws* X.903a5.

163. *agathuntheis*, modifying God, must mean roughly 'gracious'. But the addition of an iota would produce *agathuntheisi*, i.e. 'to us, after we have become good'. This might fit the structure of the sentence better, i.e. God doesn't turn away when we err, nor come back when we turn good.

164. cf. *Theaetetus* 176b2.

165. cf. H450 / D136,39.

166. A reminiscence of cap. 1, in which *hupolêpsis* is given as an example of things up to us.

167. cf. Xenophon *Memorabilia* 1.1.9.

168. The subject seems to be God, or the Pythian, mentioned in the sentence being commented on. The subject could be Epictetus, in which case *apodekhetai* will mean 'he does not approve of' etc. But this makes the *oude* difficult to construe; and it ignores Simplicius' repetition of *toigaroun* at the beginning of his sentence, in imitation of the sentence commented on.

169. cf. H260 / D37,29, H261 / D38,10.

170. Reading *adeôs* with the mss and Hadot. It seems likely that the text is in error here; Wolf's *allôs* or Schweighäuser's *ek deous* are possibilities.

171. cap. 22, lemma XXX, H301 / D58,35.

172. cap. 32 §1, lemma XXXIX, H392 / D109 – though the lemma itself does not contain the phrase Simplicius quotes.

173. *tautotês*: 'sameness'.

174. cf. *EN* 1167b7.

175. This is the second time that Simplicius has used *dia brakheôn* in place of the *di' oligôn* in modern texts of the *Encheiridion*, which may reflect a textual variant, or mere reliance on memory.

176. i.e., his warning against laughter may imply a parallel warning against weeping.

177. *Rep.* 589b1.

178. Source unknown.

179. *enstasis* again.

180. cap. 39.

181. Paxamos was a famous baker, cf. Athenaeus 9.376d (Galen 14.537 mentions a biscuit named a *paxamas*). On Thearion, see *Gorgias* 58b5-7 (and Dodds' note in his commentary).

182. cf. *Phaedo* 87d.

183. Simplicius repeats the three points made in the comparison of the carpenter and the adze at the beginning of H404 / D115,20.

184. On the ancient use of beaver-pelts, Schweighäuser cites Strabo 3.162 (Casaubon's edition) and Pliny's *Hist. Nat.* VIII.30.47. On the Seres (e.g. Chinese silk-producers) cf. e.g. Strabo 11.11.1, 15.1.34.

185. Simplicius seems to be misapplying stories of Diogenes the Cynic to the case of his students Crates and Hipparchia.

186. It would be pleasantly romantic to believe, with Oldfather, that Epictetus was 'long unmarried, until in his old age he took a wife to help him bring up a little child' (Intro to Loeb vol. 1, p. x). But there is little in this passage – and it is our sole evidence for the incident – to justify the word 'wife', or suggest that the woman was anything but a nurse for the child. In particular, Oldfather's account seems to overlook the fact that Simplicius mentions the incident exactly to illustrate when a philosopher may take on a servant.

187. cf. D.L. 6.37.

188. All manuscripts but one have *pêlikôtera* which makes little sense; one has *politikôtera*, which makes only a little more sense. Hadot accepted it, and we translate it. Schweighäuser conjectured *plêktikôtera*, i.e. 'more striking', and he is probably right; given the sequel, there is more point to a reference to the strength of this pleasure than to any political ramifications it has.

189. Simplicius' references to bits and reins convey a general reminiscence of *Phaedrus* 253d-254e.

190. Text and translation uncertain.

191. Attributed to Plato at Athenaeus 11, 507d.

192. cf. the relatively approving comments on love of honour at H278 / D47,5.

193. As at H403 / D114,50, when the subject was going to the feasts of ordinary people rather than theatres.

194. The two readings of the 'whatever' clause that Simplicius seems to be suggesting are (1) 'don't say anything about what happened in the theatre, since anything you might say about it would be irrelevant to your correction' and (2) 'you may say, about what happened in the theatre, only those things that are relevant to your correction, e.g. you may be critical of your own behaviour, of your having been excessively moved, etc.'

195. Simplicius suggests that Epictetus meant us to model our behaviour on Socrates and Zeno, not by acting just as they would have, but by acting in a way commensurate with our own lives, unpretentious, and natural – which means, in particular, exactly that we will *not* attempt to criticize rulers as Socrates and Zeno did, since we are not at their level.

196. cap. 4, lemma IX.

197. cf. *Phaedo* 83d1.

198. *sunaisthêsis.*

199. With this discussion of pleasure cf. H203 / D7,10.

200. Epictetus distinguished pleasure (*hêdonê*) and joy (*khairein*) in cap. 34, as respectively vicious and virtuous. Simplicius alters this into a distinction between two kinds of pleasure (*eidê hêdonês*).

201. Simplicius seems to be reading ahead here, and taking the *ophthênai* + participle construction from cap. 35. In that passage, the emphasis is on what others think; here the emphasis is on one's own self-appraisal.

202. The lemma differs from the standard text of the *Encheiridion* in two trivial ways; the addition of a *kai*, and a reordering of words.

203. Here the difference between the standard text of the *Encheiridion* and the text of the lemma is very significant. Epictetus mentions two atomic propositions, ('it is day' and 'it is night'), and says that the molecular proposition they form is valid in one case (i.e. if they're joined by an 'or') and invalid in another (i.e. if joined by an 'and'). In Simplicius' text, one is given a molecular proposition from the outset, i.e. 'either it is day or it is night'. This leads him to think that the issue is not how one can validly construct molecular propositions from atomic ones, but rather how one can validly construct arguments using molecular propositions as premisses. This forces him to take 'disjunction' and 'conjunction' in the lemma not as names for classes of molecular propositions, but as names for classes of arguments, i.e. 'disjunctive' and 'conjunctive' syllogisms, where these are arguments whose major premiss is a disjunctive or conditional proposition, respectively. (His assumption, standard in the logic of his time, that 'conjunction' means 'conditional' is a further source of confusion, since it is quite alien to Stoic usage). So he takes the point of the simile to be that a disjunction cannot serve as the major premiss of a 'conjunctive' syllogism.

204. Here Simplicius glosses Epictetus' word 'conjunctive' with what he takes to be its real meaning, sc. conditional.

205. The supplement <proposition> makes sense of the Stoic examples Simplicius uses, but may misrepresent what he had in mind (i.e. perhaps, the existence of objects).

206. He has previously referred to 'disjunctive syllogisms', in the plural, and in the masculine gender dictated by the gender of 'syllogism'. He now switches to the neuter singular, which would more normally refer to a disjunctive proposition, as it does in Epictetus. But it seems that Simplicius is still talking about syllogisms, and has switched the form merely to show that he is glossing Epictetus' own words – i.e. he takes it that Epictetus is using the neuter, somewhat unusually, to refer to a syllogism.

207. Something 'evidently true and in accordance with the common conceptions' might have been called a *prolêpsis* by the Stoics, but they never used the word *axiôma* in this sense.

208. Again, he uses the word in the form Epictetus did, in which it referred to a single proposition, but his comments make it seem that he is using the word to refer to a whole syllogism.

209. This sentence and the last one show us how to compose a true conditional sentence. The following sentences corroborate the sentence-construction rules by consideration of syllogistic validity.

210. Here we are given the minor premiss and the conclusion of a 'conjunctive syllogism', whose major premiss is the sentence whose truth is being corroborated.

211. Again, he seems to be explicitly glossing Epictetus' word 'disjunction' with what he takes to be its real meaning, sc. 'disjunctive syllogism'.

212. cf. *Rep.* 351c.

213. This sounds very much like a quotation. A close parallel is Simplicius' *in de Caelo*, 141.23.

214. 'Au pair' and 'professor' render *paidagogos* and *didaskalos* (the slave who takes children to school and the teacher the child is delivered to, respectively).

215. The comparison is traditional. It was made by Aristo (D.L. 7.160), and before him in a remark of the orator Demades to Philip (Diodorus Siculus 16.87.2-3).

216. *to kai axion prosôpon* (Hadot's reading) survives only in one ms. It seems likely that the correct reading was *to kai kat'axion prosôpon* (translated above), since the chapter explicitly tells us not to choose roles by their value, but by our own.

217. Simplicius interprets this chapter as a continuation of the themes he identified in the last chapter (cf. H425 / D125,20).

218. cf. H247 / D30,36.

219. cf. *Phaedo* 83d. Simplicius has already expanded on this image in his commentary on cap. 34.

220. i.e. the part of the soul that deals with beliefs (*doxa*), which is *peripezios*, literally 'lying around the feet', and so common, mundane, earthly.

221. cf. H199 / D4,40.

222. cf. *Rep.* 619b9; *Laws* 888a4.

223. cap. 33§7, lemma xliv.

224. i.e. we abandon them to their natural enemies, e.g. diseases stemming from over-eating and the like.

225. There is a lacuna here, presumably a short one since the sense is fairly continuous: walking in oversize shoes is difficult and can lead to a fall.

226. i.e. as did the foregoing caps 36-8, on Simplicius' interpretation.

227. There is some ambiguity in Simplicius' use of *gunê* ('woman' or 'wife') here. It seems likely that he is trying to interpret Epictetus' quite general account of male-female relations as a specific account of how the typically male reader should treat his own wife.

228. *kalon* can either mean 'beautiful', i.e. physically attractive, or 'morally virtuous'.

229. The language clearly refers back to the discussion of *First Alcibiades*, 128-32, which figured so prominently in the prologue (H195-7 / D3,2-55); cf. also H212 / D12,20.

230. Again, the late Platonist/Peripatetic use of 'conjunction' for the conditional, as in Simplicius' discussion of cap. 36.

231. This seems again to indicate that Simplicius thinks habituation must supplement correct belief. Cf. in cap. 5, H247 / D30,25.

232. A pun; *aphorêton* – 'unbearable' – is literally 'difficult to carry'.

233. In light of Simplicius' occasional use of *zôê* in a sense that makes it mean something like *psyche*, it is possible that this phrase adds up to something like *megalopsuchia*, i.e. greatness of soul.

234. *Protagoras* 310aff and *Theaetetus* 151b4-6.

235. cf. the story of Diogenes the Cynic, quoted above at H407 / D117,5.

236. Simplicius seems to have in mind some procedure for asking for asylum or refuge from a hostile group. Epictetus, on the other hand, is clearly referring to the ascetic practice noted at D.L. 6.23, where we learn that in the winter Diogenes the Cynic used to embrace statues that were covered with snow, in order to toughen himself up. He discusses the same practice, with the same note of disparagement, at *Diss.* 3.12.3, 3.12.11, 4.5.14. The first of these is so clear that it is hard to believe that Simplicius could have read it and still misunderstood this passage.

237. *Paroemiographi Graeci*, 1851, p. 483,15, also cited by Proclus, *de Decem Dubitationibus* 1 fin.

238. cf. H353 / D87,5.

239. *Phaedrus* 247d6.

240. cf. H352 / D86,40ff.

241. *Phaedo* 66c.

242. *Rep.* 514a-518b.

243. Simplicius apparently had a text of the *Encheiridion* in which *amathês* had been altered to *masthlês*.

244. Simplicius' lemma differs trivially, in not containing the word for 'the books' of Chrysippus. Instead it simply has the neuter plural article with the name in the genitive, i.e. 'the things of Chrysippus', which might be his books, sayings, or just his positions in general.

245. Demosthenes *Olynthiacs* II.12; Simplicius adds the word 'educational' into the run of the quotation as an improvement on Demosthenes.

246. The lemma here has the verb 'to set before' in the second person instead of the third (i.e. *protithesai* instead of *protithetai*).

247. *EN* I.6 1098a18, *Paroemiographi Graeci*, 1851, p. 79,16; p. 531,5.

248. Simplicius may well have in mind here the speech made by the personified Laws in Plato's *Crito* 50ab; the thought and language are quite similar.

249. cap. 22.

250. For similar enigmatic sayings, see D.L. 8.17ff., and Iamblichus' *Protrepticus*, especially the closely similar proverb discussed at p. 115.

251. *mê epistrephou* can mean 'pay no attention', as in cap. 50; but it could also mean 'do not turn back'; the verb *epistrephesthai* means 'to turn back, turn one's attention towards', etc.

252. *ton diairounta logon* is a phrase without parallel, and seems almost certainly a manuscript error for *ton hairounta logon*, which is a common phrase in Plato and other Stoics, and very dear to Epictetus' heart. It means very nearly what Simplicius offers as a gloss, i.e. 'right reason'. But no modern editor has adopted it, perhaps because the Greek can still be construed without the change.

253. The lemma has *oun* for the *Encheiridion*'s *eti*.

254. Hesiod *Op.* 411.

255. Lit. 'All of life (*zôê*) is one, and life (*bios*) is one, alternating etc.' On *zôê*, cf. in cap. 1 H199 / D4,40, in cap. 27 H337 / D78,40.

256. It is a natural thought, made even more tempting by etymology, that things are perfect (*teleios*) when they have reached their end (*telos*). Simplicius warns us off from one simplistic application of that thought.

257. *Apology* 21a.

258. *Crito* 46b.

259. i.e., he measures his own behaviour against the standard set by a perfect imitation of his ethical model.

260. Simplicius cites the sources for these quotations below. Their modern references are: Cleanthes *SVF* 1.527, Euripides fr. 965 Nauck, *Crito* 43d7-8, and *Apology* 30c.

261. cap. 8.

262. or: 'the present circumstances'.

263. cf. H386 / D106,1.

264. *Iliad* 5.127-8; cf. Proclus *in Primum Euclidis* 29.24-30.7, *in Rem.* 1.18.25-19.2.

Bibliography

Editions, translations, fortuna

Boter, G., *The Encheiridion of Epictetus and its Three Christian Adaptations: Transmission and Critical Editions*. Philosophia Antiqua 82 (Leiden 1999).

Dübner, F., *Theophrasti Characteres, Marci Antonini Commentarii, Epicteti Dissertationes ab Arriano literis mandatae, Fragmenta et Enchiridion cum Commentario Simplicii, Cebetis Tabula, Maximi Tyrii Dissertationes graece et latine cum indicibus* (Paris 1840, 1842).

Hadot, I., 'La tradition manuscrite du commentaire de Simplicius sur le *Manuel* d'Épictète, *Revue d'histoire des textes* 8 (1978) 1-108.

—— 'La tradition manuscrite du commentaire de Simplicius sur le *Manuel* d'Épictète', Addenda et Corrigenda', *Revue d'histoire des textes* 11 (1981) 387-95.

—— *Simplicius Commentaire sur le Manuel d'Épictète: introduction et édition critique du texte grec*. Philosophia Antiqua 66 (Leiden 1996).

—— *Simplicius Commentaire sur le Manuel d'Épictète: chapitres I à XXIX* (Paris 2001).

Hadot, P., 'La survie du commentaire de Simplicius sur le *Manuel* d'Épictète du XVe au XVIIe siècles: Perotti, Politien, Stuechus, John Smith, Cudworth', in I. Hadot (ed.), *Simplicius: sa vie, son oeuvre, sa survie* (Berlin 1987) 326-67.

Isaac, D., *Proclus. Trois études sur la providence*, vol. 1: *Dix problèmes concernant la providence* (Paris 1977); vol. 2: *Providence, fatalité, liberté* (Paris 1979); vol. 3: *De l'existence du mal* (Paris 1982).

Oldfather, W., *Epictetus*, vol. 2 (London 1928).

Schweighäuser, J., *Epicteteae philosophiae monumenta* IV & V (Leipzig 1800).

Schenkl, H., *Epictetus* (Leipzig 1916).

Stanhope, G., *Epictetus, his morals, with Simplicius his comment, made English from the Greek* (London 1694).

Wolf, H., *Epicteti Enchiridion … Simplicii in eundem Epicteti libellum doctissima Scholia* (Basel 1563; the basis for the Latin translations by Schweighäuser & Dübner).

Simplicius' life and works

Blumenthal, H., *Simplicius: On Aristotle On the Soul 3.1-5* (London & Ithaca N.Y. 2000).

Cameron, A., 'The last days of the Academy at Athens', *PCPS* 195 (1969) 7-29.

Foulkes, P., 'Where was Simplicius?', *JHS* 112 (1992) 143.

Glucker, J., *Antiochus and the Late Academy* (Göttingen 1978).

Hadot, I. (ed.), *Simplicius: sa vie, son oeuvre, sa survie* (Berlin 1987).

—— 'La vie et l'oeuvre de Simplicius d'apres des sources Grecques et Arabes', in I. Hadot (ed.) (1987) 3-39.

―――― 'The life and work of Simplicius in Greek and Arabic sources', in R. Sorabji (ed.), *Aristotle Transformed: The Ancient Commentators and Their Influence* (London & Ithaca N.Y. 1990) 275-303.

Hoffmann, P., 'Damascius', in R. Goulet (ed.), *Dictionnaire des philosophes antiques*, vol. 2 (Paris 1994) 541-93.

Huby, P. & C. Steel, *Priscian: On Theophrastus On Sense Perception* with *'Simplicius': On Aristotle On the Soul 2.5-12* (London & Ithaca N.Y. 1997).

Lameer, J., 'From Alexandria to Baghdad: reflections on the genesis of a problematical tradition', in G. Endress & R. Kruk (eds), *The Ancient Traditions in Christian and Islamic Hellenism* (Leiden 1997) 181-91.

Luna, C., Review of Thiel 1999, *Mnemosyne* 54-4 (2001) 482-504.

Tardieu, M., 'Sabiens coraniques et "Sabiens" de Harran', *Journal Asiatique* 274 (1986) 1-44.

―――― 'Les calendriers en usage à Harran d'après les sources arabes et le commentaire de Simplicius à la *Physique* d'Aristote', in I. Hadot (ed.) (1987) 40-57.

―――― *Les paysages reliques: routes et haltes syriennes d'Isidore à Simplicius*, Bibliothèque de l'École des Hautes Études, Sciences Religieuses, vol. 94 (Louvain & Paris 1990).

―――― 'Chosroès' in R. Goulet, *Dictionnaire des philosophes antiques*, vol. 2 (Paris 1994) 309-18.

Thiel, R., *Simplikios und das Ende der neuplatonischen Schule in Athen*. Abhandlungen der Mainzer Akademie der Wissenschaften und der Literatur, Abhandlungen der Geistes- und Sozialwissenschaftlichen Klasse, Nr. 8 (Stuttgart 1999).

van Riet, S., 'À propos de la biographie de Simplicius', *Revue philosophique de Louvain* 89 (1991) 506-14.

Wildberg, C., 'Simplicius' in *Routledge Encyclopedia of Philosophy* (London 2000).

The commentary

Fuhrer, T. & M. Erler (eds), *Zur Rezeption der hellenistischen Philosophie im Spätantike*. Philosophie der Antike, Band 9 (Stuttgart 1999).

Hadot, I., 'Die Widerlegung des Manichäeismus im Epiktetkommentar des Simplikios', *AGP* 51 (1969) 31-57.

―――― *Le problème du néoplatonisme alexandrin – Hiéroclès et Simplicus* (Paris 1978).

―――― 'La doctrine de Simplicius sur l'âme raisonnable humaine dans le Commentaire sur le Manuel d'Épictète', in H.J. Blumenthal & A.C. Lloyd (eds), *Soul and the Structure of Being in Late Neoplatonism* (Liverpool 1982) 46-70 (discussion 71-2).

Lloyd, A., 'Parhypostasis in Proclus', in G. Boss & C. Steel (eds), *Proclus et son influence* (Zürich 1987) 145-57.

Opsomer, J. & C. Steel, 'Evil without a cause: Proclus' doctrine on the origin of evil, and its antecedents in Hellenistic philosophy', in T. Fuhrer & M. Erler (1999) 229-60.

Praechter, K., 'Simplikios' in *Paulys Realencyclopädie* III A, 1 (1927) col. 204-13.

Rist, J., 'Prohairesis: Proclus, Plotinus et alii', in H. Dörrie (ed.), *De Iamblique à Proclus*. Entretiens sur l'Antiquité Classique XXI, (Geneva 1975) 103-17 (discussion 118-22).

Sedley, D., 'The Stoic-Platonist debate on *kathekonta*', in K. Ierodiakonou (ed.), *Topics in Stoic Philosophy* (Oxford 1999) 128-52.

Steel, C., *The Changing Self: A Study on the Soul in Later Neoplatonism: Iamblichus, Damascius and Priscianus* (Brussels 1978).

Thiel, R., 'Stoische Ethik und neuplatonische Tugendlehre. Zur Verortung der stoischen Ethik im neuplatonischen System in Simplikios Kommentar zu Epiktets *Enchiridion*', in T. Fuhrer & M. Erler (1999) 93-103.

Other references

Barney, R., 'A Puzzle about Stoic Ethics', *Oxford Studies in Ancient Philosophy* (2003, forthcoming).

Blumenthal, H., *Aristotle and Neoplatonism in Late Antiquity* (London & Ithaca N.Y. 1996).

Bobzien, S., *Determinism and Freedom in Stoic Philosophy* (Oxford 1998).

Brennan, T., 'The Old Stoic Theory of the Emotions' in Sihvola & Engberg-Pedersen (1998) 21-70.

Brennan, T., 2002a 'Moral Psychology' in Inwood (2002).

Brennan, T., 2002b 'Demoralizing the Stoics', *Ancient Philosophy* (2002, forthcoming).

Dillon, J., 'Plotinus, Philo and Origen on the grades of virtue', in id., *The Golden Chain* (Aldershot 1990) ch. 18.

Dobbin, R., *Epictetus: Discourses I* (Oxford 1998).

Cooper, J., 'Posidonius on Emotions', in Sihvola & Engberg-Pedersen (1998) 71-111.

Graver, M., 'Philo of Alexandria and the origins of the Stoic propatheiai', *Phronesis* 44 (2000) 300-25.

Inwood, B., *Ethics and Human Action in Early Stoicism* (Oxford 1985).

Inwood, B., *The Cambridge Companion to Stoicism* (Cambridge 2002).

Long, A.A., *Epictetus: A Stoic and Socratic Guide to Life* (Oxford 2002).

Schissel von Fleschenberg, O., *Marinos von Neapolis und die neuplatonischen Tugendgrade* (Athens 1928).

Sihvola, J. & T. Engberg-Pedersen (eds), *Emotions in Hellenistic Philosophy* (Copenhagen 1998).

Smith, A., *Porphyry's Place in the Neoplatonic Tradition: A Study in Post-Plotinian Neoplatonism* (The Hague 1974).

Sorabji, R., *Emotion and Peace of Mind: From Stoic Agitation to Christian Temptation* (Oxford 2000).

Westerink, L., J. Trouillard & A. Segonds, *Prolégomènes à la philosophie de Platon* (Paris 1990).

Concordance of Editions and Overview of Topics

Ench. chs	Simp. lemmas	Dübner pp.	Hadot 1996 pp.	Epict. subject	Simp. subject
–	–	1-4	192-7		introduction
1	i-vi	4-20	197-228	up to us & not	
1.1	i-ii	4-16	197-220	up to us our work	God &
1.2	iii	16	220	up to us free	determinism
1.3	iv	16-18	221-3	not up to us impeded	
1.4	v	18-19	223-7	costs of philosophy	
1.5	vi	19-20	227-8	test impressions	
2	vii	20-4	229-35	desire & avoidance	Stoic impulses
3	viii	24-5	235-8	attitude to child	
4	ix	25-7	238-42	attitude to actions	
5	x-xi	27-32	242-50	beliefs disturb	
6	xii	32-3	251-3	use of impressions	
7	xiii	33-5	253-6	sailing metaphor	
8	xiv	35-44	256-73	want what happens	evil & freedom
9	xv	44-5	273-5	physical impediments	
10	xvi	45-7	275-8	powers to use things	
11	xvii	47-8	278-80	dealing with loss	
12	xviii	48-50	280-4	attitude to slave	
13	xix-xx	50-1	284-6	reputation	
14	xxi-xxii	51-3	287-9	attitude to others	
15	xxiii	53-4	290-1	party metaphor	
16	xxiv	54	292-3	sympathy	
17	xxv	54-5	293-5	act role assigned	
18	xxvi	55-6	295-6	omens	
19.1	xxvii	56	296	invincibility	
19.2	xxviii	57	297-8	jealousy	
20	xxix	57-8	298-300	insults	
21	xxix	58	300	prior consideration	
22	xxx	58-60	301-4	mockery of philosophers	
23	xxxi	60-1	304-6	appearing a philosopher	
24	xxxii	61-6	306-16	social value of philosophy	cities & states
25	xxxiii	66-8	316-19	virtue own reward	
26	xxxiv	68-9	319-21	will of nature	*koinai ennoiai*
27	xxxv	69-82	322-44	no nature of bad	Manichees
28	xxxvi	82	344-5	others' judgements	
29	–	–	–	consequences of acts	
30	xxxvii	82-91	345-60	*officia*	relationships
31	xxxviii	91-109	360-92	piety	providence
32	xxxix	109-11	392-7	divination	
33	xl-li	111-22	397-419	behaviour in public	
34	lii	122-3	420-2	allure of pleasure	

Ench. chs	Simp. lemmas	Dübner pp.	Hadot 1996 pp.	Epict. subject	Simp. subject
35	liii	123-4	422	if act chosen, act	
36	liv	124-5	423-5	behaviour at parties	Stoic logic
37	lv	125	425-6	successful roles	
38	lvi	125-6	426-7	nail metaphor	
39	lvii	126-7	427-9	shoe metaphor	
40	lviii	127	429-30	attitude to women	
41	lix	127	430-1	attitude to gym	
42	lx	127-8	431-2	all act as think best	
43	lxi	128-9	432-4	handles metaphor	
44	lxii	129	434-5	pride in externals	
45	lxiii	129-30	435-6	judging others' acts	
46	lxiv	130-1	437-9	act as phil. not talk as	
47	lxv	131-2	439-40	recitent asceticism	
48	lxvi	132-3	440-3	3 kinds of people	
49	lxvii	133-4	444-5	Chrysippus vs. action	
50	lxviii	134	445-6	be steadfast	
51	lxix	135-6	446-9	act now	
52	lxx	136-7	449-51	ethics physics logic	
53	lxxi	137-8	451-4	4 quotations	
–	–	138	454	–	final prayer

English-Greek Glossary

abandon (to): *proiêmi*
able to (to be): *dunamai*
abuse (to): *hubrizô*
abuse: *hubris*
abusive: *hubristikos*
accident: *sumbebêkos*
accommodate (to): *sunkatabainô*
accommodating: *sunkatabatikos*
accommodation: *sunkatabasis*
accuse (to): *enkaleô*
acquire (to): *ktaomai, tunkhanô*
act (a part, role, to): *hupokrinomai*
act (to): *energeô*
acted on (to be): *paskhô*
action: *pragma*
activity: *energeia*
actor: *hupokritês*
advantage (taking): *pleonexia*
advantage (to take): *pleonekteô*
advantage: *pleonektêma*
Aeon: *aiôn*
affair: *pragma*
affection: *pathos*
aggressive: *hubristikos*
aim: *skopos*
allow (to): *sunkhôreô*
ancient: *palaios*
angelic: *angelikos*
angry (to be): *thumoô*
animal: *zôos*
animate: *empsukos*
animation: *zôtikos*
annoyance: *duskheransis*
annoyed (to get): *duskherainô*
anomalous: *anômalos*
anomaly: *anômalia*
antecedent (in conditional):
    hêgoumenon
appear (to): *phainomai*
application: *khrêsis*
appraisal: *dokêsis*

appropriate (action): *kathêkôn*
appropriate (to be): *kathêkô*
appropriateness: *oikeiotês*
argue (demonstratively, to):
    sullogizomai
argue badly (to): *paralogizomai*
argument (syllogism): *sullogismos*
argument: *logos*
arise as by-product (to): *paraphuomai*
arrangement: *sunthesis*
art: *tekhnê*
articulate (to): *diarthroô*
artificial: *tekhnikos*
assent (to): *sunkatatithêmi*
assent: *sunkatathesis*
assimilate (to): *homoioô, oikeioô*
associate (to): *koinôneô*
association: *koinônia*
associative: *sunagôgos*
attain (to): *tunkhanô*
attend (to): *prosekhô*
attention: *prosokhê*
attentive part: *prosektikon*
authority: *exousia*
aversion (object of): *ekklitos, pheuktos*
aversion: *ekklisis*
avoid (to): *ekklinô, pheugô*
aware (to be): *sunaisthanomai*
awareness: *sunaisthêsis*

bad (to become): *kakoô, kakunô*
bad: *kakos*
badness: *kakia*
be (to): *huparkhô*
bearable: *phorêtos*
beautiful: *kalos*
beauty: *kallos*
become (to): *gignomai*
being: *on, ousia*
belief (object of): *hupolêptos*
belief: *dogma, hupolêpsis*

believe (to): *doxazô, hêgeomai,
  hupolambanô*
believing: *doxastikos*
beneficial: *ôphelimos*
benefit (to): *ôpheleô*
benefit: *ôpheleia*
better of (to get): *pleonekteô*
blame (to): *memphomai, psegô*
blame: *psogos*
blamed: *psektos*
breath: *pneuma*

care for (to): *epimeleomai*
care: *epimeleia, epimeletês*
careful (to be): *prosekhô*
care-giver: *epimeletês*
carpenter: *tektôn*
cataleptic: *katalêptikos*
cathartic: *kathartikos*
cause (not the): *anaitios*
cause: *aitios (aitia)*
caused: *aitiatos*
chance: *tukhê*
change (to): *metaballô*
change: *metabolê*
chapter: *kephalaios*
character: *kharaktêr*
characteristic (defining): *eidopoios*
characterise (to): *kharaktêrizô*
choice: *hairesis*
choiceworthy: *exairetos*
choose (to): *prohaireô*
citizen: *politês*
city: *polis, politeia*
cognition: *gnômê*
cognitive: *gnôstikos*
collect (to): *sunagô*
combination: *koinônia, sumplokhê*
commensurate: *summetros*
commensurateness: *summetria*
common with (to have in): *koinôneô*
common: *koinos*
communal: *koinônikos*
compel (to): *biazô*
complete: *holoklêros, holotelês, teleios*
compose (to): *suntithêmi*
composite: *sunthetos*
concede (to): *endidômi, sunkhôreô*
conceive (to): *ennoeô*
conception: *ennoia, prolêpsis*
concern: *epimeleia*
concerned (to be): *epimeleomai*
concession: *endosis*

conclude (to): *sunagô*
conclusion: *sunagôgê*
condition: *hexis, katastasis,
  katastêma*
conditional: *sunêmmenon*
conjunction: *sumplektikos*
consequences: *episumbainô*
consequent (in conditional):
  hepomenon
consider (in advance, to): *promeletaô*
consider (to): *hêgeomai*
constancy: *tautotês*
contiguous: *prosekhês*
control (to): *krateô*
control of (in): *kurios*
coordination: *suntaxis*
corpse: *nekros*
correct: *orthos*
cosmos: *kosmos*
counsel: *boulê*
counter-impulse (to have): *aphormaô*
counter-impulse: *aphormê*
country: *patris*
craft: *tekhnê*
craftsman: *tekhnitês*
creation of the cosmos: *kosmopoiia*
criterion: *kanôn, kritêrion*
critical: *elegtikos, kritikos*
criticise (to): *enkaleô*
cure: *iama*
custom: *nomos*

deaden (to): *nekroô*
death: *thanatos*
defeated (to be): *hêttaomai*
deficiency: *endeia*
deficient: *endeês*
demeanour: *katastêma*
demiurge: *dêmiourgos*
demiurgic: *dêmiourgikos,
  genesiourgos*
demonstrate (to): *apodeiknumi*
demonstration: *apodeixis*
demonstrative: *apodeiktikos*
deprive (to): *stereô*
descent (level of): *huphesis*
desire (capable of): *orektikos*
desire (object of): *orektos*
desire (passionate): *epithumia*
desire (passionately, to): *epithumeô*
desire (to): *oregomai*
desire: *orexis*
die: *thnêskô*

differ: *diapherô*
difference: *diaphora*
different: *diaphoros*
differentia: *diaphora*
difficulties (to raise): *aporeô*
difficulty: *aporia*
disassociative: *diastatikos*
discriminate (to): *diakrinô*
discriminating: *kritikos*
discrimination: *diakrisis*
dishonour (to): *atimazô*
disjunctive: *diazeugnumai*
dispose (to): *diatithêmi*
disposition (ethical): *enstasis*
disposition: *diathesis*
distinction: *diakrisis*
distinguish (to): *diakrinô,*
    diarthrôteos, diistêmi
distress: *lupê, lupêros*
distressed (to be): *lupeô*
disturb (to): *tarattô*
disturbance: *okhlos, tarakhê*
divide (to): *dihaireô, merizô*
divided: *meristos*
divination (result of): *manteuma*
divination (to use): *manteuomai*
divination: *manteia*
divinatory: *mantikos*
divine: *theios*
diviner: *mantis*
divisible: *meristos*
division: *diastasis, dihairesis,*
    merismos
doctor: *iatros*
doctrine: *theôrêma*

educable: *didaskalikos*
education (proper, good): *euagogia*
education: *paideusis*
elemental mass: *holotês*
embrace (to): *sumplekô*
emotion (to join in): *sumpathainô*
emotion: *pathos*
emotional: *pathêtikos*
encounter (to): *peripiptô*
end: *telos*
err (to): *hamartanô*
erring: *hamartôlos*
error: *hamartêma*
essence (to have one's): *ousioomai*
essence: *ousia*
eternal: *aiônios*
eternity: *aiôn*

events: *gignomena, sumbainonta*
examination: *dokimasia*
exercise (to): *gumnazô*
exercise: *gumnasia, gumnasion*
exile: *phugê*
existence (form of): *hupostasis*
existence (to get, come into):
    huphistêmi
existence: *huparxis*
existent thing: *on*

fail to attain (to): *apotunkhanô*
failure: *apotukhia*
familiar: *gnôrimos*
fate: *heimarmenos*
fault: *hamartia*
fine: *kalos*
flee (to): *pheugô*
flight: *phugê*
follow (logically, to): *hepomai*
follow (to): *akoloutheô*
force (to): *biazô*
force: *bia*
forethought (to exercise): *pronoeô*
forethought: *pronoia*
forgive (to): *sungignôskô*
forgiveness: *sungnômê*
form: *eidos*
fountain: *pêgê*
free: *eleutheros*
freedom from disturbance: *ataraxia*
freedom: *eleutheria*
friend: *philos*
friendship: *philia, philikos*
frustration: *duskherantikos*

general: *koinos*
generate (to): *gennaô*
generated: *genêtos*
generation (the realm of): *genesis*
genuinely: *gnêsios*
genus: *genos*
gnomic: *gnômonikos*
goal: *telos*
god: *theos*
god-fearing: *theosebês*
god-like: *theoeidês*
good fortune (of): *eutukhês*
good fortune (to be of): *eutukheô*
good fortune: *eutukhia*
good life: *euzôia*
good: *agathos, kalos*
goodness: *agathotês*

stable: *katastêmatikos*
stand apart (to): *diistêmi*
state (condition): *hexis*
state (republic): *politeia*
station: *taxis*
status: *axiôma*
Stoic: *Stôikos*
strictly: *kuriôs*
strive (to): *ephiêmi*
style: *lexis*
subordinate (to): *hupotattô*
subsist (to): *huphistêmi*
subsist derivatively (to):
    parhuphistêmi
subsistence (to give): *hupostatês,*
    hupostatikos
subsistence: *hupostasis*
substance: *ousia*
substrate (to be): *hupokeimai*
sucession: *akolouthia*
suffer (to): *paskhô*
suffer emotion (to): *pathainô*
suitability: *epitêdeiotês*
suitable: *epitêdeios*
superior: *kreittôn*
superiority: *huperokhê*
suppose (to): *hupotithêmi*
symmetrical: *summetros*
symmetry: *summetria*
sympathetic: *sumpathês*
sympathise (to): *sumpaskhô*
sympathy: *sumpatheia*

take (to be the case, to): *hêgeomai*
target: *skopos*
teach (to): *didaskô*
teacher: *didaskalos*
teaching: *didaskalia*
technical: *tekhnikos*
test (to): *dokimazô*
theatre: *theatron*
theorem: *theôrêma*
theoretical: *theôrêtikos*
thesis: *problêma*
thing: *pragma*
think (to be right-thinking): *phroneô*
think (to): *dianoeô, dokeô, hêgeomai*
time (opportune): *kairos*
timely: *kairios*
tool: *organon*
topic: *problêma, topos*
train (to): *gumnazô*
training-ground: *gumnasion*

training-master: *gumnasiarkhos*
transcend (to): *exaireô, huperanekhô*
transcendence: *exairesis*
treatment: *khrêsis*
true (to be): *alêtheuô, alêthizomai*
true: *alêthês*
truth: *alêtheia*
turn back (to): *epistrephô*
turning back: *epistrophê*

unchanged: *ametablêtos*
understand (to): *epistamai*
understanding: *epistêmê*
undisturbed: *atarakhos*
undivided: *ameristos*
unfortunate (to be): *atunkhanô*
unfortunate result: *apotukhia*
unfortunate: *atukhês*
ungenerated: *agenêtos*
unhappiness: *kakodaimonia*
unhappy: *kakodaimôn*
unification: *henôsis*
union: *koinônia*
unity: *henôsis*
universe: *pan*
unpleasant: *duskherês*
unpleasantness: *duskhereia*
unstable: *astatos*
upset (being): *duskheransis*
upset (to get): *duskherainô*
use (one should): *khrêsteon*
use: *khreia, khrêsis, khrêstikos*
useful: *khrêsimos*

value: *axios*
vice: *kakia*
vicious (to become): *kakunô*
violent: *biaios*
virtue: *aretê*
vision: *thea, theama*
visual: *theatrikos*
vital: *zôtikos*

want (to): *boulomai*
weighed down (to be): *barunô*
well-being: *euagogia*
whole: *holotês, holoklêros, holos, pan*
will: *boulêma*
wisdom (practical): *phronêsis*
wise person: *epistêmôn*
wise: *phronimos*
wish (to): *thelô*
wish: *boulêsis, thelêsis*

word: *logos*
worsted (to be): *hêttaomai*

worthy of: *axios*
wretched (to be): *kakodaimoneô*
wretched: *kakodaimôn*

Greek-English Index

References are to the page and line numbers of Dübner's edition, which appear in the margin of the translation. This index covers both volumes of the translation.

adranês, impotent, 12,4; 76,2
agathos, good (divine),
  5,4.7.12.16.53; 6,1.2.4.7.27.34.40;
  11,44.45.47; 12,6; 13,43.45;
  43,4.53; 69,52; 70,29;
  71,2.9.17.22.24.40.41;
  72,7.24.27.29; 73,11.13.31.32.34;
  74,8; 75,36.41.47.48; 77,34.50;
  80,46; 81,12.13; 91,38; 100,53;
  101,36.52; 102,31; 104,12.31;
  108,33.34; good (person), 24,41;
  32,30; 36,2; 38,45; 45,26;
  60,27.30.46; 61,8.9.48; 64,38;
  67,41; 85,1; 86,36; 89,45; 95,39.46;
  102,6.14; 104,37.40.43.50; 131,7;
  good (of soul), 1,42.44; 2,10.14;
  3,49; 4,31; 6,14.51.53;
  7,2.3.5.8.9.21.23.24.28.52;
  8,25.27.49; 10,19.30; 11,49; 13,46;
  15,3.6.9.15.24;
  16,34.37.47.48.50.52;
  17,1.22.35.48; 18,6.8.12.30;
  19,23.26.29.51.54; 20,25.45; 21,31;
  22,18.23.24.40; 23,8.33;
  26,28.30.41.52;
  27,1.7.8.12.13.14.19.21.38; 28,30;
  30,28.31.52; 31,6;
  32,16.18.20.21.38.41.51.53;
  33,1.2.8.11.12.14.27.28.33; 34,31;
  36,12; 38,38; 39,17.29; 40,2;
  41,10.29.31.37.39.43;
  42,1.4.25.31.36.41;
  43,2.6.19.39.41.48; 44,3.33;
  45,6.23.53; 47,4.8.24; 48,21; 50,29;
  52,37; 55,10.34.44.48.53;
  56,27.35.41.42; 57,3.6; 58,37;
  60,15.29; 61,22.34.52.53; 62,15.40;
  63,1.33-5.37.47; 65,6.13.42;
  66,35.47; 67,7.9.11.14.21.30.37.47;
  68,22.23; 70,42; 71,3;
  73,41.42.52.53;
  74,2.4.7.16.27.28.43.44.
  45.46.48.49.52;
  75,5.6.14.16.18.19.22.24.31.43.51;
  76,13.14.18.20; 77,2.9.25.28;
  78,35; 79,9.34.47.48.49.51;
  80,15.32.43.49; 81,17.24.45.47;
  84,44.46; 85,32;
  86,1.7.15.25.36.51;
  87,4.7.18.44.49; 88,53; 89,8.20.50;
  90,7.26; 91,53; 92,10.20; 99,45;
  104,44; 105,42; 106,21.23.28;
  108,35.47; 111,6; 117,21;
  118,12.43.44; 119,14; 121,16;
  123,52; 124,1.4.5.8; 128,24;
  129,17; 131,22.50; 132,15.43.46;
  133,17.23; 134,4.17.35; 136,21.47;
  138,11; good (external; lesser),
  1,43; 4,12; 17,2.5; 18,38; 19,24;
  20,42; 28,34; 30,25; 31,5.8.11;
  32,9.12.19.23.26.30.33; 33,35;
  36,11; 38,34; 41,17.27.28.38;
  43,12.27.40.46; 54,8.15; 56,38;
  57,8.9.25; 58,5.6.29; 60,14;
  61,44.46.47.49; 62,2.51;
  63,3.9.36.48; 66,48.54;
  67,5.42.46.49; 68,32;
  75,12.31.41.50.51; 76,54;
  77,7.13.14.15.19.20.21.23.24;
  78,34; 79,22.23.54; 81,44; 86,44;
  92,3.25.28.32; 93,25;
  105,1.5.9.21.24.25.27; 109,33;
  118,47; 119,16; 123,50; 124,12;
  129,13.31

agathotês, goodness,
5,9.10.22.30.45.46; 6,4.6.33;
12,7.53; 41,22; 43,9; 60,31; 67,17;
70,35; 73,12; 75,41.50; 86,7; 93,50;
94,15.21; 100,50.53.54; 101,28;
104,8.19.22.28; 106,13; 107,33;
110,40
agenêtos, ungenerated, 12,12.16;
71,39.42; 72,38; 96,39.41.43
agnômôn, inconsiderate, 47,20;
63,39.43.49
aiôn, Aeon, eternity 71,33; 81,15;
95,37; 99,30.54
aiônios, eternal, 77,34; 100,3
aisthanomai, to perceive, 7,6; 8,49;
9,48; 10,39; 31,52; 39,19; 58,10;
102,48; 105,11; 122,51; 123,3.7;
130,11
aisthêsis, perception, 9,22; 10,38;
37,47; 68,29; 78,13; 103,5;
112,21.26; 122,54
aisthêtos, perceptible, object of
perception, 9,21; 10,38; 38,31;
123,2
aitiaomai, to hold responsible, 9,1;
30,3; 30,18; 31,49; 47,35; 79,29;
92,47; 127,23
aitiateon, to hold as cause, 11,41;
102,39
aitiatos, caused, 83,29; 84,7.22;
91,34; 137,29
aitios (*aitia*), cause, reason, 3,40;
5,13; 6,12; 8,41; 9,28; 11,39;
12,17.20.32; 13,33.43; 15,9; 16,46;
17,14; 19,45; 22,19; 24,16; 27,31;
28,4; 30,1.9.18.23;
31,7.14.23.31.35;
36,5.8.9.16.37.39; 42,5.6.26.29.34;
43,11.35.38.41; 44,2.3.5.8; 56,11;
59,30; 66,16; 67,13.36; 69,32.48;
70,1.30; 72,22.32.50.51;
73,7.16.18.24.25.28; 75,3.32.33;
76,42.51; 77,23.27.32;
79,18.20.25.31; 80,16.32.37.40.45;
81,18; 83,27; 84,6.22; 85,3.16;
86,19; 87,49; 89,1; 91,30.35.43.52;
92,7.12.14.22.37.42;
93,1.7.17.21.33;
96,2.3.4.7.9.12.30.36.37.38.42.44.47;
97,15; 98,18.44; 99,25.52;
100,2.8.28.42.46.48.51;
101,27.28.29.41; 103,53;
106,27.28; 108,32.49.54;

110,35.38; 117,51.53; 122,17;
127,40; 136,34; 137,24.29.41
akolasia, licentiousness, 17,52;
18,1; 20,34; 21,7; 32,51; 35,33;
106,29
akolastainô, to be a libertine,
116,37
akolastos, licentious, 9,4; 52,52;
89,19
akoloutheô, to follow, 2,3; 34,40.43;
36,34; 44,31; 70,37; 81,3; 95,31;
109,44; 113,29; 116,25; 121,41;
124,31; 126,48; 127,53;
128,1.2.25.29; 136,38; 137,28.38.43
akolouthia, logical consequence,
succession, 2,18; 96,12.18.29.32;
136,37
alêtheia, truth, 2,27; 5,48; 19,42;
27,16; 28,4.17; 61,43; 62,35; 66,5;
70,18.19; 72,37; 73,10; 74,48; 87,3;
88,3; 100,23; 113,3; 118,1; 119,3;
121,39; 128,20; 134,38; 138,30
alêthês, true, 3,16; 5,29; 7,7.27;
8,19.20; 9,14.18; 10,34; 11,15;
14,11; 16,35; 20,15; 23,36; 25,39;
36,46; 46,49; 48,48; 51,17;
57,11.45.46; 66,33; 68,27.35.44;
72,15; 73,9; 75,8.10; 79,46; 87,4;
88,30; 91,5; 104,39.42; 108,10;
110,47; 114,40; 120,40.43;
124,13.27.33.34; 132,44.47;
134,1.42; 136,21.43
alêtheuô, to be true, 8,20; 9,33;
13,24
alêthizomai, to speak the truth,
91,40
allotrios, not our own, 16,34.43;
17,6.21.22; 24,13; 27,14; 28,30;
32,8.11.19; 33,34; 36,49; 42,11;
44,50; 45,12.47;
47,19.25.27.34.40-2.45.48; 48,17;
51,48.49; 52,11.34; 56,41; 58,36;
59,15; 68,7; 69,42; 76,31;
83,46.49.50; 91,9; 133,20
alogia, irrationality, 30,36.53;
31,1.21.27.42; 48,28; 78,43; 117,15
alogos, irrational, 1,41; 2,4; 7,30;
30,21.33.51; 33,18; 36,46; 57,19;
63,38; 69,15; 86,33; 89,22; 112,17;
115,1; 123,46; 125,45.50.53; 126,2;
129,3; 132,19.39.53; 138,26
ameinôn, better, 103,49; 125,38
amerês, partless, 97,40; 99,29

69,36.39.40; 87,9; 90,8; 93,17;
112,7
lusis, solution, 66,49

manteia, divination, prophecy,
55,45; 109,11.18.24; 110,22
manteion, oracle, 111,16.30
manteuma, result of divination,
109,13.46
manteuomai, to use divination,
109,12.13.16.23.24.26.36.37.52;
110,3.11.13.17.23.27.53; 111,9
mantikos, divinatory, 110,40
mantis, diviner, 109,19.29.31
memphomai, to blame, 17,14.39;
42,38; 47,19.21; 91,51; 92,7.50;
93,17; 111,3; 124,2
merikos, partial, particular, 5,40;
37,17; 42,15.21; 70,20;
101,9.17.18.22.23; 136,39
merismos, division, 137,53
meristos, divided, 6,10; 86,46; 97,40;
133,5
merizô, to share, 46,17; 70,16; 94,20
meros, part, 2,40.41.43.53; 3,18;
5,42; 12,38; 37,16.17; 38,17; 39,46;
66,37; 70,40.43.51; 71,5.16;
76,7.45.48.53; 77,1; 80,54;
83,2.3.15.29; 90,45; 94,14;
97,29.31.32; 100,14.44.45;
101,7.9.11; 103,14.17.18.22.23;
111,50; 120,8; 124,54; 126,4;
134,22; 137,38.45
mesos, mean, 5,7; 6,14; 12,2; 23,12;
37,50; 38,5; 43,5; 44,11.15;
75,42.53; 76,1.5; 77,35.42; 83,35;
84,28.31; 86,32; 96,20; 106,35;
109,9.14; 111,41; 114,31
mesotês, intermediate, 10,9
metaballô, to change, 11,50; 17,53;
34,11; 36,28.41; 37,5.7;
76,7.9.36.38; 97,1.5.12; 98,54;
99,6.7; 135,30
metabolê, change, 25,12; 26,47;
36,28.41; 37,6.10.30; 76,40; 99,8
metamelei, to repent, 107,21.28;
108,14.22; 121,42; 122,1
metameleia, repentance, 19,36;
107,23.49; 108,7.11; 123,26
methexis, participation, 6,7.27;
13,46; 33,36; 54,47; 70,14; 73,44;
77,44; 97,48.52
metreô, to instil measure, 1,45;

30,33; 31,44; 48,35; 69,41; 95,7;
114,35; 115,40
metriazô, to moderate, 66,11; 129,42
metriopatheia, moderate emotional
state, 19,9
metriopatheô, moderate feeling,
24,1
metriophrosunê, moderation, 66,12
metrios, moderate, 19,47.49;
22,30.48; 27,36; 41,1; 53,3; 59,40;
66,8; 106,49; 118,54; 120,38
metriotês, moderation, 19,1; 118,25;
119,22; 128,54
metron, measure, 18,43; 54,35;
93,46; 95,6; 104,25; 121,18;
122,40; 126,29.30.31.32.44;
127,6.11
monas, monad, 5,43.51; 70,16

nekroô, to deaden, 1,31; 40,10
nekros, corpse, 3,43; 6,13; 98,43
nomos, custom, law, 7,38; 14,22;
43,24; 72,47; 79,9; 85,20;
103,37.41; 106,4;
117,22.33.41.42.45; 119,37;
130,48; 135,35
nomothesia, legislation, 95,21; 104,7
nomothetês, legislator, 103,37
nous, intellect, 50,28; 77,44; 128,4

oikeioô, to make one's own, to
appropriate, 38,16; 91,32; 107,43;
115,29
oikeios, one's own, 1,32.42;
2,10.14.23.24; 3,20.49; 5,25.36;
7,31; 9,9; 10,15.6.18; 11,23.37.52;
12,22.39.54; 14,26; 15,16.31;
17,1.4.6.21.22;
19,21.22.25.29.51.54; 22,17;
31,23.30; 32,38; 34,9; 38,20;
42,36.9; 45,10.12; 47,21; 48,38;
53,31; 59,5; 63,33; 70,44; 75,22;
76,34.35; 78,7; 79,2; 82,44; 87,39;
88,11; 90,9; 91,11; 100,16.20;
101,30; 102,34.42; 109,47; 112,13;
122,21; 126,6; 127,33; 129,31;
138,20
oikeiotês, appropriateness, 13,3;
24,22.45; 82,26; 89,54; 90,3.20;
92,24; 93,30; 94,31; 107,13
oiketês, servant, 18,30; 48,13; 49,39;
50,10.15; 52,4.6; 61,18; 64,1;
85,18; 116,21.29.43.46

Subject Index

References are to the page and line numbers of Dübner's edition, which appear in the margins of the translation. The index is cumulative, listing entries and all proper names for volumes 1 and 2 of this translation.

Lightning Source UK Ltd.
Milton Keynes UK
UKOW06f1300070815

256552UK00005B/53/P

9 781472 557360